things beyond resemblance

COLUMBIA THEMES IN PHILOSOPHY, SOCIAL CRITICISM, AND THE ARTS

Collected Essays

resemblance

ROBERT HULLOT-KENTOR

things beyond
on THEODOR W. ADORNO

COLUMBIA UNIVERSITY PRESS   NEW YORK

Columbia University Press
Publishers Since 1893
New York   Chichester, West Sussex

Copyright © 2006 Columbia University Press
All rights reserved

Library of Congress Cataloging-in-Publication Data

Hullot-Kentor, Robert.
   Things beyond resemblance : collected essays on
   Theodor W. Adorno / Robert Hullot-Kentor.
      p. cm. — (Columbia themes in
   philosophy, social criticism, and the arts)
   Includes bibliographical references and index.
   ISBN 0-231-13658-7 (alk. paper)
   1. Adorno, Theodor W., 1903–1969. I. Title.
   B3199.A34H85 2006
   193—dc22

                                  2006017599

Casebound editions of Columbia University Press books
are printed on permanent and durable acid-free paper.
Printed in the United States of America
c 10 9 8 7 6 5 4 3 2 1

Pour Odile

Contents

Acknowledgments

IT IS A PLEASURE to express my gratitude to Rolf Tiedemann, Tom Huhn, Mowry Baden, Robert Kaufman, and Richard Leppert for their friendship and for their help over the years with these many essays and to Martin Jay as well, alias g.K and sine qua non.

The author also acknowledges the kind permission from the following publishers to reprint, in some cases in revised form, "Things Beyond Resemblance," in Theodor W. Adorno, *Philosophy of New Music* (Minnesota: University of Minnesota, 2006); "Second Salvage," in *Cultural Critique* 60 (2005): 134–169; "Right Listening and a New Type of Human Being," in *RES: Anthropology and Aesthetics*, no. 44 (2003): 191–198; "Adorno Without Quotation," in *RES: Anthropology and Aesthetics*, no. 45 (2004): 5–10; "Ethics, Aesthetics, and the Recovery of the Public World," as "Past Tense," in *The Recovery of the Public World*, ed. Charles Watts and Edward Byrne (Vancouver: Talon, 1999), pp. 365–372; "The Philosophy of Dissonance: Adorno and Schoenberg," in *Semblance of the Subject,* ed. Thomas Huhn and Lambert Zuidervart (Cambridge: MIT Press, 1997), pp. 309–320; "Suggested Reading," in *Telos* 89 (1993): 167–177; "Apple Criticizes Tree of Knowledge," as "Beckett Up to Date," *Telos* 92 (1993): 192;

"The Impossibility of Music," in *Telos* 87 (1991): 97–117; Popular Music and Adorno's "The Aging of the New Music," in *Telos* 77 (1989): 79–94; "Back to Adorno," in *Telos* 81 (1989): 5–29; "Critique of the Organic," in Theodor W. Adorno, *Kierkegaard: Construction of the Aesthetic* (Minnesota: University of Minnesota, 1989), pp. x–xxiii; "Introduction to 'The Idea of Natural-History,'" in *Telos* 57 (1985): 111–124; Theodor W. Adorno, "The Idea of Natural-History," trans. Robert Hullot-Kentor in *Telos* 57 (1985): 97–110; "Title Essay," in *New German Critique* 32 (1984): 141–150.

things beyond resemblance

Introduction

Origin Is the Goal

There is only the question: When will I be blown up?
—WILLIAM FAULKNER, Noble Prize speech (1950)

WRITTEN IN THE IMPERATIVE IN 1989, the essay that leads this collection—"Back to Adorno"—urged renewed interest in the oeuvre of
a philosopher and social critic who had been consigned to temporal
backwaters both in Europe and the United States. In Europe Adorno
had by that year already undergone two decades of a second exile, not,
as in his own lifetime, as a Jew from Germany but as a posthumous exile from European political and philosophical consciousness: in a matter of months after his refusal to support the revolutionary student ac-
tivism of *soixante-huit* and having summoned the police to clear the
university halls of demonstrators—followed soon after by his death—
the masses of students who had for years considered his work and pronouncements in awed attentiveness, and practiced its epigrammatic
phrasings as if proclaiming the open sesame of history itself, would
hardly acknowledge these same writings and words except with bitter
dismissal. In the United States the situation was opposite yet in a sense
identical: for though Adorno's work had never been broadly studied
and had certainly never experienced a period of centrality to social and
political thought as in Europe, the journal—*Telos*—that had most substantially introduced his work to the United States and provided his
major interpreters was no longer motivated by his thinking. A consen-

sus existed that whatever might be found in the corpus of Adorno's writings had already been sifted and was not of first or much importance at all. At the same time, poststructuralism had, for more than a decade, occupied center stage. This was puzzling, since structuralism itself had never been so established in the United States as to plausibly motivate such widespread and detailed criticism here. But there was no mistaking the appeal with which its associated linguistic gestures spread endemically across a rigidifying pragmatic heartland. In decades when the engineering differential—*stress*—excluded in one sweep from public reference the psychodynamic concept of *anxiety*, academia's contribution to a nation always wanting to get things done as with hammer and saw, rather than by invoking intellect, was to provide *reading* to dislodge *interpretation*, *rewriting* to take the place of *conceptualization*, and the handy toughness profiled in any announced *deconstruction* to easily trump weak-willed *critique* and the fragile mentalism of *insight*. At elite universities those presentations succeeded that made nostrils flare at any *privileging* that had dared take place off campus. It was a minor detail, but one relevant here, that during this period the scholarly journals attached to those universities often enough rejected work concerning Adorno with an accompanying note that this was a topic that in some distant past had already long come and gone.

Nineteen eighty-nine itself is in any case not so remote that much is required to present the situation in which "Back to Adorno" was written. But the reason for this brief history is not to affirm the essay's impulse unreservedly, whether in its first moment or now. For even if instance after instance from the history of philosophy were amassed to ballast the claim that philosophy has progressed almost as a rule under the flag of one kind of return or another—whether as "back to Kant" or as Kant's return to Plato, as Husserl's return to Descartes or as Heidegger's return to the pre-Socratics—this would not justify promoting the same under the banner of a return to Adorno. On the contrary, Adorno's philosophy took shape in dread recognition of the reversion of society to the primitive, a dynamic from which he only with luck preserved his own life. The problem that marks the center and circumference of his thought was the effort to comprehend and perhaps even circumvent this logic of progress as regression. Without a doubt the preeminent reason that his work must now be of vital concern in the United States is for what precisely can be learned from it in a nation that has so palpably entered primitive times. The vindication of torture, the desiderated abrogation of due process while utilizing its protections for its destruction, the paranoiac assault on thinking, the fixed denial of reality, the gangsterism of secrecy, the strategic humiliation of opponents, the cowering press, the trumpeted urge for sacrifice in the name of nation, the effort to legislate mystification in the sciences, the vengeful transformation of the judiciary, the coded speeches addressed to the faithful, the claim to divinely sanctioned autarchy by a president who speaks, reads, and writes only with difficulty and who is plainly incapable without a sworn cabal of advisers: these are contemporary trappings of phenomena as anciently recurrent in history as the steady exhalation of a desert wind.[1]

The country now leans heavily into this ancient breeze in the name of a return to national origin. But while the history of this development is more than complex, the event underway is stereotypical in key regards because the forces that incise its lineaments themselves pattern the stereotypy of history. Consistently, what appears unique turns out to be the remnant of defeated individuality: the president's much remarked eccentric posture—the facial muscles flexed, the head thrust forward, the shoulders pressed up and back, the pelvis restrictedly tensed—is a primordial startle response to fright, heavily muscled in a preoccupying exercise regimen directed against the recognition of the internal source of the characterologically established danger, which he perceives on all perimeters as "bad people." His easily triggered hypertonic deportment is a variant of the spasmodic salute and the forcedly stiffened marching limbs in which across centuries the ranks of the authoritarian acknowledge uncomprehended historical shock and greet one another in muscle-bound admiration. The life of this president could not be made interesting except insofar as all that is important in it were seen to be the opposite of the biographical.

I

Urging forward ho, backward to Adorno, advised considerable misdirection to an oeuvre that is fundamentally a critical study of the dynamic of historical regression. Certainly, had "Back to Adorno" presented its own intention in terms of what was actually to be achieved, it would have taken a different stance and found an apter title. But does not the aphorism with which this introduction is concerned—"Origin Is the Goal"—simply redouble the misdirected salvo of "Back to Adorno" and seek to reinflict a misunderstanding that has supposedly just been cleared?[2] The whole of Adorno's writings, it might seem, could be construed in its accusation. For Adorno asserts that history stands in thrall to regression—that progress necessarily re-emerges as a vestige of the primitive—so long as the principle of history remains the domination of nature. And the claim to origin is itself the act in which domination insists that, where rights are to be determined, priority must be ceded to what has come prior. As Adorno writes in *Negative Dialectics,* the category of origin is the "seigniorial, the confirmation of him who stands first because he was there first; of the autochthon against the immigrant, of the settled against the migrant."[3] In the concept of origin, then, nature is dominated in its own name.

To demonstrate this thesis in North America, Thoreau may be chosen from among many, especially since in a single sentence he ably carves to the exact point where the invocation of the primeval proves to be usurpation: "I wish to speak a word for Nature, for *absolute* freedom and wildness."[4] While this invocation of nature prepares the eye for the encompassment of trees, sky, and virgin field, it is the seigniorial tone of his *absolute* claim—echoing from the old world as it resounds afresh on untrodden continent—that deserves closest attention. By speaking in the name of origin, its freedom, its wildness, the newcomer to the woods establishes an inviolable right, as if the manor house of nature had always been his.

Thus, if "origin is the goal" means that the goal is to arrive back at the origin, the epigram effectively insists on pursuing Thoreau's path in his saunters; as an axiom, it commands the way back as the only way forward. The aphorism, then, must fall to Adorno's critique of origin as the fundamental device of domination—and fall as well to this critique's further implications. For even if one assumes to have long ago soberly jettisoned primogeniture, Mayflower, and polo blazon—even if Adorno's critique seems as self-evident as the concept of origin, itself the very model of self-evidence—still, any apparently perspicacious understanding of origin may be brought up short when it sets out pragmatically to get on with life as it happens. Knowingly or not, the impulse of industriousness is itself lived in the sweat of a brow that lays claim to origin: "The raging ethos of labor," Adorno writes in the same passage of *Negative Dialectics* quoted above, is evidence of origin's perduring spell.[5] History, as the course of presumptively unremitting labor, proves to be obligated to origin since labor is the assumed penalty for an initial deviation from truth in the sense of the given precedence of origin.

In quick evidence of this thesis, Adorno might have cited scriptural authority, which stipulates perpetual labor as the toll levied on the *felix culpa* by which return to edenic origin is commanded. Or, equally apt and more contemporary, Adorno could have referred to the logic of Thoreau's notoriously penny-pinching, survivalist home economy, by which the primordial Yankee sought to nestle back into the redoubt of his wooded origin. But where Adorno did in fact turn to demonstrate the relation between life as the research of origin and life as the lived penalty of labor was to Karl Kraus, the Viennese poet and language critic who first gave stamp to the motto "origin is the goal." For Kraus coined the apothegm with the surly confidence of a satirist in the eternal foundedness of his principles. Under this aphorism he marshaled the battalions of his considerable wit and equipped them with the modernist weaponry of a starkly unornamented style. The battle he envisioned was a decisively apocalyptic struggle for the recovery of a prelapsarian purity of expression in opposition to the comically deplorable forsakenness of journalistic chatter. Kraus no more doubted the origin to which he appealed than that the battle for its recovery would have to be waged with a daily relentlessness to match the appearance of every next day's newspaper, line by line, *in perpetuum*.

Kraus's aphorism, "Origin Is the Goal," then, desiderated a utopia of expression situated somewhere prior to the primordial linguistic transgression, to be achieved by modern means. And in the first of three remarks in Adorno's *Collected Writings* (his *Gesammelte Schriften*), where he touches directly on Kraus's epigram, Adorno would therefore draw plausibly on the motto to help explicate the idea of the modern as a power for the restoration of the archaic—as a conservative optic for magnifying the perception of the primitive in the modern. Thus, in a discussion of Thorsten Veblen in *Prisms,* Adorno uses Kraus's motto, and its dialectic of the modern and the prehistoric, as a backdrop against which he could revealingly project the archaic intention of Veblen's technocracy: "Karl Kraus, the critic of the linguistic ornament, once wrote 'origin is the goal.' Similarly, the nostalgia of Veblen, the technocrat, aims at the resurrection of the most ancient."[6]

But, however plainly Adorno at one point recognized the conservativeness of Kraus's aphorism, he came to perceive more to it than that. For when Adorno returned a second time to the epigram, years later in *Negative Dialectics*, it was to acknowledge a transformation in its meaning: "The conservative-sounding phrase of Karl Kraus, 'origin is the goal'"—Adorno found—had come "to express something of what it scarcely meant in its own time and place: that the concept of origin must relinquish its static hauntings." Adorno went on to explain his new sense of the motto as meaning that "the goal is not to be recovered in the origin, in the phantasm of a good nature, but rather origin devolves from the goal; it is only from the goal itself that origin is first constituted. There is no origin save in the life of the ephemeral."[7]

Thus, while in its own moment Kraus's motto asserted the claim levied by origin on goal, in the epigram's development it could be seen sloughing this demand to take sides with the claim of goal on origin. And, in doing so, there is no doubt that the epigram has lurched toward the inscrutable. It presents a conundrum on the order of— rather than deciding to walk a mile in ten minutes—wanting to walk ten minutes in a mile. Reveries of this kind may even involve scattered elements of a critique of mathematical commutation that is genuinely apposite to the transformation that Kraus's aphorism experienced, which must have something to do with the fragile irreversibility of its word order. But as if concerned that only its elusiveness will prevail when there really is something being said, the epigram makes an exceptional effort at its own clarification by providing self-exemplum: in having escaped itself, the imperiousness of its own assertedly unbudgeable origin, it criticizes the "static hauntings" of its conservative husk, modeling origin in "the ephemeral," its own transience, as the goal.

The phrase, however, can be elucidated still more closely: Origin, in any philosophical sense—the epigram now seems to say—wants to relinquish the research of genesis for that of arriving at the new.[8] And if the motto's conservative trappings, even to this moment, prohibit it from asserting the new outright, this is with some advantage because the new that the phrase anyway seeks is the goal in the sense of what has acquired the quality of being the source. Thus, while it would be

sophistry to want to wring argument from epigram, by its own implication "origin is the goal" translates directly, if incompletely, into possible vernacular expression such as that life lives from the new, and
only that, and wishes it were that altogether. As such the phrase stands
in refusal of longing for another world, another start, as if the difference between what is and utopia—the genuinely new—were the
greatest, rather than the smallest, step. Even in its traces the new is
better indicated with an eye and ear—for instance, Cézanne's and
Berg's—for the smallest transitions and, where a vernacular placeholder is needed for the new, is best stated not in the futuristic but in
the most modest, such as in wondering what it would be like if one's
head cold had vanished: in considerations, that is, that derive from
sensing the exact weight of things, not from supposing that the little of
what we can bear, let alone know, of history had never happened.[9]

II

> True conquest is the causing the calamity to fade and disappear.
> —EMERSON, "Circles"

The transformation undergone by Kraus's epigram has the unim-
peachable objectivity of the involuntary; it is as sure a thing as that—
when and if Johnny ever comes marching home, again, this time from
Iraq—few voices at the parade will be singing "We'll all be gay ..."
Much that this Civil War lyric now has to say would itself be worth
considering, but the most important aspect in the transformation of
Kraus's motto remains to be stated. And it is this: the epigram presents
a critique of origin that rejects the facile dismissal of the concept. It
differs fundamentally from the unmasking of origin as convention—
from the demonstration of the coercive imposture of a socially constructed second nature as first nature. What this distinction amounts
to begins to be evident in the recognition that insight into the fraud of
origin vastly antedates the idea that origin is the goal. The former is
indeed of the greatest antiquity and legitimately counts as progress's
first discovery. Liberal example might be marshaled, for instance, by
illustrating the development of Cycladic technique.

A relic, however, more germane to this discussion would be a fourteenth-century dispute between nominalists and realists at the faculty

where Luther studied. The nominalist thesis that language presents the *flatus vocis* of convention, and not an existing universal or form, necessarily came to odds with the realist underpinning of teleology. Against it, nominalists argued characteristically, and with ingenuity, that since only the real particular exists, a bird can not—for example—be said to build its nest in order to lay eggs in it, for at the moment of that construction the eggs, yet to come, must logically be excluded from reference.[10] It is not haphazard that this nominalist insight spans centuries with all the spunk of a practical joke—akin to denying having pulled the chair out from under someone, since he had not yet sat down on it. The cunning coiled up in this nominalism, which served the emancipation of individuality in the protestant reformation, reduces what seemed to be first nature to a spurious abstraction of schoolmen. Every further contemporary insight into what is now known as the social construction or invention of childhood, language, or mores, etc., continues to depend on varieties of nominalism for its critique of origin. The thinking achievement is hardly to be scorned. The attention that it brought to the individuality of the "real particular" contributed profoundly to the development of historical perception and reasoning as well as to the scientific comprehension of nature. However, in its rejection of origin *tout court* it remains blind to the origin for which its cunning unconsciously speaks and is, as a result, ultimately no less obtuse to history than to nature.

The full scope of Adorno's work can begin to be described as a study of the origin that is asserted in the radical critique of origin. With the somewhat lighthearted locution of his lectures, for instance, he might have characterized that fourteenth-century nominalist ruse as "textbook dialectic of enlightenment." His elucidation of this dialectic of enlightenment is, however, in fact the most serious contribution that Adorno can make to understanding the contemporary situation in the United States. But the little that has so far been said about this dialectic—on one hand describing it as an insistence on a return to origin that sets history in thrall to regression and on the other hand as the forward vector of progress by which history achieves an identical result—may seem confused. It is not. It indicates that the two directions are importantly the same. Yet while the pivot of domination around which these two directions turn in relation to each other is better developed than summarized, what causes these images to appear to conflict illogically in the first place is the result of the spatialization of nature produced by mechanization. This post-seventeenth-century development set the framework for a historicism in which it became possible and necessary to imagine travel from one historical period to the next, as if changing rooms, because time itself was subsumed to the constraints of this spatialization.[11] It is the accompanying and unavoidable concretization of the temporal metaphors that, in this essay, produces a sense of jumbled temporal geography in which apparently opposite Euclidian directions, not located on a circle, are said to arrive at the same spot. Obviously, this development is not to be outwitted in this essay by any kind of sifting or terminological asceticism, and neither would it be productive to try, since the images, however confusing their overlap, reveal genuine forces of mind and society.

With regard to the concept of regression itself, however, it helps considerably to grasp the dialectical relationships that are at stake in Adorno's work if it is recognized that the spatial extension, along which the timeline of regression is almost instinctually imagined, deceives entirely. For while Adorno's concept of regression invokes an immense literature in history and philosophy, from Hesiod through Spengler and Toynbee, that has struggled to comprehend social decline and barbarization, Adorno engaged this body of thought most of all psychoanalytically, in the technical meaning of the concept of regression. Some orientation to the concept is gained, then, by reference to psychological experience in which nothing is more obvious—however common sense balks at it—than that earlier and later are not spatially separate in the course of a life. The traumatic return of the repressed covers no spatial distance, but it does "arrive"—and with an uncanniness bearing an inescapable familiarity, as if it had always been in front of the mind's eye where, in fact, it had always been, though without conscious perception. Regression, then, as Adorno occasionally points out, is not to be understood concretely, as traveling back to an earlier period, but as the manifestation of conflicts that were never resolved in the first place. In this, Adorno agrees with Freud in emphasizing that the infantile past of the individual and of humanity itself remains active within both the individual and society in conflicts that continually reemerge in moments of crisis that reveal the ongoing failure to solve these conflicts.[12] Regression, then, certainly as Adorno conceived it, could be described as the enduring situation of the reproduction of incapacitating conflict. Faulkner's comment that "there is only the question: When will I be blown up?" now blooms fresh on the stem—as if he mistakenly wrote these words for 1950 when they speak so appositely in 2006 to stepping on or off subway or bus in city after city—because traumatic repetition fragments the consciousness of historical continuity in which the repetition would be recognized.

III

> True conquest is the causing the calamity to fade and disappear. . . .
> The way of life is wonderful; it is by abandonment.

Adorno was among the first to address the philosophical dimensions and implications of psychoanalysis.[13] His early appropriation of Freud was so complete and formative of every aspect of his thinking that during his years in the United States, mostly the 1940s, in spite of the fact that he had no clinical training in the field, he credibly presented himself as a psychologist—then meaning a psychoanalytic researcher—in letters of introduction and in his participation on research projects such as the *Authoritarian Personality* (1950). Not only does his theory of regression require for its understanding visceral familiarity with Freud, but the central idea of the *Dialectic of Enlightenment* that progress is regression plainly derives from the psychoanalytic theory of symptom formation as puzzle structures in which the conflict between gratification and self-punishment have taken shape as continually inhibiting "compromise solutions" in the individual. The emancipatory interest in Adorno's development of a paratactical style, the nonsubordinating structure of clauses in his essays that is experienced by some readers as directionlessness, has origins not only in Walter Benjamin but in the specific emancipatory claims of psychoanalytic techniques of association. Adorno did also criticize free association for its absence of conceptual rigor, but this does not deny the role it had in the development of his thinking. *Aesthetic Theory* (1970) begins with the most detailed criticism of psychoanalysis for reducing literature and the arts to the neurotic inspirations of its makers, but the whole of the work plainly develops the relation between the unconscious history of human suffering and art that forms this experience as a relation between id and ego. And again: Adorno compellingly rebuffed the whole of ego psychology as conformist.[14] But the founding volume of ego psychology, Anna Freud's *Ego and the Mechanisms of Defense* (1936), which introduced the idea of identification with the aggressor, must be acknowledged as Adorno's vade mecum in the centrality of this idea to the *Dialectic of Enlightenment* (1944) and throughout the theory of artistic making in *Aesthetic Theory*. It is among the lesser ironies, but revealing nonetheless, that Adorno's most famous essay, known in English as "The Meaning of Working Through the Past"[15] seems to have been penned by a psychoanalyst wanting to recommend to social history the analytic intention of "working through"[16] conflicts with an individual patient. But the German title itself is not psychoanalytic at all.[17] On the contrary, in that essay Adorno was criticizing a phrase, popular after the war, that promoted an approach to the past that aimed at "being done with," "drawing the balance line," "clearing away," or "finishing off" the past, that is, its *Aufarbeitung*. All the same, however—and this must have impressed the English translator—what Adorno recommends to German society in opposition to this *Aufarbeitung* of its past indeed has much in common with the psychoanalytic approach of pursuing the conflicts of a life through to their end rather than thinking one could be done with it all by slamming the door.

But whatever the origins of Adorno's thought in psychoanalysis, it is remote from this essay to argue that his thinking remained identical to these origins. It would be more relevant to his work to notice the considerable injustice he might be said to have done those origins while embracing them. For if Adorno was by his own lights profoundly nuanced in his psychological observation, especially in *Minima Moralia*, when he employs psychoanalytic reasoning directly, as he does extensively in his study of Stravinsky in *Philosophy of New Music* (1948), his thinking can lack discernment. In *Philosophy of New Music* in particular the typology of neurotic and psychotic symptomatology established for Stravinsky's music is concocted almost right off the page from a quick study of Otto Fenichel's *Psychoanalytic Interpretation of Neurosis* (1945) and, deprived of clinical differentiation, employed with the schematic amateurishness of the worst of what Adorno consistently deplored in his acerbic characterizations of psychoanalytic condescension and cocktail-hour interpretations.[18]

It would not be difficult to go through Adorno's writings and demonstrate repeatedly that his theory of identification with the aggressor, his concept of regression, and his ideas on homosexuality, just for starters, fall considerably short of the relevant psychoanalytic literature and expertise.[19] Yet, although the criticism catalogued would matter to the detail of some of Adorno's observations and pronouncements, it would ultimately have little bearing on his work. For in spite of the many psychoanalytic sources of Adorno's thinking, he was not at all interested in being a psychologist and only found himself in that role in the midst of the constraints of immigration. And while his social philosophy has many psychological implications, relevant, for instance, to the bland characterology of the president of the United States, in its full development Adorno's thinking is more opposed to psychology than otherwise. No doubt, however, this tempts misunderstanding in that Adorno's relation to psychology differs uniquely from the history of the philosophical critique of psychologism—as it is known, for instance, in Husserl and Heidegger—by the fact that what is antipsychological in Adorno's thinking is, paradoxically, not only opposed to psychological reality but also affirms it.

This complex relationship to psychology could be concisely expressed as dialectical, since in this instance what is oppositional is not in any way reduced as such by the fact that it also involves affirmation. But the concept of dialectics is one of the central ideas in Adorno's work that presently warns away from its quotation, except *faute de mieux*. And the alternative that is, indeed, available at this point is to give evidence of a standing antagonism in Adorno's work and then show that this nonidentity of the thought with itself fails to disqualify it but on the contrary deepens its grasp of reality. It should, then, be noted that while Adorno's thinking is antipsychological, the *Authoritarian Personality* characterizes the authoritarian itself by a strict antipathy to introspection and a general refusal to acknowledge the ambiguities and contradictions of its own psychological dimension. And to ensure that this figure is recognizable, without needing to return in historicist-dense evocation to the epoch in which Adorno collaborated on that study, it may be remarked that the current governor of Florida, sworn to *acta non verba*, laconically provides a contemporary model. Notice, in a moment, his manner of warding off any would-be challenge to the claim on nature that he lodges for the habits of his family. Notice, too, that the strength of his stance draws on a nation's felt authority in any contemporary conversational reference to the "hard wire" of the mind. Expressed in his asserted *on/off* controls and *modes* is a country's unyielding determination not to know the truth of itself, as if even to imagine that possibility were to run the absurd and repulsive risk of disgorging its own insides: "It's not nature for us [the Bush family] . . . to turn on this reflective mode and somehow spill our guts."[20]

Thus government speaks for nature's nation. What specifically the governor would fear to reveal could be studied psychologically and detail would emerge. But his succinct statement has already disclosed much more than it would ever knowingly have allowed itself to speak; in his assertion of family allegiance, indeed, he has already betrayed family and given the lie to the claim of its primordial solidarity. For the governor's words are a statement of extreme mistrust and suspicion on all sides. This goes far beyond the bounds of the family life to which the governor of a state would like to restrict the comprehension of reality. The antagonism, whose powers the governor both subserves and employs, not least in confident opposition to himself, leaves behind the stereotype and bare rudiments of individuality audible in just his few words.

The abrupt dynamic of this antagonism cannot finally be studied psychologically or by means of any social psychology that would presuppose some kind of harmoniously nested Parsonian arrangement of human spheres. This is why, Adorno held, psychoanalytic approaches are seen to fail most perceptibly when they seek to understand the genuine barbarians of history who arrive on the hour to take over the reigns of nations in crisis—even of those countries that are so preoccupied with the tit for tat of buying and selling that they are only with the greatest intermittence aware of their circumstance. The psychological studies of these governors, presidents, and those chancellors that became dictators, necessarily assemble interchangeable materials from reports of concealed rantings and tantrum, coerced allegiance, pervasive suspicion, and ominously enforced protocol—including the well-documented anxious need of one Texan to be in bed right after dusk if not to wake up once again alcoholic at dawn. What is not understood, in other words, in the psychological studies is what their publicly elected subjects of research most have in common, which appears starkly in the banality of the discoveries that can be made about them. While these clues to personality are completely familiar to psychoanalysis, it is unable to follow them in the direction of the force of abstraction that carves their collective profile unless the science were to destroy the boundaries within which it helps people as best it can. Psychoanalysis's functional position in the division of labor is hardly able to resist repeatedly establishing itself in its systematic claims as a science of origin with a locus restricted to the individual.[21]

This begins to explain why Adorno's concept of regression—which remains to be presented—is psychoanalytic but not a psychological concept and why, as he uses it, it need have little responsibility to the whole of psychoanalytic research. In this it exemplifies Adorno's general approach to concepts, which can be described with partial but useful exaggeration as a rigorous pragmatism that in its emancipatory aim is strictly antipragmatic: As it requires them, Adorno's critical theory breaks concepts out of the systematic structures in which they were developed and where they subserved the purpose of self-preservation in the mastery of the object. Separated from the constraint of their origin, which obligates them to the self-identity of the system— its self—concepts become available for an association as they are associated in the object itself. Note should be made of the psychoanalytic source of this idea of an association that, freed from its defensive purpose, allows ideas to come into a potentially liberating order. But the psychoanalytic idea of association has been transformed, for it has become a philosophical concept insofar as it has been subordinated to the primacy of the object. The concept is no longer directed back toward the self, and its systematic order, but rather, on the contrary, to what the thinking self can achieve that is other than itself by surpassing itself in its object as what escapes the claim to identity. This intention transforms the function of transitions in the presentation of the material, which become paratactical in order, in a sense, to test the actuality of the middle point around which the concepts are organized: this does not dismiss the demands of sequence but heightens them in recognition that—contrary to eighteenth-century assumptions of the association of ideas—it is exclusively because one thing does not follow the last that sequence is revealing. It is well-known that Adorno called these associations of concepts constellations—as named by Benjamin, who represents, along with Hegel and Nietzsche, other origins of Adorno's thinking.

These other figures could, of course, be valuably developed as additional foci of this discussion, but the question here is necessarily whether Adorno's prismatic use of concepts successfully escaped these and, in fact, the sum total of its origins. One measure of this might be the sense, on entering any one of Adorno's essays, that even in their very first words one has already arrived too late to find out for sure what any of the concepts mean—a feeling that is not relieved by studying the entire rest of his oeuvre. This perpetual entry in *medias res* is not epical but philosophical: it is the thinking feel of being in the midst of the object, sometimes at the height of its antagonistic conflicts. The meaning of the concepts is, in other words, in the bindingness of their insight and nowhere else. This is, once again, a transformation of psychoanalysis. But the nature of this bindingness must be clarified and insisted upon, for it could easily be passed over even though it amounts to the topic of this essay in that it is a variant of the recognition that the epigram "origin is the goal" is important only because it critically recuperates origin itself. The point is this: Adorno's critique of systematic reason is not—as has been indicated—a dismissal of thought's claim to bindingness, but, on the contrary, having rejected compulsion as the standard of consecutive thought, it means to gain a more demanding and compelling bindingness on the basis of what in it is radically true. In his aesthetics it is in just this sense that Adorno would discern the actual progress in Schoenbergian composition over any earlier form. But, to present what is at stake here in the most general terms, the critique of domination necessarily remains another form of domination—and hardly rare in that the gesture of emancipation as domination comprises the whole of ideology—unless there is the possibility in domination itself of recuperating it from its own destructiveness. What Adorno wanted to comprehend was the capacity of thought—of identity itself—to cause reality to break in on the mind that masters it. This concept of emancipatory reason can calmly be stated as the most important idea in Adorno's philosophy and the one most needing exposition and critical examination. It can also be stated as the idea of how the critique of even the sum total of origins would require the recuperation of origin and ultimately nothing less than the reconciliation of reason with myth—with what has always been—if the critique itself is not to be the furtive assertion of origin. One implication of these ideas is that, since no systematic presentation of Adorno's thinking is possible, the only way of proceeding is in further combination of its concepts for what there is to be discovered in the material itself.

IV

> True conquest is the causing the calamity to fade and disappear as an
> early cloud of insignificant result in a history so large and advanc-
> ing. . . . The way of life is wonderful; it is by abandonment.

The life of the adamantly trouble-free governor is certainly a matter
of psychology and family life, but in its every aspect as progeny of
the form of national epic that Emerson presents. In the essayist's vision this national panorama unfolds with buoyant imperturbability.
History's masterful advance controls the rhythm of the brightening
day, unsealing the horizon across a landscape brimming with success.
Where advance encounters its only impediment in the vestige of mis-
fortune, veridical dominion disperses that vestige with no more memory of its blemish than the sky remembers a cloud that momentarily
marred its blue dawning. History emerges in the triumph of this pristine sky as a spontaneous force of abandonment whose wonder is extolled for tolerating no trace of what might have discouraged it, for
recognizing that whatever might have gotten in its way was inherently—in the passage's most startling expression—of "insignificant
result."

The chanting eloquence and brutal high spirit of this fairy tale of
national origin was to goad, enthuse, and restore to its labors a colonial
nation still in its coonskin cap. But while the caps have changed,
Emerson's big bellied, pristine sky, in its spontaneous incapacity to acknowledge its gut fill, hovers in steady familiarity over the course of
American centuries. It perdures legitimately as tradition, though certainly not as evidence of an exceptionally American tradition but—as
is now starkly visible from whatever angle the country is regarded—
as the tradition of the progressively generic itself. Emerson's presentation of this tradition's concept aimed to be definitive for his idea of *true
conquest* only secondarily concerns how it is exemplified in one particular nation, even if in the passage itself the definition ultimately over-
whelms the example provided. In his condensed success in this presentation he ably contributes to a general understanding of conquest's
own form: The second nature in which history establishes itself as
pristine sky is manufactured out of a first nature that it consumes exclusively as raw material. This is the single event of Emerson's few
lines, and by its power of abandonment it succeeds in carrying this out

in a single moment: what disappears is indifferently gone. But there is more to it than that, for the passage can only recommend this expeditious gesture of dismissal as a worthy, genuine power by demonstrating its work as an open secret. Thus, even as it conceals, it patiently illustrates the legerdemain of its power of abstraction, though certainly it carries out this exposition without itself having any understanding of how it actually happens: the big beaker of *calamity*—the demonstration begins—can confidently be poured into the little beaker of *insignificant result*—the demonstration proceeds—and that beaker made to vanish with a wave of the arm into the pristine sky given that in the process the former, the content of the big beaker, agrees not to make the slightest peep.

Emerson himself in his prodigious proselytizing, crossing the stretch of the country in all directions with as little complaint in his travels as St. Paul in his, could not have entered more directly in this nation's primordial landscape. Its logic, which he captured in the genius of his own rhapsodic thinking, would have prohibited him, ultimately, from denying that when he castigated what he called the "hypocrites" of his own age who battled for the lives of the "masses"— lives, he said, that were "not worth preserving"—he stipulated the strictures of the only possible form of self-affirmation that this landscape tolerated and in its name he pronounced final judgment on the worth of his own life. Likewise in their rough but bland obliviousness and a posture that once froze in a cringe, the emphatically trouble-free governor and the early-to-bed, early-to-rise, tongue-tied brother are themselves part of the manufacture of a sacrificial landscape of conquest whose sky beams wherever its enduring tradition is fulfilled: in the ability to demand and receive offerings brought to it in silence.[22] These men's piety is authentic, and their psychology no less narrow. The conquest they continue to mobilize has in just several years successfully jettisoned from public iconography every image of the edifices of democratic deliberation, national administration, and any kind of sculpture of liberty, with the only remainder an omnipresent flag whose one assertion is conquest. Of necessity, whether as forward ho or this way back, its exigency is regression because as the assertion of the primordial form of identity—bare self-preservation—conquest can only be the progressive development of the principle of necessity. By its own structure inured to any perception of what is occurring except as an intrusion on its thinking, it has no alternative but to reproduce the conflict that motivates it in steadily impending, explosive self-antagonism.

V

> What help from thought? Life is not dialectics. We, I think, in these times, have had lessons enough of the futility of criticism. Our young people have thought and written much on labor and reform, and for all that they have written, neither the world nor themselves have got on a step. Intellectual tasting of life will not supersede muscular activity.
>
> —EMERSON, *Experience*

"What help from thought?" In the rhetorical gesture the first words call it quits with the improbable stuff. But, immediately on its rejection, the passage proceeds to draw up a semblance of argument and conclusion: "We, I think . . ." The contradiction is a truth: The passage insists that thinking may advance only in its denial. It gains the capacity for this denial in self-hypnosis. A listening *we* is summoned to attend to the moment when the red herring is held up directly in front of the apostrophized many, and "since none of you"—the passage essentially continues—"have seen what I hold up to your vision, I rightly invoke you and whomever some day reads these words in the presumption that it was never there." The puppeted empty eyes bestow blessing, confirmation, and strength on the puppeteer himself. In the name of *we* he may now treat the object—thought itself and the reality it purports—with the authority of the convened assembly to ignore whatever complaint this object might raise. It is a gang of one and a gang nonetheless. For the passage would not have its coherence if the imaginings were arbitrary. The conjured *we* is the factual social reality of the day in its economic solidarity against labor and reform. These citizens are as real as their unity is abstract. Under the authority they have provided for the incapacitating of thought, the writer who speaks for them will go on to inflict their vengeance. The passage thus continues on to easily win its pretense of an argument, which in any case only amounted to having taken a moment to draw its supporters round to prove that it had what it needed to enforce what was presumed in its first words. The troublemakers and their cause, labor and reform, will be dispersed: *we* have had enough of "futile" youth. Nothing will stand—certainly nothing these young people have "written" as excuses—between the intention of this *we* and the muscular activity that will now take action as it sees fit.

But however provoked this *we* has been by the "lessons" it has had, its dismissal of a gourmandizing "intellectual tasting" in favor of "muscular activity" has much to teach. A war against thought has turned out to be a war against pleasure, which Emerson, with the exactitude of an allergy, has sensed lurking back of the impulse of criticism. The passage militates the sum of its confidence in the certainty that this—probably effeminate—wile can be mocked without it finding any recourse. Here then, again at his best, Emerson provides as supplement to his theory of conquest a no less concise demonstration that asceticism—the rejection of "intellectual tasting"—is fundamentally a restriction of thinking. If thinking were permitted to continue unchecked, he has perceived, the outcome sought would not relinquish its claim to pleasure until it had unhinged the rote pragmatism of the struggle Emerson has already engaged. The implications of the passage here become imposing and begin to run directly counter the grain of its own momentum, carving in deeply. For in his thesis on asceticism Emerson implies that the inefficacy he has claimed to identify in thinking, as grounds to demand its halt at what the citizenry had anyway already planned to do, is solved not in less thinking but in more. For, when not called to a halt by narrow purpose, the principle of identity potentially becomes the critique of that principle's imposed hardship, one that would not otherwise be able to rest even when every last molecule on earth had become grist for the mill.

Thus, followed beyond the limits imposed by a pragmatism that has by its own restriction and taboo absorbed all possible ends into their stipulated means, identity becomes the critique of identity in freedom to the object. What can appear in this thinking altogether more than vacant ratiocination is, on the contrary, the translation of second nature back into first nature. This would not make first nature blossom any more than the discernment of Emerson twisting his own arm back of his own shoulder is a garden vision. Rather the traces of what first nature surrendered, with ostensible spontaneity and actual brutality, could be made evident as what it needlessly underwent long after the achievement of the moment when, as second nature, it could have come to its own assistance. Thought wants to shape itself to the instant when this recognition is made binding in thought itself, without compulsion, in such a fashion that this recognition could not be lifted from any face in which it has been thought. In this the epigram "origin is the goal" is wrested from any possible service to the pristine and becomes a teleology of nature that makes good on its nominalist and Kantian critique by rejecting any providentialism, as if what needs to be done is to follow the way that has been secured by its preexistent end. On the contrary, "origin is the goal" indicates an objective teleology of the new insofar as the new is the source from which origin devolves, that is, insofar as the goal is experienced exclusively as it takes shape in the comprehension of what has been suffered.

This concept of teleology is the central idea of Adorno's *Aesthetic Theory* as he develops it, for instance, in his theory of composition as the technical obligation of the critical eye and ear as it follows word, note, or color "where it wants to go." Only in art—Adorno held—can the material be shaped to "where it wants to go." For this reason Adorno wrote, the third and last time he touched directly on Kraus's epigram: "*Origin is the goal* if anywhere, then in art."[23] The comment occurs in the midst of the discussion of art beauty in relation to natural beauty, and the thinking is this: "What natural beauty itself longs for but cannot achieve in deprivation of the principle of identity, art beauty gains as the plenipotentiary of the new in the form of memory of nature in the dominating subject whose capacity for domination has become that of emancipation."[24] The experience of this form of memory, critically comprehended and developed in concepts, is what Adorno counterposed to historical regression as the only alternative to barbarization. No doubt he considered memory of nature in the subject to be a kind of "intellectual tasting of life," but not as the preoccupation with the pleasures of the table where *les gourmands* demonstrate to perfection their taste—as the ascetic essayist mockingly casts it—but where second nature recovers its own qualitative dimension so that it can be experienced. Hewing to the smallest transitions, art seeks the primacy of the object where it can be made to "break in on the mind that has mastered it." Where this occurs it is as considerably more than a peep: it is the translation back out of the pristine sky of every last thing that supposedly vanished into its fantasy. This is a making that is potentially its—every last thing's—ally not least in refusing to deny the irremediableness of a history in which the sky itself—the one not to be seen back of Emerson's close-fisted fantasy but

the only one that ultimately is not a fetish and can possibly be loved—
has been transformed into unprecedented storm while an incapacitated thinking continues to plan for making it irreversibly something
like cinder.

VI

The essays on T. W. Adorno collected in this volume, including one
translation, are drawn from work completed over the course of more
than twenty years. Beyond many minor amendments, including the
correction of earlier misprints, the essays here—with several exceptions—have not been substantially rewritten. Assurance does not need
to be given that the author could hardly be more familiar with their
limitations, all that he would do differently now and the many points
on which he now thinks differently. But the assembly of these essays,
keyed to the idea that *origin is the goal* goes some way to taking the
thorn out of the proverbial hoof, and from the start this has been part
of the motivation for collecting them here for republication. If "Back
to Adorno," for instance, is no more to be repaired retrospectively
than the rest of history, the form of criticism that it and the other essays here have wanted to represent is that in which something more
can possibly appear than what was exactly put there to start with. The
intention of this introduction has once again sought to explicate this
form of criticism as it is implied in the development of an epigram
while, at the same time, wanting this epigram to draw the work assembled here into a constellation around itself. In this construction
what the reader will find that is repetitive in these essays, and contradictory as well, will have a different meaning than simply repetition
and contradiction: they will supplement and correct each other.

What is certainly not part of the intention here, however, is any
claim to have blown breath back into a distant Austro-Hungarian epigram, as if its own lungs would then engage to move its respiration
forward. The past now reaches deeply through its syllables as it does
through every word and concept that ever found its way into
Adorno's writings, disintegrating ideas and whole phrases and passages. Much could be said about why even the briefest quotation from
Adorno's writings has acquired something of the comical about itself.
And how it can be that, all the same, there is still no coming away

from their pages without the sense that they could hardly be more true. The contradiction shapes a productive puzzle in which something like a critical tradition might legitimately be sought. This puzzle needs to be heightened and made more distinct. What is now only half readable in Adorno's writings indicates the impulses of its criticism. No alternative is available, then, to casting in with Adorno's thesis that there is nothing important except by way of forgetting. If the transformation these years are constantly completing on Adorno's thinking is ignored in the interest of any kind of resuscitation, the possibility of following it where it wants to go—the contrary of dismissal and a labor of criticism—is necessarily forfeited.

Back to Adorno

The mind is the most terrible force in the world principally in this
that it is the only force that can defend us against itself. The modern
world is based on this pensée.

—WALLACE STEVENS, *Adagia*

THE ONLY LEGITIMATE "back to" is one that calls for a return to
what was never reached in the first place, which is the case with
Adorno's writings. In America, his life work was born into a bottle.
While this bottle may be about to burst, to date every conceivable reason has contributed to the delay in his work being better known here,
from the pall that has fallen over the knowledge of the German language since WWII, to the unfamiliarity of the idealist tradition, to the
decline of Marxism. Not least in importance has been the overshad-
owing vogue of deconstruction, which has done inestimable damage
to critical thought. Hard-won insights into class structure, surplus repression, and conformism have been passed off in favor of the refine-
ment of techniques of avoidance and the glamorization of a sort of
punning that used to be dismissed as the last resort of a washed-out
imagination. Just where this genre of imagination fits in best happens
to be right at the top. If by a quirk of fate one ended up looking
around Harvard this past season—winter 1989—it was possible to
come across a whole crowd of people who had written books and essays with the word *difference* in the title, nestled around a Christmas
tree, scores in open hands, caroling hard, primarily worried whether
every part was covered. Their ironic glances, claiming to put it all at a

distance, testified to how they put themselves at home. If, however, cracks have appeared in formalism's lacquered surface, any return to Adorno must still contend with the damage done to his writings by their inadequate translation and the blunting of his thought by the ensuing decade and a half of misunderstanding and neglect. New translations are needed. This is particularly true in the case of *Dialectic of Enlightenment,* a seminal work that has been especially lamed in translation.[1] Any attempt, however, to take a new look at this book—even if a completely dependable translation were available—must also come to terms with Habermas who, as the result of a terrifically unlucky historical mismatch, has emerged as the preeminent representative of the Frankfurt School on this side of the Atlantic.

Dialectic of Enlightenment Reintroduced

Dialectic of Enlightenment was coauthored by Adorno and Horkheimer in California between 1941 and 1944. It was first circulated under the title *Philosophical Fragments* in a limited mimeographed edition among members of the exiled Institute for Social Research. In 1947 this manuscript appeared in book form, bearing its present title and significantly revised. Obscurities were edited out; capitalism and totalitarianism, previously conflated with fascism, were differentiated. But, very importantly, Marxist terminology was replaced by more neutral economic and sociological expressions: *proletariat* became *worker, capitalist* became *employer,* and *exploitation* became *suffering.* This hedging, the immigrant authors hoped, would speed the manuscript past federal authorities whose anticommunism they had every reason to fear.[2] What needs to be explained, however, is why, years after the war and the authors' return to Europe, the volume was once again masked and in a substantially more drastic fashion. Once the original edition was sold out—in the late fifties—no further publication was permitted. In spite of the broad interest in the book, the repeated urgings of insiders to the reestablished Institute for Social Research (such as Marcuse), and the circulation of a pirated student edition, a new edition was only authorized several months before Adorno's death in 1969.[3]

Though it has never been generally known, the reason for the protracted delay in republication was a major disagreement between its authors. Adorno himself had reservations about the book, but he supported a new German edition,[4] and in his lectures openly complained that the text still had not been translated into English. It was Horkheimer who repeatedly blocked any republication. This disagreement over the book's fate was not an isolated incident, but involved fundamental differences between the two authors. Whereas all of Adorno's later writings reach back to this book, quoting and citing it, Horkheimer was not interested in the reappearance of a work whose stridency and radicalism were far from the thinking of his later years, and which, even in the context of his early development, marked a lacuna. Except for several essays written while *Dialectic of Enlightenment* was being drafted, the work fits uneasily into Horkheimer's oeuvre. Horkheimer was, after all, the person who had been instrumental in the rejection of Benjamin's professorial dissertation (*Habilitationsschrift*) on Baroque drama, who in the course of his life was increasingly drawn to Schopenhauer, and who at the end of his life expressed himself vehemently against birth control and dissonant music. He certainly had an oblique relation from the start to a text that owes much to Benjamin and whose undercurrents are those of erotic freedom and aesthetic radicalism. Horkheimer stood at a much greater distance from Adorno than might be guessed from the reputation of their friendship and the book's joint signature. This raises the issue of who actually wrote which of the book's essays.

Authorship

The editor of Horkheimer's collected works, G. S. Noerr, has made a detailed study of the essays' typescripts, the files where they were stored, and the handwriting of those who revised the manuscripts. Though painstaking, such positivistic philology is not of great use here because, as Leo Lowenthal and Gretel Adorno have pointed out, the essays were the result of collective dictation and intensive conversation. The typescripts Noerr examined are densely mediated documents. More is to be learned about the work's origins from stylistic comparisons. With regard to just this issue, Habermas has claimed it is obvious that Horkheimer wrote the volume's lead essay "The Concept of Enlightenment."[5] Unfortunately, Habermas is so sure his claim is self-evident to any careful reader that he furnishes no support for it. Yet he inadvertently provides counterevidence elsewhere by citing some of the well-known formulations from the lead essay: "Every attempt to break out of nature's power by breaking nature only results in deeper subordination to nature's power"; "Men and women have always had to choose between subjection to nature or the subjection of nature to the self"; "Just as the myths already realize enlightenment, so enlightenment with every step becomes more deeply embedded in mythology."[6] Habermas did not choose the most startling lines from the essay, though it would be overly picky to complain about any selection from an essay in which every sentence has acquired a reputation. Each is crucially memorable and—in revenge—sure to be cited into oblivion.

This quality of the lead essay, however, casts doubt on Horkheimer's primacy in its composition. With few exceptions there are no comparable lines in the rest of Horkheimer's work; neither before or after did he formulate such compelling ideas. In contrast, the elasticity of thought, the rhetorical ingenuity and aphoristic trenchancy of the essay characterizes all of Adorno's writings—from his first book on *Kierkegaard* to the last lines of *Aesthetic Theory*. Comparing the volumes Horkheimer and Adorno wrote independently of one another while they were working on *Dialectic of Enlightenment* is like juxtaposing Spinoza and a TV philosopher: Adorno's *Philosophy of New Music* is written on the same level as *Dialectic of Enlightenment*, whereas Horkheimer's *Eclipse of Reason* is akin to valuable though diluted culture criticism of the same period.[7]

A transcript of a conversation that occurred early in the first year of their collaboration in California gets at the truth of their styles. During a strained moment in their discussion, Horkheimer said, "Our linguistic differences could be summed up as follows: in your work the consecrated appears in many passages, in mine what appears is the cozy [*das Gemuetliche*], the simplification. If we kept this in mind, we would do better." This is not a compliment. Divinatory language did not impress Horkheimer. And to deliver this sting he also had to hurt himself: however accurate the self-characterization, a cozy style for a man who readily compared himself to Husserl could not have been an ideal.[8] Horkheimer was drawing a boundary against his collaborator, not embracing his special talent. His remark was not a moment for things to begin to improve in a conversation, and indeed Horkheimer went on to attack Adorno's style with certainly the most damning sociological epithet of the Hitler era:

Adorno's language—he continued—was based on analogies and thus bore the "form of petty-bourgeois thought, that something always means something."[9] Adorno retaliated, expressing in a nutshell what undoubtedly many have sensed—if not explicitly—as what does distinguish their styles: "I would object to your writing that it has an element that conspires with the *status quo*. Your writing is beneath the experiences that you want to communicate, my writing is above what I am able to communicate."[10]

Just from the few lines quoted from *Dialectic of Enlightenment* by Habermas, it is obviously the latter form of writing that prevails in the lead essay as a whole. This is not, however, reason to reverse Habermas's claim and argue that the lead essay—or the book—is exclusively Adorno's work. What Habermas, for reasons yet to be discussed, does not want to consider is that the book really was, as the authors themselves repeatedly claimed, an act of collaboration. Though the construction of the book shows Adorno's hand at every turn, it is far from unalloyed Adorno. Something has been mixed in. The lead essay, for example, by beginning with a quote from Francis Bacon, shows Horkheimer's propensity for the history of ideas, which runs throughout the essay. But even the Odysseus essay, which many—Habermas included—have taken to be exclusively Adorno's work, at points shows what Horkheimer called his simplifying style. It relaxes Adorno's grip and lets one catch one's breath before being swallowed up by the next line. There is also an occasional glibness that otherwise never occurs in Adorno's own writings. The book is throughout a hybrid.

Habermas and *Dialectic of Enlightenment*

Habermas's "Postscript" is an important key to the current situation of *Dialectic of Enlightenment* in Germany. He insists that it is necessary to intervene to save the great work from the very dialectic of progress as regression that the text analyzes. The book is threatened by its own success: students have become possessive of it, and this possessiveness runs contrary to its truth: "its radical character threatens to disappear." For the good of the book it is necessary to work against the "falsely possessive relation to the penetrating truths of *Dialectic of Enlightenment*."[11] However, the analysis of the cunning of reason presented by *Dialectic of Enlightenment* knows more about Habermas than does Habermas about the book: the opening gestures of his essay mimic those of his opponent in order to be in a better position to defeat him. Yet Habermas's ruse is badly staged. If he had been Odysseus escaping from Polyphemous's cave, he would have ridden on top of the sheep, and that would have done it for Western civilization. His efforts to feign the book's salvation while condemning it make one rub one's eyes as one reads. Habermas's critique of possessiveness goes no farther than awarding "The Concept of Enlightenment" to Horkheimer: "In it, Horkheimer developed the basic ideas of a critique of enlightenment that today is on everyone's lips."[12] As for that radical character and those penetrating truths in need of refuge, none are discovered. On the contrary, for Habermas the book is a monstrosity, a Nietzschean attack on reason that claims enlightenment is irrevocably destructive: "It is no longer Marx, but Nietzsche who points the way. It is no longer a theory of society saturated with history, but a radical critique of reason denouncing the union of reason and domination."[13] It is a critique mired in the aporia of being unable to account for the grounds of its own criticism: "If enlightenment is caught up in an unstoppable process of self-destruction, where then would such a critique, which made this diagnosis, have a right to such a diagnosis?"[14]

To dismiss a thought on the basis of insufficient "right" is a meager hermeneutic, whose picket-fence mentality betrays its limitations in its simplified understanding of Nietzsche. But, in any case, the "radical critique of reason" cited by Habermas is not in any way Adorno's position. He never considered the self-destructiveness of enlightenment a necessity. On the contrary, this necessity is, in the strongest sense, an illusion, which is not to say that this illusion is without consequence. How to break this illusion is the key problem of the whole of Adorno's philosophy. But, if Habermas's interpretation is correct, how did Horkheimer—whom Habermas considers a man of reason—get involved in such an irrational project? According to Habermas, Horkheimer's participation was the result of being isolated with Adorno in California. In these conditions an otherwise reasonable interdisciplinary scholar fell to dark thoughts:

The end of the journal,[15] his extraction from the interdisciplinary context of the Institute and the beginning of an exclusive relation to Adorno: these are the circumstances that signal both the final break from an offensive, materialist theory of society directed towards change and withdrawal into speculation—a transition to a deeply pessimistic, wait-and-see philosophy of history aimed at making it through the winter.[16]

Overlooking for a moment the theoretical aspects of this criticism, it is worth responding to the recurring *idée reçue* of Adorno the pessimist that underlies this description of a good-natured, progressive materialist tangled in the web of a speculative mind's depressiveness. Habermas's portrayal is a distortion. And the need for distortion can be read out of the criticism itself: The charge of pessimism betrays a narrow consciousness that characteristically associates the hazard of moroseness with "absorption in speculation," with slipping into that uncanny region where, when left to itself, thought seethes, coils, and uncoils. A rigidity vis-à-vis what is under the surface motivates Habermas's comment. The charge of pessimism is more pessimistic than the pessimism it claims to perceive.[17] Even pessimism is dialectical, and especially in Adorno's case the relentlessness of his life's work can hardly be attributed to a lack of hope for change, but only to the most naive optimism, which was continually transformed—by the refusal to compromise—into an instrument of cognition. This dialectic of pessimism was opaque to a whole group of people who worked with Adorno at the Institute for Social Research and who commented often on how strange it was that someone who wrote "like that," who worked with such intense seriousness, could at other times be so *albern* (silly, absurd). Without any further research, those who found this combination puzzling would be self-described "optimists."

Habermas's depiction of Horkheimer and Adorno is confuted by the same transcript discussed earlier. In it Horkheimer contrasts his own recurrent depression with Adorno's optimism, whose naïveté bothers him. The following conversation so fully characterizes the discussants that it deserves quoting at length:[18]

HORKHEIMER: . . . You never say anything about the positive object of negative theology, yet you leave no doubt that such a theology exists. . . .

ADORNO: . . . I have no secret doctrine. I believe, however, that I have an eye for picking up from things the reflection of a source of light that could not be the object of intentions and thoughts.

HORKHEIMER: Can one really do anything with these sorts of ideas? My difficulty is that I always get exactly as far as we have gotten today, that is, as far as objective despair. . . .

ADORNO: What gives knowledge the stamp of authenticity is the reflection of possibility. This is what my fundamental philosophical experience is as well as the origin of your critical energy. . . . I believe that there is a certain sort of concrete insight [*Erkenntnis*] with a force that—even in its particularity—contains the possibility of the whole. The fragmentary concrete. [Adorno gives an instance of what he means.][19]

HORKHEIMER: You have a pundit's eye for everything. . . .

ADORNO: . . . My comment [the example of the fragmentary concrete] has been criticized as naive. Is not this criticism already an admission that one no longer believes in happiness? Is not this naïveté a higher form of knowledge than the unnaive knowledge of analysis?

HORKHEIMER: I have not given up the claim to happiness, but I do not believe in happiness. Whoever really believes in happiness is in the worst sense naive.

ADORNO: We must be at once more naive and much less naive.[20]

"Look What I've Got for You"

Why would Habermas want to manipulate the exclusive attribution of a work he thoroughly dislikes to the author he seems to prefer?[21] By ascribing the heart of the book to Horkheimer and then showing that the book itself is an aberration in the life of a once reasonable man, Habermas can arrange for Horkheimer to disown the work in reason's name. Habermas is not concerned then with possessiveness versus truth; rather, he wants to knock the book out of the hands of those previously mentioned students. The maneuvering here is part of an ongoing struggle in Germany between the heir apparent of the Institute for Social Research and its most important figure. The relative forces in this struggle are currently not in doubt. In Frankfurt Adorno is virtually forgotten.[22] And, as Habermas has become more powerful, he has become increasingly confident in making implausible claims about Adorno. His assertion, for example, that *Dialectic of Enlightenment* is a Nietzschean repudiation of reason runs up against the fact that the book is throughout explicitly concerned with the recuperation of reason. The preface to the book states as its intention the conceptualization of a "positive concept of enlightenment."[23] To reconcile this repeatedly stated aim of the book with his own thesis, and after having already claimed that the book is fundamentally an attack on reason, Habermas abruptly throws in that Horkheimer wrote the good lines, Adorno the bad:

> In the text . . . the points of reference for this position [the recuperation of enlightenment] can only be found in those chapters that betray Horkheimer's hand. I mean that the insistence on an almost eschatologically potentiated power of theory; the belief in an antiauthoritarian tendency in enlightenment; and finally, the conjuring of a self-transcendent enlightenment. Other passages, which I would attribute rather to Adorno, stand in cross contradiction to these positions.[24]

If there is anything stylistically obvious, it is that the phrase "cross contradiction" makes a noticeably big lump on the page. Even if one suspected that every explicit argument for reason in the volume was from Horkheimer's hand, it would only be necessary to open up to any page of Adorno's many other works to realize that this is mistaken. Here is a remark from a lecture course entitled "The Philosophy of History"— a course important in this context because in it Adorno explains many of the central ideas of *Dialectic of Enlightenment:* "Whether history has meaning, depends on whether humanity is able to constitute itself as humanity; whether humanity achieves this or not will depend on whether reason—as a force of the domination of nature—is able to gain control of itself, to reflect on itself."[25] The concepts of humanity and reason are identical here, and there is no question where Adorno stands on the matter. He is pursuing a critique of reason by way of reason. How this is possible is not obvious; if it were, it would not have occupied all of Adorno's life. But Habermas missed the point. Adorno, he insists, became entangled in a radical denunciation of reason that could not ground itself. Realizing this, the best Adorno could do was to ignore the contradiction. This was possible in Adorno's case because he could distract himself with art: Adorno "showed greater equanimity [than Horkheimer] towards the *aporia* of the self-referential critique of reason because he could bring another motif into play. . . . The aesthetic experience of modern art had opened itself up to him as an *independent* source of insight."[26]

Just under the surface of Habermas's misleading description of Adorno's relation to modern art is Habermas's pride that modern art has not opened itself up to him. This comment fits tightly with other remarks in the "Postscript." His suspicion of speculation is of a part with a broader disdain for any objectification of the imagination. He draws a line this side of a sphere that gains its truth by way of non-communication, by resistance. In its wooden response to the ambiguous, the philosophy of communicative action would score poorly on several scales of the *Authoritarian Personality*. Habermas styles himself the keeper of reason's flame, but, in his relation to the aesthetic, more evident is reason's fury.

Reason, Aesthetics, and Enlightenment

The division between reason and the aesthetic, which Habermas seeks to establish in Adorno's work, is a division drawn and insisted upon by Habermas, not by Adorno. Paradoxically, by insisting on this division Habermas separates himself from the Enlightenment tradition. For throughout the German Enlightenment, and especially since Kant, the defense of reason has been conceived not just as inseparable from but ultimately as dependent on the aesthetic. *Dialectic of Enlightenment*—and Adorno's work as a whole—is the modern successor of this tradition. Showing just how tightly bound to this tradition Adorno's work is will help counter Habermas's interpretation of Adorno as the enemy of enlightenment. This is best approached from the perspective of the problem of the dialectic of enlightenment as conceived by Adorno.

In the "Introduction" to *Dialectic of Enlightenment* the authors present the familiar figure of this dialectic: "The fallen nature of man today cannot be separated from social progress."[27] Adorno's writings and lectures are filled with variations on this idea. In a lecture, for example, he stated: "Precisely in that freedom represses nature, freedom falls back into mere nature."[28] In these comments "social progress" and "freedom" are synonymous with reason or human spontaneity as domination, progress in the control of nature results in regression to nature. The dialectic of reason is a dialectic of natural history, of history progressively embedded in a fallen nature from which it seeks to escape. This idea has been the object of a long reflection in the West since the biblical conception of the relation of self-assertion and disaster, of the mastery of nature and regression to it as labor and death. In Kant this dialectic of enlightenment is formulated in epistemological terms: "The paradox of knowledge is that the more articulate and objective it becomes, the more it covers over and obscures reality as it is in-itself. The same human imagination which generates appearance casts an impenetrable veil over being itself. As the end product of the cognitive process, the phenomenal object stands as a permanent barrier before the thing-in-itself."[29] Knowledge is the process of becoming embedded in nature, for Kant a nexus of gapless necessity. His epistemology was itself the result of the effort to recuperate reason from empiricism and the reduction of reason to nature. Yet the Kantian critique of empiricism resulted in the delimitation of experience to the empirical, which is functional in the system of the Kantian *felix culpa* because, as an epistemological equivalent of the biblical "through a glass darkly," the obscurity of what is beyond inspires a longing for it. And thus this obscurity was for Kant a rational goad to the course of infinite self-perfection. At the same time, however, the radicalness of this epistemology threatened to darken the glass altogether, challenging the recuperation of reason. Reason, by its own concept, must be realizable. However, experience limited to the empirical is unable to instantiate the possibility of this realization. The third critique is a necessity of the project of the recuperation of reason, because in the harmony of the mental faculties the judgment of taste is the perception of the possibility of the realization of reason. Aesthetic experience is the "as if" perception that the world exists for us, giving assurance that reason can be realized, but without threatening the ethical rigor of the Kantian system by bringing this goal within grasp. It is important to have in mind—in terms of the tradition of thought in which Adorno stands—that here, as aesthetics becomes the key to the recuperation of reason, this form of judgment is not separate from reason, but is the play of reason itself.

Kant did not foresee that writing the third critique, rather than simply completing the system, would ultimately draw the other two critiques into its own orbit as a sort of second Copernican turn. Yet Schiller's *Letters on Aesthetic Education*, the next major aesthetics, was conceived from the start with the idea of the dependence of reason on the aesthetic. And this aesthetics is a pivotal point between Kant and Adorno. As will be immediately evident to those already familiar with Adorno's work—and as will be elucidated later for those who are not—every element of Adorno's analysis of the dialectic of enlightenment and its relation to aesthetics has its precedent in Schiller's aesthetics, beginning with the natural historical figure of the dialectic of enlightenment itself. As Schiller writes, "We disown nature in its rightful sphere only to experience its tyranny in the sphere of morality, and by resisting the impact nature makes upon our senses, we receive from it our principles."[30] Reason, the principle of unity, excludes what is other than itself—nature—and thus regresses to nature. The measure of the failure of the development of reason is that it is sacrificial: "It will always argue a still defective education if the moral character is able to assert itself only by sacrificing the natural."[31] One result of this faulty development is that society has not brought about sociality, but egotism: "In the very lap of the most exquisitely developed social life egotism has founded its system, and without ever acquiring therefrom a heart that is truly sociable."[32] Though it might be hoped that egotism would at least be matched by fearless individuality, the opposite is the case. This egotism is conformist: "The fetters of the physical tighten ever more alarmingly, so that fear of losing what we have stifles even the most burning impulse towards improvement, and the maxim of passive obedience passes for the supreme wisdom."[33] Whereas Schiller took sacrifice to be the measure of regression, in *Dialectic of Enlightenment* sacrifice itself is the form of progress as regression. And, whereas Schiller thought that egotism becomes conformity as a result of a fear of a loss of ease, for Adorno self-assertion as self-renunciation is the route by which the self adapts to the status quo.

Odysseus or Reason and Aesthetics

Schiller took the side of reason against reason, intending to counter the dialectic of enlightenment by way of aesthetics. Aesthetic semblance, which he conceived in terms of Kant's free play of reason, is to recuperate reason. To restore those narrowed by the dialectic of enlightenment, Schiller writes that it is necessary to "surround them, wherever you meet them, with noble, great and ingenious forms and encompass them about with the symbols of excellence, until sem-

blance conquers actuality, and art triumphs over nature."[34] Echoing
Schiller, Adorno wrote in his earliest aesthetics that the problem of art
is "to change the world by the strength of an image."[35] Adorno's writings follow Schiller in the specific sense of conceiving the solution to
the dialectic of enlightenment, the realization of reason, as dependent
on aesthetic semblance. Just as for Schiller the aesthetic is the play of
reason, so Adorno conceives of reason as inextricable from art. In
"Odysseus or Myth and Enlightenment" the relation of the two is developed programmatically, and their inextricability could not be more
evident: the essay is the study of an art work whose protagonist, in his
struggle against myth, is the model of the origin of reason. The inner
process of the *Odyssey* is, literally, the process of reason. Odysseus's
struggle against mythical powers in the achievement of self-identity
becomes the order of the epic's self-identity, its organization of the
mythical legends into a whole.[36] The fate of reason, however, differs
in the two cases: in the former, reason regresses; in Odysseus's struggle
against myth, it is myth that prevails: "the inexorable force that he
[Odysseus] commands, ironically triumphs in that he himself returns
home an inexorable force, the judge and avenger of the legacy of the
powers from which he escaped."[37] On the level of the epic, however,
this process becomes the production of semblance by a caesura in the
text: "by virtue of this caesura the semblance of freedom lights up,
which ever since civilization has not succeeded in extinguishing."[38]

Adorno's essay is thus constructed on several levels at once: One
level concerns the origin of reason that, on another level, becomes the
structure of the epic. But there is a third level, one that Habermas disregards. He claims that those essays of *Dialectic of Enlightenment* in
which Adorno predominates—such as the Odysseus essay—do not
have comments on the need to recuperate reason. Here Habermas is
right. Such statements cannot be found in the Odysseus essay. But to
suppose that the point of the essay is not the recuperation of reason
would be like claiming that Hegel is only dialectical when he talks
about dialectics. Habermas ignores that the Odysseus essay is—as it is
titled—an "excursus," and specifically in the sense that it pursues in
detail the "positive concept of enlightenment" developed in "The
Concept of Enlightenment." This positive concept of knowledge is
one that would no longer be the domination of nature, but the dissolution of domination and thus of natural history.[39] The essay does not
talk about the recuperation of reason, but aims at the recovery of a

content (the previously mentioned caesura) that is aesthetic—a content to which reason is essential and without which reason is devoid of reason. Just how Adorno conceived of this aesthetic caesura, how it reformulates the recuperation of reason through the relation of reason and aesthetics, is what now needs elucidation. But to do so first requires a discussion of his theory of the relation of sacrifice and reason in the Odysseus essay.

Cunning, Sacrifice, and the Origin of Reason

In the collected transcripts of the discussions between Horkheimer and Adorno, Adorno's first mention of the intention that would direct the writing of "Odysseus or Myth and Enlightenment" actually refers to Oedipus rather than Odysseus: "There is a mythical category, which one would need to analyze carefully: cunning. Humanity pulls itself free of nature through cunning. Oedipus eliminates the puzzle of the sphinx by a trick, he does not actually solve it.[40] This is a proposal to study the primal history of subjectivity (*Urgeschichte der Subjektivitaet*), the origin of the intellect by which a physically overwhelming force is outwitted. Adorno ultimately focused this study on Odysseus rather than Oedipus because, while both are classical figures of heroic intellect, Homer stands on the border of Western civilization between history and prehistory in a way that Sophocles does not. When Adorno planned this study of Odysseus he had already developed the rudiments of a philosophy of the history of cunning in his book on *Kierkegaard* (1933). But his comment to Horkheimer points back to the origins of both the Kierkegaard study and the Odysseus essay. A reconstruction of the origin of Adorno's insight into the form of cunning will help explain why he conceived it as the cipher through which progress becomes regression. Horkheimer, in reply to Adorno, recognized that the basis of Adorno's project was a critical transformation of Hegel: "In Swabian dialect 'thinking' and 'cunning' are the same word. If one holds to this Swabian motif, then Hegel's cunning of reason acquires a whole new interpretation. Or is perhaps that which Hegel calls reason nothing else than cunning?"[41]

As often in the transcripts, Horkheimer acts primarily as a sounding board, announcing as discoveries and extrapolations what are actually fundamental to Adorno's thought in the first place. Adorno's project is unthinkable except as a critical transformation of Hegel's doctrine of the ruse of reason, which Hegel condensed most succinctly in the *Encyclopedia* when he wrote that "reason is as powerful as it is cunning."[42] This doctrine of the cunning of reason was Hegel's solution to history. He knew better than most that history "forms a picture of most fearful aspect and excites the profoundest emotions and the most hopeless sadness." Yet, when this vision compelled him to ask "to what principle, to what final purpose, have these monstrous sacrifices been offered?" his answer took the form of a justification of these sacrifices. The principle to which these sacrifices are made is unity: the self-conscious unity of spirit with itself. The creation of this unity is a perpetual act of cunning. The developing whole achieves higher levels of self-consciousness by way of its unwitting elements. World-historical individuals and nations pursue immediate passions and interests, but in this pursuit unknowingly fulfill the aims of reason. In the moment of this realization their life comes to an end:

> Once their objective is attained, they fall off like empty hulls from the kernel. They die like Alexander, they are murdered like Caesar, transported to Saint Helena like Napoleon. . . . They were fortunate in being the agents of a purpose which constituted a step in the progress of the Universal Spirit. But as individuals . . . they were not what is commonly called happy, nor did they want to be.[43]

The irony of this description is that, whereas the Hegelian spirit is modeled on individuality, here the process of the realization of spirit, the living individual, is supererogatory. This amounts to the sublimation of the "monstrous sacrifices" of history in the apotheosis of the progress of spirit. Divested of this theodicean veneer, however, Hegel's theory of the cunning of history became Adorno's fundamental insight into the dialectic of enlightenment: the unity of the self is the work of a sacrificial cunning. Just as Adorno argued in his first formulation of the dialectic of enlightenment that the Kierkegaardian dialectic of the self is a sacrificial process that is effectively the Hegelian dialectic turned inward, in the first excursus of *Dialectic of Enlightenment* he shows that the movement of Odysseus toward self-unity is a movement of self-sacrifice. To preserve himself—whether in his encounter with Polyphemus, Circe, or the Sirens—Odysseus must at every point renounce himself. Cunning is control through sacrifice, and progress is regression because the form of progress is sacrificial.

Odysseus is a small-scale model of the developing whole of world spirit.

On the basis of this insight Adorno reconstructed the primal history of subjectivity. Cunning originates in sacrifice. Odysseus's cunning escape from mythical powers has its paradigm in the deceptiveness of mythical sacrifice, which in every instance aims to exchange as equivalents something less valuable for what is more valuable: the hecatombs exchanged for victory in war. Adorno shows that the overturning of sacrifice, and the movement toward the development of cunning inheres in the dialectic of sacrifice. In carrying out the deception, the supplicated deities are at the same time overthrown: "All human acts of sacrifice, methodically carried out, deceive the god to whom they are offered: they subordinate him to the primacy of human purposes and dissolve his power."[44] Cunning develops as progress in sacrificial substitution. The power to substitute an ox for a human sacrifice is no different from the power of the employer to substitute the labor of others for the employer's own. "The Concept of Enlightenment" develops this theory of progress through sacrificial substitution to explain the development of discursive logic as a form implicit in mythical sacrifice: "Substitution in the course of sacrifice marks a step toward discursive logic. Even though the hind offered up for the daughter, and the lamb for the first-born, still had to have specific qualities, they already represented the species. . . . Substitutability reverses into universal fungibility."[45] The unity of knowledge sought by physics is the epitome of the ruse of reason in that this unity is the result of the sacrificial abstraction of the particularity of the world as a whole. The pivotal point at which myth becomes enlightenment and enlightenment becomes myth is sacrifice, and the transition from myth to enlightenment is progress in the power of substitutability. Whereas "The Concept of Enlightenment" follows out this dialectic particularly in regard to logic and the sciences, "Odysseus or Myth and Enlightenment" explicates it with regard to the history of the self. The unity of the self originates in the internalization of sacrifice as renunciation. Civilization begins with the sacrifice of the self to the self and the power of the self develops as its power of renunciation: "The history of civilization is the history of the introversion of sacrifice. In other words, it is the history of renunciation."[46] The actual form of Odysseus's cunning, whether with Polyphemus or Circe, is his ability to dominate himself, that is, to renounce himself in the service of his own self-preservation. Cunning resists nature qua myth, but in its sac-rificial order it becomes myth.

Reversal of Domination

Dialectic of Enlightenment thus presents the origin of reason in sacrifi-cial cunning, and, because progress, in the form of domination, is sac-rificial, this dialectic recreates the mythical world of sacrifice from which it wanted to escape. If this were as far as Horkheimer and Adorno went in their study, however, it would still go beyond Haber-mas's claim that *Dialectic of Enlightenment* is "a radical critique of rea-son denouncing the union of reason and domination."[47] Drawing a boundary always implicitly crosses that boundary. Insight into this Hegelian dialectic, however, is as anathema to Habermas as it is a con-stant source of Adorno's reflection throughout the Odysseus essay. One variant of this dialectic takes shape as the central concern of the Odysseus essay with the possibility of domination transcending domi-nation—an idea that at every point and in the most paradoxical ways constantly seems to threaten to return Adorno's work to theodicy. The modern conception of the reversal of mediation, of course, was neither Hegel's nor Adorno's but one of the fundamental events in the mod-ern history of the concept of the relation of technique and nature in German thought.[48] Beginning in the eighteenth century, with the reintroduction of Aristotle's concept of nature, the long predominant idea of the antithesis of technique and nature was rejected for the idea that technique can recreate nature. This is fundamental to Kant's aes-thetics: The imagination "is very mighty when it creates, as it were, another nature out of the material that actual nature gives it."[49] Simi-larly in Schiller, who was the first in German letters unequivocally to take the side of the liberation of technique in art, one reads, "It is, then, not just poetic license but philosophical truth when we call beauty our second creatress."[50] It would be possible to follow this idea of the rejection of the antithesis of nature and technique throughout modern German thought and show its centrality to Marx and social-ism as well as how this idea developed as a possible solution to natural history. History is not necessarily natural history if history can—in some fashion—transform nature as the production of a second nature. In Adorno's work the possibility of an end to the dialectic of enlightenment depends precisely on the production of a second nature. Adorno makes this plain in a discussion of the division of labor and the alienation that is its result: "It is not the goal of a true society to destroy the division of labor and to revoke alienation, but rather to perfect the division of labor and thereby mollify suffering. The great philosophers have all known perfectly well that through alienation, through this return of the subject to itself by way of the social division of labor, an infinite amount of good has accrued to humanity."[51] Every formulation in the first excursus culminates in terms of this idea. Thus: "Marriage is indeed part of the mythical bedrock of civilization. But its mythical hardness and fixity emerges from myth like a small island from the infinite sea."[52] Or, again, property: "Although the fixed order of property, which is an aspect of settledness, is the basis of alienation from which all homesickness and all longing for a lost primordial condition originates, it is nevertheless at the same time only by way of settledness and fixed property that the concept of homeland develops."[53]

These reversals of marriage and property are only instances of the basic issue of the possible reversal of mediation with which *Dialectic of Enlightenment* is concerned: the reversal of subjectivity from the domination to the liberation of nature. Given Adorno's concept of domination as sacrifice, this reversal is necessarily formulated in theodicean, almost Christological terms of the overcoming of sacrifice through sacrifice: "Odysseus is at the same time a sacrifice for the abrogation of sacrifice. His masterful renunciation, as a struggle against myth, stands in for a society that no longer demands renunciation and domination: one that masters itself, not in order to coerce itself and others, but for reconciliation."[54] Self-sacrifice goes beyond itself because the self that is the internalization of sacrifice becomes the critique of sacrifice. The internalization of sacrifice is the establishment of the principle of identity as the principle of the self. This self-identical self can no longer be sacrificed in that, as self-identical, it is inimitable and therefore cannot be substituted: "The self is precisely the human being to whom the magical power of substitution is no longer attributed. The establishment of the self severs that fluctuating unity with nature that the sacrifice of the self claimed to achieve."[55] The development of the principle of self-identity involves not only the rejection of human sacrifice but the origin of the standard for the critique of all sacrifice. Cunning emerges from sacrifice as reason, the idea of the free unity of

the general and the particular, in other words the principle of reconciliation: "Reason means, according to its own form, something like
the idea of the reconciliation of the universal and the particular."[56]

Cunning goes beyond the sacrifice from which it emerged and becomes implicitly the critique of sacrifice. The "positive concept of enlightenment" elucidated in "The Concept of Enlightenment" is therefore not an invention of the essay but the dialectical development of
the new out of the old: as the principle of identity, reason is in its origins the critique of the vitiation of the particular by the whole. This
potential of reason, however, is limited by what made it possible: "The
enmity of the self to sacrifice involved self-sacrifice because the price
of this enmity was the denial of nature in men for the sake of domination over extra-human nature and over other men."[57] The inimitable
self is beyond human sacrifice, but in the achievement of this non-sub-
stitutability the self becomes totally other than nature and forfeits its
telos: "In the instant in which men sever the consciousness of themselves as nature, all of the purposes for which they struggle to preserve
themselves, social progress, the intensification of material and intellectual forces, indeed consciousness itself, are vitiated."[58] The principle
of identity becomes the autarchic reduction of the world to itself in order to control it. This nexus of identity becomes a second nature that
appears as a context of absolute determinacy as all-encompassing as
the nature that reason hoped to master. If freedom is embedded in nature by its distance from nature, in memory of itself as nature it would
escape nature as a web of total determinacy: "Precisely reason that no
longer takes itself to be absolute, that recognizes itself as nature and no
longer as something absolutely opposed to nature, precisely this reason that is conscious of itself as nature, ceases to be mere nature."[59]
The intention of the Odysseus essay—itself an act of organization and
control—is the recovery of the telos of reason through memory of nature and is therefore the most emphatic effort of reason conceivable.

The Cunning of Art and Memory of Nature

It is naive to say so, but there is no art without reason, e.g., no symphony orchestra without the invention of that ingenious axle that allows the fluttering articulation of one or several keys on woodwinds;[60]
Francis Bacon throws paint onto his canvases, but nothing would
appear in these splashes without the constructive technique that is

brought to bear on them; anti-intellectualism characterizes more poets manqués than otherwise. And there would be no *Odyssey* without the mind of Odysseus: Adorno writes, "the venerable cosmos of the Homeric world, charged with meaning, reveals itself as the work of ordering reason."[61] The idea that art is "independent" from reason must be Habermas's own, because it cannot be found anywhere in Adorno. Adorno's aesthetics are a continuous reflection on the idea of the possible reversal of domination into liberation. The *Odyssey* is composed of mythical legends as an epic in which novelistic elements begin to appear, but this work of organization is not conjuration: "What epic and novel in fact have in common" is "domination and exploitation."[62] The Odysseus essay takes the side of this domination. And this defense of one of the first literary art works of the West develops as an affirmative study of the emergence of the novel—of prosaic narration—in opposition to mythical chant and legend.

Adorno develops his parti pris for the *Odyssey* as novel vis-à-vis various critics whom he names, but importantly also vis-à-vis one who goes unnamed: Benjamin, and the *voelkish* organicism of his appreciation of the story form in opposition to the novel in "The Storyteller." In that essay Benjamin criticizes the novel by deriving from its dependence on the printing press the idea of a narrative form cut off from living speech. This new form, Benjamin claims, is occupied exclusively with the perplexity of the isolated individual and the incommensurability of the protagonist's experience. Every novel ends with the question of the meaning of life; and the only form of hope it offers is memory. The story form is opposed to all this: it is a work of living speech, a craft work of social solidarity; it is passed on from hand to hand, bearing the traces of all those who have held it; contrary to the perplexity of the novel's protagonist, the story form is sedimented wisdom and advice for living, for the linking together of one story with the next. A work of the people, it is part of the earth: the story form "resembles the seeds of grain which have lain for centuries . . . and retained their germinative power, to this day."[63] This power is the ability to counter myth—the antagonistic relation of nature and humanity—by cunning. "The wisest thing . . . is to meet the forces of the mythical world with cunning and with high spirits." The story form learned this lesson from the archetypal storyteller, who, as Benjamin writes, pointed the way to the "happily ever after" because he was a teller of fairy tales: "The first true storyteller is, and will continue to be, the teller of fairy tales."[64]

In the Odysseus essay Adorno takes issue not only with Benjamin's undialectical theory of cunning—for Adorno, cunning is itself mythical—but, most insistently, he takes issue with Benjamin in the last line of the Odysseus essay. For Adorno, the "happily ever after" is not the work of the story, but of the novel: "Only by first becoming a novel does the epic become a fairy tale." This idea hinges on Adorno's theory of sacrifice. In art, domination is able to become liberation, the truth of the whole, because the same process of the domination of nature that society carries out occurs within the art work; the same sacrificial act of reason is carried out by art through its construction. The dialectic of enlightenment is the inner process of the art work, and explicitly so in the Odysseus essay in which Odysseus appears as the allegorical figure of this process. However, whereas the sacrifices required by self-preservative reason in the actual domination of nature are silenced by the semblance of necessity woven by the principle of identity, art mourns the sacrifices it carries out. Art undoes its self-identity by the same process through which it establishes its self-identity. This is the form of art's cunning: "Homer's story of Penelope, who every evening pulls apart what she wove during the day, is an unconscious allegory of art: what the cunning woman does to her artifacts is what art actually does to itself. Ever since Homer's poem, this episode is not what it is easily mistaken to be, an addition or vestige, but rather a constitutive category of art: through this category art absorbs the impossibility of the identity of the one and the many as an element of its unity. Art works, no less than reason, have their form of cunning."[65] Art works take themselves apart as they put themselves together, and as they do so the progressive Hegelian dialectic is brought to a standstill in a moment of expression. Art becomes memory of nature in the mourning of its caesuras. This theory is presented in Adorno's *Aesthetic Theory;* the Odysseus essay is the presentation of the experience of this caesura: after Odysseus's victory over the suitors, Telemachus—in the name of civilization—has the women who regressed to prostitution in his father's absence hung. Homer describes how their feet kicked, but "not for long." Adorno continues: "But after the 'not for long' the inner flow of the narrative comes to a halt. The gesture of the narrator . . . is that of a question: Not for long? By

bringing the account to a halt, the gesture prevents the forgetting of
the condemned and reveals the unnameable eternal torture of the second in which the maids struggled against death."[66] This caesura is art
at its most cunning, a moment that Adorno's critics would presumably cast as "pessimistic." For Adorno, however, "by virtue of this
caesura the semblance of freedom lights up, which ever since civilization has not succeeded in extinguishing." In the possibility of remembering what has happened, the coldness and *impassibilité* of the novel's
narration is transmuted as memory of nature. This memory has two
aspects: it contains not only what was undergone but the possibility of
the fairy tale's long ago and far away, which predicates the happily
ever after. In reflection on this dialectic at a standstill, the necessity—
pace Habermas—of the world's derring-do dissolves, and possibly enlightenment comes to terms as the consciousness of the futility of sacrifice. In this consciousness, reason may recover its telos. Here
Adorno, whose maxim was the Socratic impulse to lose arguments in
such a way as to convict the other side of its mistakenness, would want
Habermas to have the last word of his opponents' idea of enlightenment. Thus Habermas: "How can these two men of the Enlightenment (which they both remain) be so unappreciative of the rational
content of cultural modernity that all they perceive everywhere is a
binding of reason and domination?"[67]

Things Beyond Resemblance

Toilers of the world, disband! Old books are wrong. The world was
made on a Sunday.

—VLADIMIR NABOKOV

EVEN AFTER TRANSLATION INTO ENGLISH, T. W. Adorno's words
still seem to want to linger at least half in German, as if continuing to
long for something in the original that they cannot find in this language. They have good reason: acute and ancient differences in the intellectual experience that these two languages have undergone continually obliges philosophical translation at crucial juncture to choose
between meaningless fluency and the indecipherably meaningful.
This division in experience, however, must certainly not be imagined
as traveling down some central boundary, parsing carefully to the left
of German and to the right of English, but as shooting off along such
complex fault lines and in so many directions, carving the world up so
unexpectedly, that it is finally hard to say what lies on which side of
what line. Consider, for instance, *Philosophie der neuen Musik* and
other key works in Adorno's oeuvre such as *Dialectic of Enlightenment*
and *Minima Moralia*. By whatever degree of remoteness vulcanized
against English translation, these are solidly American writings. Indeed, in the years they were written—mostly the 1940s—they were
works of an American citizen, whose "complete and true signature"—Theodore [*sic*] Adorno—endorsed his Certificate of Naturalization on November 26, 1943.[1] If this seems to concoct a trick photo-

graph in which, under the pressure of emergency residence, a stubbornly monadic intelligence is seen forcibly posed up against a spec-
trally implausible red, white, and blue backdrop, no doubt to Adorno
himself his life in the United States did sometimes feel that way. But
even after his return to Germany the whole of his writings would be
marked by aspects of his American experience. This is certainly evident in all the works that were primarily completed here. *Dialectic
of Enlightenment* and *Minima Moralia,* for instance, are dense with
American realia: the hairstyles of film stars, the latchless close of re-
frigerator doors, and the pathless landscapes abutting the highway
system. And if on this continent the German inscription to the opening pages of *Philosophie der neuen Musik*—"Los Angeles, Kalifornien,
I. Juli 1948"—seems to tilt almost by its own inertia into English, the
statement of place and date may well have caused its first European
readers, as they took the book in hand, to query the haphazard course
by which this remote North American work had finally arrived in
Germany.

"I still hear . . ." and the Question of Music Appreciation

American experience is, indeed, at every point so central to the whole
of *Philosophie der neuen Musik*[2] that in lieu of it the work would have
taken an altogether different form. Yet the place of this American experience is more difficult to perceive in this volume than in any other
major work Adorno finished here. Hardly a single direct reference to
North America is to be found in its pages. Still, an eye aware of the
many subterraneous branchings of American experience through this
German work—and confident as well that demonstrating the pattern
of these branchings would provide an introduction to what may otherwise seem a remotely alien text—is initially restricted to directing
attention to the eccentric traces of these branchings. The most revealing are those of the fracture struck by the stamp of the work's own
moment. For the physiognomy of this moment is so characteristic
that, as *Philosophie der neuen Musik* is rotated angle by angle, the
works of other writers that were caught in the same temporal percus-
sion are refracted in it as if they can be read out of its surfaces equally
well. It is in this sense that one surface in particular shows itself etched
with a scene from *l'amérique profonde* circa 1947, and when turned

forward for examination, that surface serves incomparably to illuminate for a contemporary American readership what is homey in what might otherwise be taken for an opaquely obscure work of German aesthetics. The inscribed scene—it will be observed—gestures directly to matters of aesthetic doctrine, is preoccupied by questions of beauty, conformity, and the relation of art to nature, and is apparently fully conversant with Adorno's studies of jazz and the commodity fetish:

> Mentally, I found her to be a disgustingly conventional little girl. Sweet hot jazz, square dancing, gooey fudge sundaes, musicals, movie magazines and so forth—these were the obvious items in her list of beloved things. The Lord knows how many nickels I fed to the gorgeous music boxes that came with every meal we had! *I still hear* the nasal voices of those invisibles serenading her, people with names like Sammy and Jo and Eddy and Tony and Peggy and Guy and Patti and Rex, and sentimental song hits, all of them as similar to my ear as her various candies were to my palate.[3]

This is European Humbert Humbert's reverie on the difference between inner and outer as observed of an American girl to whom his, in some sense, physical longing is bound. He has much to contemplate in the mass market of Lolita's inner nation. On this page he begins to construe his observations of his girl companion and does so in homology to his thoughts on the external allure of a ravishing music box as it differs from those innards he begrudgingly nourishes: As girl is fed with gooey fudge sundae, so is machine with common coin and these bodies reciprocate in comparably nondescript kind, radiant of an inner life of which Humbert can no more discern what there is to listen to in the "disgustingly conventional" Lolita than he can find what there is to hear in the indifferently conventional jukebox songs that remain inert to his ear. Many layers of experience become available to readers at this point. But since the proximate cause here for the examination of this passage is the mysteries of music appreciation, focus must lodge with the protagonist's own condescending meditation on the fact that the jukebox presents its musical monism just to him, a European who happens to be preoccupied with whatever threatens to steal away the heart of the girl he has himself captured on a yearlong tour of American motel and highway life. And it is only to help magnify this puzzle of music appreciation that it makes sense to postulate how bewildered Humbert Humbert would have been if, made to live far beyond his own years and tricked into interests equally transcending his fixation, he somehow had to consider that now, fifty-some years later, the list of artists he cited as those same-sounding Sammy, Eddy, Patti, and Guy would have metamorphosed into such distinctly familiar, durable national landmarks that many contemporary readers can survey these dolmens and menhirs and call up the apposite surnames as a matter of confident second nature. The songs that sang just to Lolita, indeed, may occasionally still sing to thee. And who knows how many stalwarts of swing might want to butt in right this moment, however long after the fact, to explain to Lolita that if it is true, as Humbert reports, that she never bothered with the difference between sweet and hot jazz, these were once—and remain—causes to die for.

But, in spite of the urgencies of jazz enthusiasts, in spite even of the likes of a Nietzsche who claimed that a future that had just a fraction of his feeling for Wagner would be another world, in spite, finally, of Adorno's many claims throughout his oeuvre of the utter necessity of Schoenberg's compositions, the scene under discussion between girl and predator provides for any American readership the requisite approach to Adorno's *Philosophie der neuen Musik* because its ironic study of music appreciation casts such a heavy shadow across the credibility of any kind of devotion to music. This shadow is made to descend the moment Humbert Humbert conjures the simplest, most evident fact of musical experience, one that is nevertheless extraordinarily hard to isolate credibly. Here that fact can, however, for once be directly examined when one realizes that what this mismatched couple each heard in the music of the day, one dismissing it, the other entranced, was more alike than otherwise. The proof of which is this: in the passage cited, Humbert is writing his confessions decades after the event, yet the music that was indifferent to him earlier is as sealed in his fur covered ears as he himself is ensconced in prison, for he continues to hear the music distinctly in its several different voices: "*I still hear* the nasal voices of those invisibles serenading her." These voices are singing to the once aloof no less than they did to the once enthralled. And it must be some aspect of how this sound perdures that what Humbert in earlier years haughtily spurned as "sentimental song hits" has become the sentimental content of his own life. For note: he addresses elegiacally the voices that return to him when he goes to think of the girl he lost: *"I still hear . . ."*

In other words, Humbert Humbert is not only a fictional character but, like all flesh and blood, is as much obliged to find locked in his head the music that is put there as is anyone who has ever been followed home by a song—from who knows which store—that would not stop playing. For musical memory, as among the mind's preeminent powers of sensory reproduction, is involuntary in the highest degree. Its obliging dictum, fluently engaging rhythmically nodding head and gesturing limb, is the simplest: the more any music is heard, the more there is a need to hear it again whether from loud speaker or left hemisphere. Who knows what proportion of Americans now hear subsecond fragments of Christmas music through all four seasons in the unvoiced hummings that provide the waking day's rhythmical underwebbing of unremarked transitions. Even if musical memory amounted to nothing more than the rote concatenated knowledge of advertisement jingle by the self-proclaimed unmusical, this aptitude for commercial glue-all would rank in any other application of thought as a prodigious talent. Because musical memory is so profoundly and capaciously involuntary, it is also the most exactingly trainable form of human memory. Among the musically skilled this involuntariness is organized in such a fashion that, both hands on the piano in the midst of a labyrinthian twenty-minute recital of Olivier Messiaen, the pianist can only partially let himself know what he is doing until he rises from the bench to take some kind of credit for the genuine mystery of the accomplishment. Likewise, the ominous pride in being a music lover may be a complex object, but it may be nothing more than identification with the inhabiting irrefragability of rhythmical, vibrating memory in the ecstatic convergence of obedience and self-assertion. Such was certainly the spiritualized self-regard of Nazi battalions marching in striding chant through occupied French towns—while the beauty of those voices to this day remains unreconcilable in the ears of the formerly dominated. In an Alzheimer clinic a round of "Happy Birthday" will lift heads off of chests and cause even those lips to move whose voices do not know where to follow. Musical memory is a primordial reflex, often enough—and increasingly so—establishing in the nervous system the Pavlovian other that residually spans self and reflection with the elegiacal cloak of *"I still hear . . ."* regardless whether, beyond that sentiment, much if anything is being remembered. If there is truth to the philosopheme that *il faut aimer*—then above all *il faut aimer la musique*.

Imperious Taste and Inflicted Souvenir

Exotic Humbert Humbert's experience with swing, the return of the vacuous as the long lost, discredits the presumed primacy of taste over tune, as if tune serves only at the sovereign's pleasure and must withdraw when the master wearies. Discernments of taste are hardly at issue when sound is so narrowly inflicted to start with. In this regard, if asked why it is only swing he remembers, Humbert would have had to reply that that was all the jukebox was playing. Today the selection is by magnitudes more restricted in terms of the actual, drilled imposition of commercial music. What played nationwide in American restaurants in 1947 now plays ubiquitously—and on just one small part of the mechanism of reproduction—as part of a diversified MTV on 94 channels in 164 countries. It characterizes a situation that is at every turn difficult to take seriously because of the disproportion between the modest object consumed and the devices of its distribution. Displaying a bracelet of charms and skulls, the barely composed music—much of it dissociated ballad and erotically dramatized repetition—verges on the imaginatively neutral while the aggressive expansion of the music's economic organization is systematically predatory almost beyond imagining. Recently this single American brand of music—MTV—consolidated its European holdings by acquiring its only competitor in Germany for a people it pursued as "the world's second-largest television market in advertising revenue, behind the United States." The company announced its success by warning away possible challengers who might make a lunge on the bloody claim struck to a scrap of the perceptual functioning of teenagers: "Our intentions for the German market are long-term and permanent"—as if holding something clenched between locked teeth could never be grip enough.[4]

    Music's economic integration and particular vulnerability to commercial consolidation depend in part on the social functions that music has virtually always had as well as on those functions that emerged with the industrial development of techniques of mechanical and electronic reproduction. The latter have contributed to the commercial primacy of music among the arts not only in the sheer number of socioeconomic functions it was and still is now made to serve, but as the only art that performs functions that have become socially sine qua non. Neither movies nor—certainly—the plastic arts can possibly inculcate themselves as commercial necessities in the everyday structure of life on the scale of music, whether in the ease with which music's intensities of sound, feeling, and rhythmical order can be mobilized in the promise of expressive immediacy, accompanying presence, ecstatic transcendence, sexual assertion, devoted obedience, registered complaint; whether as regression in the service of the ego; whether as a dogmatic rhyming wisdom literature for the otherwise unadvised, as a carping-thumping motivational device for suppressing expression, or for cocooning and masking painfully disruptive psychological states.

Commercial music is truly the snake oil of adolescence, and, given the absurdity of what the bottle dispenses—the music itself—its broad application would be comic were it not meant to salve the most legitimate and urgent needs a person may have. The range of these urgencies, indeed, and the manner in which the music is internalized in response to them, indicate that commercial music has succeeded at arrogating to itself, as a simplified vehicle of identity, the inward transport of richly disguised, recently undomiciled Penates. This has occurred in an almost century-long process, now in sharp relief, of the manufacture of a globally generic youth, a fragment of a new division of labor predicated on permanently hobbled family patterns of individuation. In this regard the economic consulting firm that recently commented on the conditions for MTV's acquisition of an expanded advertising market proved genuinely knowing while passing a numb hand over a considerable swath of reality: "German media is evolving from a predominantly family-owned, fairly parochial market into a part of the global media marketplace." The outlook is good: "With an upgrade, this could be a really vibrant market."[5] There would be reason to join in this optimism if the music did not so substantially fail at providing what is so urgently sought in it—and if it did not colonize musical memory while depriving its listeners of actual musical experience.

The Universal Musical Prodigy

An internally directed "Did you hear that?" is implicit to all musical audition, and, if it were not, no amount of musical reminding, whether played on a violin or transmitted by radio, would ever amount to memory. This reproductive capacity is felt as an individual genius even in the falsetto rendition of an irritating tune nobody in the car, including the clowning adolescent yelling over his friends' voices, wants to hear. Yet the talent as such is as universal as the capacity for speech, and must be, since at some historical threshold it first tutored speech into existence.[6] Otherwise singing would not have the ability to tutor back the capacity for speech after cerebral accident has damaged it. Nor would each individual voice be shaped in the first place by lifting words off of adored lips and then—as naturally as if there were no other language in the world to speak—returning them again in recognition. All mental repetition may be essentially musical. Of all the senses, the organ of musical perception is—in the words of another age—"beyond question the most intricate and the most wonderful."[7] The eardrum is so acutely sensitive, even to slight variation in air pressure, that if the musculature of the neck provided sufficient cranial dexterity, rhythmical, minimal modifications in the altitude of the head would have permitted the invention of *Luftdruckmelodien* antedating Schoenberg's *Tonfarbenmelodien* by millennia.[8] The ear is so capably antipathetic to missing a note that it itself produces fundamental tones in spontaneous relation to upper range harmonics so that the sounds of baritone and double bass are factually audible even on radios—such as those built in the late 1930s—that transmit no frequencies below middle C. Aural differentiation is capable of distinguishing the simultaneous soundings of six, eight, and even twelve notes individually and of becoming so restless out of the desire for greater differentiation as to have prompted experiments with fifty-two-note octaves. The extent of this capacity for differentiation is unknown. But the necessity of reproducing what is heard—which can be an absolute power of musical discovery in the ability to follow the music where it most wants to go, in listening for what Adorno calls the *tendency of the material*—is so vulnerable to music that insistently goes nowhere that, trapped by the latter, the ear may be as little able to recognize the difference between twelve simultaneously sounding notes and the sounding of one note as it could disdainfully care less what difference this limitation could possibly make.

Sounding Allegiance and Musical Quality

The ear, in its capacity for musical audition, is now the most stupidified and exploited of the senses. It is only one measure of its abandonment of this capacity that, while the toe taps apace, critical studies focus credulously on a supposed primacy of verbal and visual culture. But this disregard should not prohibit recognizing in Humbert Humbert's experiences of music the involuntarily self-confirming allegiances of musical memory. Nor should it prohibit perceiving an implication of this involuntariness: that there is no necessary relation between these allegiances and the quality of the compositions. Emphasizing this discernment has been the primary motivation of this essay, not, though, with the expectation that arriving at its statement would transform all as with a wave of the wand, since, obviously, so much is not to be transformed with any kind of gesture: the tunes, for instance, that irremediably fill every ear are, if anything, soon to be more encompassing and louder. Still, the intention here of urging forward the shambling figure of musical quality, half cloaked as ever in the dubious attire of the aesthetic standards and absurdly empaneled contests of past centuries, may at least serve to cast a salutary and even expanding shadow over felt musical allegiances and interrupt, however momentarily, the ready insistence that life is to death what sweet is to hot. Even if in its implications the concept of musical quality is immediately a conundrum, it may at the same time initiate a starkly Dickensian meditation as to whether all those words and tunes, remembered with such autonomic self-certainty, are not somehow the wrong ones.

If even at this point in this essay, however, thoughts of this kind still cannot be contemplated, Humbert Humbert's musical experiences in the New World, in whatever way enscrolled across one surface of *Philosophie der neuen Musik*, have hardly contributed, in the work's North American introduction, to mollify an expectably balky readership. For the topic of Adorno's work is the central most difficult problem of music aesthetics: that of musical quality, in the sense of compositional right and wrong as it is known in the most intimate experience of any composer in deciding to set—or not set—one note next to another, and as compositional right and wrong determines musical quality insofar as compositional decision successfully, or unsuccessfully, lives from the potential import of any particular composition. *Philosophie der neuen Musik* ultimately means to respond to the demand that each composition makes: that its own import be known for what it is, or is not, and that anything less than this comprehension is less than listening. Musical quality then, as Adorno understood it, is finally a matter of knowledge. Indeed, for Adorno, music became new music in that moment when the entire development of Western music finally sought to shed its immediate sensuous sonority in favor of knowledge itself. *Philosophie der neuen Music*, as if in acknowledgment of music having cultivated the capacity for speech, wants to reciprocate by providing music with the capacity of the concept. In acknowledgment of this undertaking, Adorno has rightly been called the first philosopher since Pythagoras to have had something new to say about music.[9] The claim, however, settles for hyperbole when an even greater exaggeration would accelerate hyperbole directly into blunt fact: for, in all of history—Pythagoras included—Adorno is the only philosopher of world importance whose musicological expertise was in every regard of a caliber equal to his philosophical capacity; Nietzsche would by comparison be an amateur. If Adorno is not the only philosopher of music to have known what he was talking about, the *niveau* of musical comprehension in his writings now makes it seem that way. These are portentous estimations, no doubt, but it should be noticed that by its title alone *Philosophie der neuen Musik* itself makes an almost unsurpassable claim.

Unpublishable Manifesto

The new translation of the *Philosophie der neuen Musik* is preceded by two earlier versions in English. The more recent of the two was a musically knowledgeable and occasionally felicitous edition published as *Philosophy of Modern Music* in 1973, at a time when the vast corpus of Adorno's writings was otherwise still inaccessible to English readers.[10] The translation made a seminal work familiar to a generation of students. Over several decades it helped prompt extensive scholarship on

Adorno and thus indirectly motivated many other translations since made of Adorno's works, now amounting to almost all of his most important writings. But if increasing familiarity with Adorno's thought has necessarily been matched by comparable recognition of that translation's substantial and even prohibitive deficiencies, the decision to present a new translation of *Philosophie der neuen Musik* also gives occasion to recognize gratefully the important contribution *Philosophy of Modern Music* has made.

The translators of the 1973 edition could not have consulted or even known of another English translation made more than thirty years earlier. This was Adorno's own undertaking in 1941, the year he moved from New York City to Los Angeles. The manuscript from which he worked, then bearing the slightly variant title *Zur Philosophie der neuen Musik*, consisted of the Schoenberg portion of the volume, variously amended.[11] The English text had been solicited by the philosopher and editor Dagobert Runes for publication in the recently founded *Journal of Aesthetics and Art Criticism*. Adorno responded enthusiastically to the request. As a refugee needing to make his mark, he had urgently sought publication of his work in English and had in fact bitterly failed at this desideratum during his several years in New York.[12] This rejection of the translation, however, only marked the initial objections to *Philosophie der neuen Musik*. So much has been adduced against it over the years that speculation curious to discover those first editorial protestations could conclude without hesitation that, since then, they have doubtlessly been instantiated many times over. And if speculation, reviewing the dense expanse of objections lodged, became curious to account for the many varieties of animus the work has attracted, that puzzle would not last long either. For, whatever its substantial complexities, every reader who has vigorously taken up arms against *Philosophie der neuen Musik* has correctly understood that this is a work that has long been up in arms against the world. The challenges that it poses verge on the absolute. The reason, in other words, that it has so often been attacked is that it is itself so antagonistic. Its stark "for" and "against," originating in an age of revolutionary political struggle, means to leave no doubt: this is a manifesto.

This combative form can be followed right into the revisions that the tendentious initial essay underwent in 1948 when Adorno— tentatively in expectation of his own return to Germany—prepared it for publication there. He sharpened the structure of the text as if even a philosophy devoted to a second immediacy would tolerate nothing less than self-evidence. As any reader of the new edition will easily notice, the major event was the addition of the Stravinsky section. While that addition and the inclusion of a separate introduction deprived the Schoenberg essay of sole claim to a distinguished title, the earlier essay in return took pride of place in a manuscript now sufficiently enlarged to hold its own ground as an independently published volume. The main sections were titled in argot of the Paris Commune "advance" and "reaction," that is: as "Schoenberg and Progress" and "Stravinsky and Restoration." These alternatives define a drastic historical conflict conceived not as one conflict among many but as *the* conflict, the one in which all other antagonisms in the contemporary situation of music were immersed and on which their solution depended. This is a critical epistemology that seeks to polarize the extremes of a situation and draw the terms of the conflict as tautly and distinctly as possible. Since it conceives no other way out than through, it measures the knowing self by its capacity to tolerate the tension of the reality grasped, to look it directly in the eye. Unflinchingly confident that it alone was the match for its historical moment, the title of the volume was amended minutely but decisively: deleting the *Zur*—the "On the"—from *Philosophie der neuen Musik* transformed the work's claim of being one contribution to the topic at hand into an announcement of being the philosophical voice of the topic itself.

This uncompromising manifesto, however, while claiming to grasp the musical landscape whole, is unaccompanied by any plans to occupy the mapped terrain with forces of its own. If prepared to challenge and lead the way, it makes no provision at all for rank and file. Unlike the aesthetic manifestos of expressionists, dadaists, and futurists, which in the early decades of the century imitated political aspirations with the verisimilitude of a hand sketching a crowd surging forward, the political image traced by *Philosophie der neuen Musik* is of a Europe in the decade following the signing of the Hitler-Stalin pact, shattered and devoid of any conceivable revolutionary cohort. The boulevards and public squares had only just been cleared of masses marching in costumed, patterned demonstration of a solidarity of will that, in the years since it had forced Adorno to flee, was responsible for acts that would be the first in history to require laws prohibiting the denial of their occurrence. The problem Adorno faced in his music-theoretical manifesto was hardly the mobilization of individuals in collective initiative; rather, he sought to understand the compulsion to which an entire nation had capitulated—a nation that in living memory had been marked by a distinctness of social structures, self, place, language, and custom to which it would be difficult to find adequate American parallels—and to conceive an individuality that might withstand a dynamic whose terminus was hardly perceptible. Although today a student looking back through one end of history's telescope, consulting dates, might conclude that the armistice marked the last day of fascism in Germany, this was not how the situation and its probable future appeared to anyone close to that moment, and certainly not to Adorno and Max Horkheimer. For years following their return to Germany, both prudently retained their U.S. passports and citizenship in expectation that fascism would rekindle and perhaps spread worldwide. There is not, in fact, a single sentence in *Dialectic of Enlightenment* that its authors could have cited in expectation of any other development. For Adorno, then, any kind of shoulder to shoulder could only have meant lockstep. Under the weight of bodies heaped in bulldozed graves, human warmth itself succumbed to taboo. Resorting to aesthetic barricades in sometimes tumultuously pained language, *Philosophie der neuen Musik* inches forward only by sequentially rejecting every ally it had first summoned to it along the way. When, soon after its publication, Schoenberg read the book— which would just as soon acquire the reputation among those who have never read it of being the quintessentially dogmatic statement of serialism—he himself described *Philosophie der neuen Musik* as an "act of vengeance." In a letter to the eminent musicologist H. H. Stuckenschmidt he fumed in outrage at Adorno's apostasy: "He attacks me quite vehemently in it. . . . Now I know that he has clearly never liked my music."[13]

Marginal Translation

For what it might have meant even marginally to the development of American thought and aesthetics, it is regrettable that Adorno's draft translation of *Philosophie der neuen Musik* was not revised and published as Runes promised. But, not only did the draft not enter American thought and letters at that moment, it did not even make its way into Adorno's posthumous papers, which is exceptional since from early on Adorno saved drafts of almost every page he wrote. And if that draft is somewhere, it is not to be found in Frankfurt. In this regard, it may be significant that Adorno was hardly pleased with his work. He was well aware that his recently acquired English was still inadequate to the task and, in addition, in the close society of middle-European refugees in Santa Monica, California, where he frequently found himself together with Schoenberg, he felt constrained to reduce the tendentiousness of the manuscript: "I've translated the music essay into pigeon English and so fundamentally castrated it that Schoenberg will not be able to be mad about it, without however being able to avoid that he will be if I don't succeed at hiding the publication from him."[14]

The unrevised draft, then, was a substantially compromised manuscript, and it may be just as well that it went missing, accidentally or not, for its vanishing plausibly spared unavailing arguments over authenticity and precedence of translated statement. But one would still like to know at least how Adorno treated the title. For its translation is, in fact, not obvious, though this may come as a surprise to many, since even without a word of German anyone who reads English can directly see that *neu* means *new* in *Philosophie der neuen Musik* and can easily find this confirmed in any German-English dictionary, none of which will offer to translate *neu* as *modern*. This does not prove, however, that without meddling translators languages would be mutually transparent to each other. The 1973 translation of the title as *Philosophy of Modern Music* was thoughtfully correct in idiom: "Modern Music" is the exact English equivalent of the German *Neue Musik* in the two most important senses: as the correct term for the music produced by the radical group of composers—treated in *Philosophie der neuen Musik*—whose music broke from tonality in the first decades of the twentieth century and as the decisive division in music history in opposition to the music of the Middle Ages and antiquity, in German *Alte Musik*—in English often *early music*.

But recognition of the title's idiom is not definitive of its translation since the idiom itself is problematic. In German and English, for all else that it is, *modern* is the period of the *new* and as such—in one of its aspects—by establishing the new as something fixed militates against it. The *modern* as the lingeringly recent, the diluted new, is what Schoenberg disliked in the idea and why he rejected it as meaning merely fashion, preferring to it the *new* as effectively synonymous with art that is art: "I personally do not like the term 'Modern' very much. It has too much the meaning of fashion. . . . To me art is: new art. That which has never been said or done before–only that can be art. . . . This is the minimum requirement–to be new in every respect."[15] However many topics Schoenberg and Adorno could have disagreed on, the linguistic sensorium that perceived the distinction of the new and the modern as a difference between the sounding music of what had never before been heard and the sounding of the latest thing that was already too late was theirs in common. If this was not by a long shot all that Adorno understood in the relation of these concepts, still in the longing for the new as the epitome of art as art, as what alone could catch up in its hands the dense fabric of the ever same and rend it open in that instant as if no other source of light were known, it is the motivating pathos of *Philosophie der neuen Musik.* Music, Adorno thought, had come to the point where, to be music at all, its measure was a single quality—in composition as in its import: the utterly new. For this reason *Philosophie der neuen Musik* is rightly translated as *Philosophy of New Music.*

But citing the new is no magic bullet, as if the title redux, free at last to travel under its own flag, will now surely win the day. On the contrary, the title may emerge from its restoration corrected but appreciably grayer, as if a book on "new music" were itself the sort of fad that Schoenberg scorned as merely "modern," to be ranged alongside of volumes marked "new age music" and other catalogues of the space age Gregorian. For the appraising eye and ear are now obliged to note that "new music," when cited as such, no longer spontaneously invokes the modern, while "modern" wants to shift directly into the "contemporary" or "postmodern," as if the new were only of tangential relevance. The new and the modern may be in the midst of disentwining from each other, as if the new could not possibly be thought of as founding the modern and subsisting in it as the motivation of a period that inveterately seeks the new. Pried apart, the concepts are reciprocally withering. This is confirmed by the fact that thirty years ago the title—*Philosophy of Modern Music*—spoke self-evidently of the new in a way that it no longer does, just as Arthur Rimbaud's dictum—*il faut être absolument moderne*—can not now be stated except in historical quotation. If the opposition of the modern to the new on which Schoenberg focused is in one regard self-evident, it is also clear that a museum of modern art would considerably fail the claim of its appelation if it insisted on being redubbed a museum of "new art."

Lawfulness and Regression

Adorno acknowledged with Schoenberg something in the modern inimical to the new, but his auscultation of the concept registered this element as the dialectic of enlightenment: the dynamic in which the possibility of the new is consumed in the modern's reproduction of itself as the recurrently primitive. The thesis that Adorno developed, initially elaborated in his book on Kierkegaard,[16] is that the primordial effort to overcome the struggle for self-preservation and its familiar habitus, red in tooth and claw, fails because self-preservation must seek to dominate an initially overwhelming nature but in consequence succeeds less in preserving the self than in preserving domination. For the weaker is unable to overcome the stronger other than by conforming to that force and adoring it. Whatever self-preservation gains for the possibility of the new is consumed by the ever same demand that it be relinquished in sacrifice to the principle of domination that the self, with constantly augmenting technical capacity, asserts in opposition to both internal and external nature. What continually transforms progress into its opposite, then, is lawfulness itself: "No rule"—Adorno writes in *Philosophy of New Music*—"is more repressive than one that is self-promulgated."[17] The mastery of nature converges with catastrophe because the development of the self is restricted to nothing more than a system of self-imposed order, and thus fetishes of control are surrogated for the object of which it has been deprived. The greater the control over nature, the more the self is incapacitated by its remoteness from its own object, and the more it is ultimately obliged to discover that the world on which it can inflict virtually limitless power is at the same time progressively beyond its actual control. Progress as domination is therefore inextricable from domination as regression—not, however, regression in the sense of a movie running backward but as the choiceless return to what was never solved in the first place: the struggle for self-preservation.

With this as background, it is apparent why Schoenberg violently disliked *Philosophy of New Music.* For as Adorno points out in the preface to this study, it was written as an extended excursus to *Dia-*

lectic of Enlightenment.[18] And, in the first essay, "Schoenberg and Progress," Adorno demonstrates musicologically how the possibility of the new in the tendencies of the musical material of the Western tradition were developed by Schoenberg and the Second Viennese School in the early decades of the century and then juggled away, as if under a spell, in favor of the fascination for techniques for the self-imposed manipulations of serialism. In the name of emancipated composition, Schoenberg established a technique for the domination of the musical material that resulted in the extinguishing of the subject, on one hand, and a completely abstract compositional material on the other: "By virtue of setting music free to undertake limitless domination over the natural material, the enslavement of music has become universal."[19] All that can be heard in the serial works, Adorno observed, is the ordering principles of serialism itself raised superstitiously to the status of object of veneration. Portrayed thus, Schoenberg found himself in the role of the modern precisely in the sense of what is inimical to the new. It is not surprising, then, that he hardly thought anyone needed to study Adorno's presentation of his work, and he in fact insisted that readers could just as well put the book aside with these, its first words, since *ab ovo* it was completely discredited by its title:

> Through the formulation of the title, his book has lost the claim to be taken seriously. Grammar would have to ask: "whose philosophy?"—answer: "that of the new music," or: "what does the new music do?"—answer: "it philosophizes." Only a nonsensical formulation of a question can provoke such a nonsensical answer.[20]

But here Schoenberg is certainly mistaken: the title is not nonsensical question and answer. It names a manifesto of the primacy of the object. In this form alone *Philosophy of New Music* struggles to sink heel into turf against the massive slide of history. It is the comportment of a subjectivity that, instead of establishing itself as a sacrificial temple to itself, achieves, in refusing to renounce itself, its object. *Philosophy of New Music* conceives this comportment in both musical composition and philosophy by showing that they have an affinity predicated on their distinction, not by subverting music as a thinker in disguise. Only because music is nonconceptual in its structure is the dialectic of construction and expression, which transpires within it, able to bring the dialectic to a halt in shaping the thing-itself as the unconscious transcription of historical suffering. The musical material has a *tendency* in just this sense: lodged within it, as its own dynamic, is the need of history—what nature has undergone—to speak for itself, which it can do, however, only on condition that subjectivity intervenes to compose it. The compositional ear must test for the difference between right and wrong if it is to shape the import of the material's tendency in opposition to every countervailing tendency of convention in the material and to every incapacity of the composer, who, the more radical the music, must proceed almost cluelessly. As Adorno writes, in one of his most profound appreciations of Beethoven's achievement, truth cannot—as a power of illumination—be gained in any other way than subjectively, and not merely as a subjective truth apologetically secondary to scientific certainty: "Objective is the fractured landscape, subjective: the only light in which it glows."[21] The potential of art, then, is the ability to restore to nature the qualitative, historical, dimension that subjectivity, enthralled with the spurious objectivity of its own lawfulness—a considerable act of imagination that claims to be its opposite—deprived nature of in the first place by dominating it and transmuting it as raw material. Conventional music is what raw material sounds like. What is appreciated in it— whether it wails or pleads—is what it takes to silence history; the music is compelled by its own subjective insufficiency to follow the trace of the market where it leads, not where the material most wants to go. Compositional right and wrong can therefore be criticized from the perspective of the import gained or sacrificed. The only intensity that any eye or ear can perceive in the possible liveliness of an art work— whether in the difference between the colors framed on the wall from the same colors of the coats hung in the corner or in the difference of what one composed note can resonate from the miscellaneous wandering of empirical sound—is how color and sound may take the measure of the weight of history. The extent to which art succeeds or fails at taking this measure, Adorno thought, is the degree to which the old is transformed into the new and, for what things are to date, the utter limit of the new. *Philosophy of New Music* at every turn demonstrates the primacy of the object in the history of music, first, by showing how developments in the material are instantiated as the increasingly compounded puzzles that history presents to the composer and, second, by seeking to interpret the import achieved in the compositional answers given in order, finally, to understand why it is—as any contemporary ear must still acknowledge—that new music has yet to become any more than peripheral to the listening ear. To the extent that Adorno succeeded in this study, Schoenberg might as well have turned his criticism of the title of Adorno's work against Gustav Flaubert for writing *Madame Bovary* without including in that title the warning that the views provided were exclusively those of the author.

Tendency of the New

The idea that the musical material itself has a *tendency* to which composition responds is as familiar as the everyday event of discerning the direction of a sentence and completing it with the word that has momentarily escaped one's interlocutor's command. The puzzle of modern composition, however, as described by Adorno, would oblige nothing less than providing not the vocable intuitively implied by convention but the one word that would reveal what initially obstructed remembrance. Conjuring the presence of the forgotten, it would shatter the coherence of the sentence. In sentences of just this kind, in which forgetfulness intervenes to reveal itself as involuntary memory's deepest ally, Schoenberg in his late works developed a technique for eluding the domination of the material and protecting the spontaneity of composition. Insofar as sentences that seek to take advantage of their own possible forgetfulness are hardly sentences anymore, Adorno likewise claims that Schoenberg's late compositions can no longer be called "works" since their own dynamic sloughs off the claim to compositional wholeness. The technique becomes capable of responding to the tendency of the material precisely there where the caesuras and interruptions of the late Beethoven found their limit. In these moments, in Beethoven's late works, silence diffuses over the landscape as the compositional subject frees itself, leaving the musical phrases behind in fragments: "The mystery," Adorno writes in *Philosophy of New Music*, "is between these fragments."[22] This distance between the fragments is potentiated in late Schoenberg in compositions that employ the lawfulness developed in serial composition to destroy the lawfulness of the work, the nexus of meaning that establishes its semblance of wholeness. What first fractured the surface of the integral art work in Beethoven's late style now cracks down through the bedrock of the composition itself. The semblance of wholeness, in which the listening ear recognizes its own unity and finds its image confirmed, is demolished, and what deepens between these fragments is that which the power of likeness gains for the unlike. These compositions are a kind of metaphor that says: "You are to this what this is not to you."

The most important artists of the late nineteenth and twentieth centuries, from Stéphane Mallarmé to Virginia Woolf and Wallace Stevens, experimented with procedures of this kind, and they help elucidate what Adorno understood in the technique of the late Schoenberg. Wallace Stevens in particular, whose work often provides a North American concordance to Adorno's thinking, clarified with the greatest succinctness what is at stake in this technique in "Prologues to What Is Possible," a poem of his late style:

> The metaphor stirred his fear. The object with which he was
>   compared
> Was beyond his recognizing. By this he knew that likeness of
>   him extended
> Only a little way, and not beyond, unless between himself
> And things beyond resemblance there was this and that
>   intended to be recognized.[23]

This is how in Stevens his ruddy, heroic imagination takes the brunt of what he called the weather and how at that imagination's boundaries it hears a foreign song that sings "without human meaning."[24] If these lines, however, were cast simply as a triumph over human meaning, if the monumental tone did not tremble at its own solemnity, they would not quote Wallace Stevens's poetry. A related procedure is what makes something other than human intention comparably evident in the dense, rhythmical groupings of Paul Cézanne's brush stroke, composed so that the way into the brush work never permits exit by the path of entry. Instead, elusive gates continually open transitions between the bunched strokes so that the eye passes consecutively, plane to plane, beyond its own intelligence, at every point coherently arriving where the eye would never have had mind to go on its own, catching its breath while the restlessly static object insists that the activity is entirely its prerogative. Stevens, whose own work often originated in the developments of French painting, himself presents this activity of the eye, but in transposition:

> As he traveled alone, like a man lured on by a syllable without
>   any meaning,
> A syllable of which he felt, with an appointed sureness,
> That it contained the meaning into which he wanted to enter,
> A meaning which, as he entered it, would shatter the boat and
>   leave the oarsmen quiet
> As at a point of central arrival, an instant moment, much or
>   little,
> Removed from any shore, from any man or woman, and
>   needing none.[25]

These experiences with "things beyond resemblance" are elucidated—and themselves comprehended—by Adorno's analysis in *Philosophy of New Music* of the sounding resonance of Schoenberg's late work: "The man who surrenders to tears in music that no longer resembles him at the same time allows the stream of what he himself is not—what was damned up back of the world of things—to flow back into him. In tears and singing the alienated world is entered."[26] But what is damned up back of the world of things? What do these metaphors of unlikeness, which Walter Benjamin called allegory, reveal in giving onto the alienated world? Adorno in the last lines of the section "Music as Knowledge" explains that what yawns open in the impersonality of Schoenberg's late works—having destroyed the immediate semblance of wholeness, the meaningful coherence of detail—is how "the earth reclaims Eurydice."[27]

Blares Silently

If *Philosophy of New Music* prompts many questions of itself, it poses no fewer to the place where it was written. Among the most difficult is whether an ear that is fully preoccupied by sound, whose force of self-evidence owes ultimately to its ability to exploit the ancient antagonism between individuals and the society they somehow constitute, can possibly win away from that music's resonance a critique of culture that reaches beyond what presupposes the failure of culture ever to become a human one.[28] It is, after all, more than a curiosity that what blares silently in every inner ear gives no indication of ever becoming part of thinking that conceives an alternative to what transpires. Yet the naïveté that is determined to stay up all night, as if in studied decipherment of scrolls recently recovered from the Dead Sea itself, transcribing lyrics intentionally garbled under drum amplification, deserves encouragement. Music is that capacity for knowledge—but not if listening itself has been deprived of every discernment; and not if that listening is left to founder by a critical theory that can itself only think to weigh in as the hero of every battle against the injustice done by what claims to hear a difference between music that is emphatically composed and music that is not. *Philosophy of New Music* provides more than just indications for cultural criticism that, rather than falling into step with claims for a toothless otherness in the cause of a pluralism of *musics,*[29] is critically alert to the impulse to shun "what has become alien to men . . . the human component of culture, its closest part, which upholds them against the world."[30] The question remains what strengths there are to sense the new, to compose it, and to comprehend it as what cannot in any other way be said. But whatever might be found of importance in Adorno's work, it is not to be expected that such thinking would somehow be greeted by allies gathering from all corners now—when the sky itself is in danger of turning straightaway to ash—any more than in the emergency of Adorno's own decades. It is to the point, then, that though *Philosophy of New Music* was written with only the sparsest reference to the place of its composition, this was certainly not out of obliviousness to a situation that so startled Adorno that it prompted him to coin the phrase *culture industry* to describe what—as he once commented—he could never have imagined had he not found himself here as a refugee. Living here he came to understand, as he writes in the introduction to *Philosophy of New Music*, that radical music itself developed in "antithesis to the spreading of the culture industry" into music's own domain. This stance, "together with the socially manufactured predisposition of the listener, brought radical music into complete isolation."[31] This is clue enough for any reader to discern that every page of this volume, concerned with the possibilities and impossibilities of radical music, is riven through by what it resisted as by the capacity for determinate negation.

The Philosophy of Dissonance

Adorno and Schoenberg

THEODOR W. ADORNO AND ARNOLD SCHOENBERG are two of the most uncompromising figures of the twentieth century. Photographs of them in old age witness the clenched stubbornness of an African fetish reappearing in their faces. The intensity of this spirit shaped and penetrated every detail of their work. In his *Theory of Harmony*, for example, it compelled Schoenberg the educator to disclaim the book's massive pedagogical effort. After four hundred pages of careful and sometimes bombastic instruction, reasons for the book are increasingly met by counter reasons, until the two sides come to grips in a locked tangle. At one point Schoenberg goes so far as to reject craft—the entire content of the book—as a standard of composition. Authentic technique is, on the contrary, he says, occult knowledge. He confronts himself with the challenge that this hermetic ideal poses to what he has written: "Someone will ask why I am writing a textbook of harmony, if I wish technique to be occult knowledge. I could answer: people want to study, to learn, and I want to teach." Having driven himself into a cul de sac of his own manufacture, the only escape route he permits himself to imagine is further self-resistance.[1]

This is an eccentric process, but the passage tips the hand on Schoenberg's occult knowledge, which he clearly did not consider unteachable. In fact he constantly demonstrated his basic sorcery in composition class. Once, for instance, having demolished, phrase by phrase, the blackboard exercise of the precocious teenage composer Dika Newlin, he turned to the other students to explain the logic of his coup de grace, as he wiped out a final measure of eighth notes. Class, "do you know why I do not let her use eighth notes? . . . Why, because she *wants* to use them!"[2] Schoenberg thought this funny, and in its own way it was, and still is. But the technique recommended— which permits giving only under the auspices of taking away and requires that one hand always be ready to undo the work of the other—is keyed to the most rapacious demands of twentieth-century composition. For it is not possible to do justice to the experience of this century without knowing how, literally and in the same instant, to block the scream as it occurs. In Schoenberg's "A Survivor from Warsaw, for Narrator, Men's Chorus and Orchestra" (opus 26, 1947), German soldiers, before dawn, throw open the sewer where Jews, asleep, are hiding. But even the first moments—the orders shouted, the searchlights—are hard for the ear to follow, let alone describe. The narrator provides the only report of the event, which he relives as one of a haggard crowd as it is driven out of hiding and provoked into a stumbling fast march in the street. He does not know what is or is not dream as the soldiers wade into them and he is clubbed down. The chaos and shattering of the narrator's own perceptions deprive the listener of any objective recourse. Listening becomes the realization that one's head has been grabbed from behind and dragged underwater. Everyone having been knocked to the ground, the sergeant—maybe to save bullets—orders their heads smashed. In the concussive instant that the rifle butt strikes the narrator's head, however, we do not, and could not possibly, hear a scream. The subjective form of the report prohibits the event being registered externally. Instead, the sound that must have occurred is documented only by a muffled, suddenly slack and hollow peacefulness that suspends the recurrent heart-spasming alarm motif that functions throughout the cantata in ostinato. There is perhaps no other composition, no other art work, in which fright and hope become comparably identical in the moment that they vanish. The power of the composition depends on this moment. The panicky inconsolableness of history ignites in this stifled, imploded instant, whereas any scream would have provided the rationalization that it might have been heard.

I

Schoenberg's intransigence is easily lost from sight in America, where the edifice of New Music—to estimate its cultural magnitude—would be diminutively tented by the League of Professional Bowling, itself one of the lesser sports. Yet Adorno's work is on this same horizon even more recondite than Schoenberg's, and as a person he was ultimately more self-protective and austere. Compared to the many vignettes that circulate about Schoenberg, funny classroom stories do not seem to exist about Adorno. Likewise, where Schoenberg's letters have been a major source regarding all aspects of his life, Adorno took considerable precaution to keep his personal correspondence out of public hands for decades after his death, when—as he rightly feared—it would be used biographically to dilute his work. He spoke by starting at the top of a full inhalation, which he followed down to the last oxygen molecule left in his lungs, and his written style perfected page-long paragraphs hardened to a gapless and sometimes glassy density, as if the slightest hesitancy for an inhalation or any break for a new breath would have irretrievably relinquished the chance of completing the thought. Every one of his stylistic peculiarities was defined by the effort to maintain a moment of critical, historical self-consciousness in opposition to mass culture. This is why his work consistently draws the animus of cultural resentment. For, without flinching, he unmasked the substitute gratifications and betrayals of contemporary society. A population that knows perfectly well that it lives in the service sector of the culture industry will not soon forgive him for putting his finger on what people jockey for as they crowd in line for a new film—"people watch movies with their eyes closed and their mouths open"[3]—or for revoking the sensed prerogatives of stardom—mass culture's universal bestowal—by showing that what scintillates in glitter is powerlessness: "he who is never permitted to conquer in life conquers in glamor."[4]

II

Adorno and Schoenberg of course are related more integrally than comparisons demonstrate. In *Philosophy of New Music* Adorno marshals the resources of the entire theodicean tradition of German idealism—the Kantian justification of empirical, practical, and aesthetic judgments, the Hegelian expansion of the transcendental deduction to comprehend the rightness of the universe—on behalf of the justification of an irreconcilable music. He shows that this isolated music had, in the strength of its isolation, become a singular repository of critical historical experience. Adorno does not deduce this position. On the contrary, his thinking originates in this musical experience, and he devoted his life to its elucidation. What distinguishes Adorno's efforts in this from almost the whole grim genre of aesthetics is that, whereas it generally demands either systematic philosophers who are deaf and blind or effusive admirers of Beethoven's triumph, *Philosophy of New Music* is a defense of Schoenberg's work that presents New Music's own philosophy; the study aims to carry out conceptually the historical reflection implicit in the music and to raise this reflection to the point of the music's self-criticism. Insofar as Schoenberg's music is a dissonant order, Adorno's work is fundamentally the philosophy of dissonance. Only because Adorno was constantly following the traces of his own sensorium through this music was he able to complete this Hegelian project.

III

The central thesis of Adorno's aesthetics is that art becomes the unconscious writing of history through its isolation from society. In *Philosophy of New Music* Adorno details the immediate object of aversion from which modern art and Schoenberg's music withdrew. There he writes that just as abstract art was defensively motivated by its opposition to photography—the mechanical art work—Schoenberg's music developed in "antithesis to the extension of the culture industry into music's own domain."[5] In that Adorno took the side of this music against the culture industry, it can be assumed that he would hardly have made himself more popular at a rock concert than at a conference on Schoenberg entitled "Constructive Dissonance." His Krausian ears would have recognized in this title the intention of providing sounds that literally dug a moat around themselves—music that will never be heard in any hotel elevator—with the requisite positive glow of popular culture. Just as the latter makes sure its monsters turn out cuddly, "Constructive Dissonance" puts a finger out to give a tickle under the chin: "See, those nasty sounds aren't so bad. You don't put them on to play at bedtime, but they want to help, too." Whatever this conference's intention to hear and think Schoenberg anew, in *Philosophy of New Music* Adorno writes that the conciliatory gesture—such as is unmistakably lodged in the phrase "Constructive Dissonance"—was the sign that led the historical retreat from Schoenberg's music: "Such conciliation to the listener, masking as humaneness, began to undermine the technical standards attained by progressive composition."[6]

Adorno's criticism would not have stopped with the title. The conference brochure itself documents the formula for the translation of modern art into mass culture; there in the center of a paste-up of photographs of famous people meeting famous people, Schoenberg cavorting with Kokoschka, a picture of Schoenberg playing table tennis, is a photo of the composer seated in front of a wall of his paintings. While the effort of these well-known paintings is to break through the visible world, to defeat its webbed replicative patterns of illusion, the steady narrative distance of perspectival space, and in opposition present a deposition of isolated subjectivity, the photograph—the amateur and illusory medium par excellence—with its limited powers of focus, contrast, and construction, its unshakable normalization of optical distortion, patches over this content with a melodramatic, stereotypical image of Schoenberg's face, half in darkness, half in light. And however much the paintings themselves struggle to force their way into the present, the photograph embalms each moment with stasis as a dull sign of an irretrievable past.[7] This irretrievability is a fundamental source of its mass culture appeal, because the past that is shaped is anecdotal and sentimental. Every photograph is equally old—even one snapped a second previously—and calls for the same identical tear to be shed on its behalf, the "I knew you when" that all photography hums. An amnesiac's historiography is created: the need for continuity in time is fulfilled while assuring that the impulses of time remain at a neutral, unshifting distance. If popular music sings of sentimental journeys, the conference brochure photography promises a sentimental conference. And this promise is made good by the actual conference organization into three parts: contexts, interactions, and reception—which could be deduced from the advertisement. "Contexts and Interactions" are to provide a photograph of Schoenberg in the historicist "back then." This is followed, plausibly enough, by dredging for bodies, that is, with "reception," a concept that, however the phenomenologists doll it up, surfaces on the palate with such en-

thusiasm and legitimacy only because it derives from the sensorial order of radio and television.

IV

Glossed by mass culture's carefully managed populist eye, the continuous claim throughout Adorno's writings to emphatic musical
experience—particularly that of Schoenberg's music—has often been
grounds for shrugging off his social criticism as elitist. This is only secondarily because of mass culture's allergy to New Music. More impor-

tant is that both New Music and Adorno are assumed to be representatives of the world of the symphony hall. Insofar as this is the perception, the rejection is not altogether unjustified. If music becomes important as the voice of the voiceless, its symphony hall performers, sponsors, and auditors occupy almost exclusively social positions that gain from the voiceless remaining so. Symphony hall is not shy about this class allegiance, with its playbill of aperitifs and perfumes, an audience of scions in swagger fashions, opera lovers coasting by like ocean liners wrapped in camel-hair overcoats, and a conductor who, whenever he circles from the orchestra to deliver his bows, reveals his aristocratic bearing to be that of a majordomo. Any doubts as to whom these performances are for is dispersed by the San Francisco Symphony, which each year offers subscribers a selection from the Mercedes Great Performers Series and the opportunity to attend BankAmerica Foundation preconcert talks. Popular music fans correctly recognize that they are not invited to these events. But the resentment felt blocks recognition of how much the two worlds have in common, from the sequined dresses to the fame of powerless dukes, kings, and princes, to the inevitably glossy, repetitive performances. Symphony hall and popular music are not the different substances their audiences are encouraged to believe them to be, but different layers of mass culture.

It is only because so-called classical music has been progressively absorbed as one layer of popular culture that it is difficult to realize that Adorno took the side of emphatic music against symphony hall, where he found this music neutralized. He did not, however, consider this neutralization simply adventitious. On the contrary, through its beauty, emphatic music participates in its commercial neutralization, and Adorno wanted to show how the direction of music itself was toward overcoming this neutralization through its internal critique of beautiful semblance. Schoenberg was, in his opinion, the key figure in this transformation of music.

V

A recent San Francisco Symphony performance of Mahler's Sixth Symphony condenses these issues and makes a bridge to Adorno's analysis, in *Philosophy of New Music*, of Schoenberg's achievement. At a BankAmerica preconcert talk, in fall 1991, the contemporary composer Christopher Rouse—who is a pop music aficionado—introduced Mahler's Sixth Symphony, a work, as Rouse mentioned, of special importance to Schoenberg's group. Rouse's introduction is of interest for what is characteristic in it, much of it owed directly to Mahler's own programmatic comments. Only a condensed sentence of fragments from his introduction, taken up in medias res, needs paraphrasing to bring this familiar genre of music appreciation to mind: In the theme of the third movement, Rouse explained, Mahler announces his towering love for Alma. And in the finale, the hammer blow of fate sounds for the third and last time, presaging the final disaster that would befall the composer the following year.[8] Just as moviegoers watch their stars illustrated by the role performed, this introduction to the Sixth Symphony obeys the constitutive limits of mass culture—simulation and portrayal—and converts the music into a snapshot of the great man's life. It sets the music as an event back behind the white border of that never-never land where fame keeps its trophies.

The music itself, however, is hardly content with the role of portraying Mahler's life. And it is possible that members of the post-talk audience sensed something of this as they craned their heads above their seats to see these blows of fate struck. In Mahler's Sixth these sounds are performed not by the plausible kettle drums but by a sledge hammer. This is, of course, not one of the spiritualized instruments of the symphony orchestra, for the percussionist cannot help but emphasize the struggle to fit the blow of a fifteen-pound hammerhead to the beat. Yet these three blows, programmatically conceived as three blows of fate, go beyond the programmatic. The hammer blow of fate becomes fate the hammer blow; no longer the portrayal of fate but the leveling impact itself. And whatever the force delivered to the subjectivity that stirs in the music, this extra-aesthetic sledgehammer delivers a blow to the fictional order of music altogether. If the various introductions of sections of the orchestra seem to occur without reference to actual time, the three hammer blows break through the autonomous temporality of music each with the intention of notching the clock face itself.

VI

This act, in the decades surrounding the symphony's composition, was only one of many similar events that transformed art into modern art. In drama it has common origins with the untempered shock dealt by August Strindberg's chamber plays; it has affinities with Georges Braque's and Pablo Picasso's *tableaux choses,* with Isadora Duncan's effort directly to objectify the inward, and with Wassily Kandinsky's rejection of illusionistic space. The sculptor and dramatist Ernst Barlach formulated the Platonic antimimetic, antiart direction of modern art: "I do not represent what I for my part see, or how I see it from here or there, but what is, the real and the truthful. . . . The world is already there, it would be senseless just to repeat it."[9] Throughout these decades art moved fundamentally against fiction, against portraying or representing the world, and toward essence. Adorno shows in his major study of Schoenberg that he carried out this project in the medium of music, extending the illusion-shattering intention of Mahler's hammer blows to the total musical structure. This was a radical transformation of musical expression. Whereas music since the seventeenth century had simulated subjectivity and dramatized passions, producing images of expression, Schoenberg's break from tonality achieved a depositional expression, a docket of the historical unconscious that registered impulses of isolation, shock, and collapse.

This depositional capacity depended in the first place on the decline of tonality and the resulting possibility of a free manipulation of the musical material. But, second, for expression to be expression, it must be necessary; what occurs must have the quality of needing to be as it is. And what Schoenberg discovered—according to Adorno—was that the impulses sedimented in the material could be bindingly organized according to a principle of contrast. Dissonance, the bearer of historical suffering, would be the rational order binding together melody and harmony. Harmonic simultaneity would be that of independent contrasting voices. As a result, in Adorno's words, "the subjective drive and the longing for self-proclamation without illusion, became the technical instrument of the objective work."[10] This transformed musical time: whereas the constitutive repetition of traditional forms makes music indifferent to time and susceptible to the background function required of popular music, in Schoenberg's music the repetition of the *Grundgestalt*—the basic shape—must become new. It answers the dialectical question of how the old can become new at the same time that the music refuses to hold its even distance from the listener. Rather, in the words of Adorno's Kafka description, it races toward the listener like a freight train. Schoenberg emancipated dissonance, but, more important, he made dissonance necessary.

Adorno's understanding of the significance of this technique needs to be understood in the full context of *Dialectic of Enlightenment*, the companion text to, and written in part contemporaneously with, *Philosophy of New Music*. Whereas, extra-aesthetically, subjectivity translates phenomena into examples of a subordinating concept and thereby consumes the potential of expression, in Schoenberg's music subjectivity organizes the nonidentity of the universal and the particular; it is an organization that, in its dissonance, constantly surpasses its own organization. The ideal that inheres in this music is a transformed subjectivity that, rather than dominating its object, gives it binding expression. Necessity in this case really is—for once—freedom in that inseparable from the bindingness of this music's historical deposition is the sounding implication that what has transpired historically did not need to have happened and does not need to continue.

Critique of the Organic

Kierkegaard and the Construction of the Aesthetic

A thousand lamentable objects there,
In scorn of nature, art gave lifeless life.

—SHAKESPEARE, "The Rape of Lucrece"

THIS IS AN UNLIKELY SPOT FOR A YIDDISH STORY, but nevertheless: the chancellor rushes into the throne room and informs the king
that the harvest has been infected; whoever eats from it falls insane.
He urges the king to seize what untainted stores remain and rule a
mad people sanely. The king refuses; he will not be separated from his
people. "Instead" he tells his chancellor, "we will make signs on our
foreheads so that when we are mad we will know what has happened." The idea of a mark that would awaken them from history
turned disaster bears some interest, but it is not beyond suspicion. For
the mark on the forehead is of sacrificial lineage and recurrence to it in
difficult times is not a thought to crack open history, but its most dependable reflex. The struggle to win control has always had the form
of sacrifice, not because domination has been mismanaged, but because sacrifice is the dialectical truth of domination. This is the point
of Adorno's *Dialectic of Enlightenment* (1944). Domination does not
contingently imply sacrifice, but is structurally sacrificial: the ego
"owes its existence to the sacrifice of the present moment to the future";[1] abstraction, the modus operandi of scientific control, is nothing
other than the sacrifice of the particular to the universal. Adorno's aim
in tracing out this dialectic was to show that the historical effort to es-

cape the compulsions of nature fails to achieve human autonomy because the nature that self-preservation is to preserve is destroyed by
the logic of self-preservation. History is therefore a process of its own
transformation into nature or—in Adorno's alternate formulation—
into myth, the condition of necessity from which it meant to escape.
This analysis of the dialectic of enlightenment implies an aesthetics,
and here the interest of the mark on the forehead returns somewhat
transformed: Adorno's aesthetics attempts to locate an image that
would awaken history from its self-consuming progress as the compulsion to sacrifice. Such an image, however, would not be simple
mimicry of the logic of sacrifice, but neither is it dialectically conceivable that the image would circumvent sacrifice. Rather, as Adorno
wrote in one of his last formulations, it would be sacrifice that would
become memory of nature as the expression of sacrifice: "All that art is
capable of is to grieve for the sacrifice it makes and which it itself, in its
powerlessness, is."[2] *Kierkegaard: Construction of the Aesthetic* was the
first major philosophical study Adorno published; it appeared in
bookstores on February 27, 1933, the day that Hitler declared a national emergency and suspended the freedom of the press, marking
the transition from chancellor to dictator.[3] References to this moment
in the appearance of *Kierkegaard* generally note this as "ironic." But
there is nothing ironic about it: *Kierkegaard* is the study of the unconscious reversal of history into nature, Adorno's first analysis of the dialectic of enlightenment. According to Adorno, sacrifice "occupies the
innermost cell of his [Kierkegaard's] thought."[4] The process of his
philosophy is a sacrificial struggle against nature: "through sacrifice he
asserts his rule,"[5] which nevertheless succumbs to nature because "sacrifice is itself mythical."[6] Although the ostensible claim of the philosophy of existence was to overcome the abstractness of idealism, abstraction remains its unwitting course in its sacrificial progress through
Kierkegaard's hierarchy of the "stages on life's way": the aesthetic, the
ethical, and the religious spheres. "Existence" itself turns out to be a
pure abstraction of which nothing can be predicated, and the re-
doubtable leap of faith is not an act of transcendence but the despair-
ing culmination of self-sacrifice. The truth-content of "existence," on
the other hand, is in the sphere that "existence" rejects by its own
progress, the aesthetic sphere of semblance: the sphere of melancholy,
fragmentation, transience. In aesthetic semblance, existence passes
away as the wish for a reality without sacrifice; it is the sphere of the

memory of nature. *Kierkegaard: Construction of the Aesthetic* intends to recuperate the sphere of the aesthetic from the dialectic of existence: "not to forget in dreams the present world, but to change it by the strength of an image."[7]

Early Adorno

Although *Kierkegaard: Construction of the Aesthetic* was Adorno's first published philosophical work, this is not the work of a novice. Adorno had already written more than a hundred articles—mainly on music—as well as two extensive philosophical studies: a doctoral dissertation, *The Transcendent Thing and Noema in Husserl's Phenomenology* (1924), and a professorial dissertation, a *Habililationsschrift*, *The Concept of the Unconscious in Transcendental Psychology* (1927), an analysis of the concept of the unconscious in Freud and Kant. This latter work should have qualified Adorno for a professorship at the Johann Wolfgang Goethe University in Frankfurt, but its neo-Kantian sponsor, Hans Cornelius, rejected it—frankly hedging—as an "unworthy topic." Three years later, Adorno, age twenty-seven, submitted the Kierkegaard study, this time successfully, under the direction of Paul Tillich. The order of these projects of course does not document when Adorno became interested in them. As far as the Kierkegaard study is concerned, it was not exclusively written in the three years following the completion of the Kant/Freud study. Its gapless density depended on a visceral familiarity with every word of Kierkegaard 's extensive oeuvre. From a letter of Siegfried Kracauer to Leo Lowenthal, dated 1923, it is evident that the twenty-year-old Adorno was already completely familiar with Kierkegaard's writings and perhaps spoke an adolescent Kierkegaardese: "If Teddie one day makes a real declaration of his love ... it will undoubtably take such a difficult form that the young lady will have to have read the whole of Kierkegaard ... to understand Teddie at all."[8] Kierkegaard, then, was one of Adorno's earliest interests, which is not surprising. In the early 1920s German philosophy was in the midst of a Kierkegaard renaissance, as it was called, and almost every major development in philosophy depended on how Kierkegaard was appropriated: the emergence of existential philosophy in Jaspers first publications, the "dialectical theology" of Barth and Tillich, and, later in the decade, Heidegger's *Being and Time*, all drew on Kierkegaard's concept of existence as antidote to idealism. In this historical context the contentiousness of Adorno's decipherment of Kierkegaard's philosophy as the apex of idealism becomes evident. Although political turmoil and the war dissolved this context, Adorno's interest in Kierkegaard continued through the war and after. In 1940 he gave a talk, later published in English as "Kierkegaard's Doctrine of Love,"[9] to a seminar convened by Paul Tillich in New York City, where both had emigrated several years earlier. Whereas the *Construction of the Aesthetic* dealt exclusively with Kierkegaard as a philosopher, the 1940 lecture extended the analysis to his religious writings. In 1963, six years before his death, he wrote "Kierkegaard, One More Time," a study of Kierkegaard's last publications, their political implications, and his polemic against the established church.[10] Apart from works directly on Kierkegaard, and there are several smaller pieces not mentioned here, Adorno's writings bristle with reference to him, often explicitly, frequently as *sous-entendu*. And in another sense all of Adorno's works draw arcs out from his involvement with Kierkegaard because it was in this first major work that Adorno developed the fundamental ideas and forms of everything he ever wrote after it. Passages from Kierkegaard could be transposed seamlessly to his final works, as well as the reverse. In his review of the book, published only several days after it appeared, but after he had already fled the country, Benjamin was prescient: "In this book much is contained in little space. Very possible that the author's later books will spring from this one. In any case the book belongs to that class of rare and peculiar first-works in which a winged thought appears in the puppation of critique."[11] The image, however, Adorno would dispute: the organic was not the measure of his work.

Enlightenment and Myth

Whether they admired the book or not, the other early reviewers of *Kierkegaard,* like most since, found it impossible to summarize. F. J. Brecht wrote: "To discuss this book is difficult; to sum it up without distorting it, impossible,"[12] and then Mr. Brecht seized the reviewer's prerogative to shoot and run and panned the book in half a page. Helmut Kuhn found the study brilliant but flawed: "Its deficiency ... is that its energetic and adroit thought does not solidify into binding and definitive concepts; rather it rolls by in expressive and polished formulations that are frequently overwhelmingly successful but also hovering and fragile."[13] Another complained that the reading was fatiguing: "the peculiarly swirling and swimming" text made understanding difficult.[14] Karl Loewith called the book insightful in spite of its "dictatorial, ranting and mannered style:"[15] if he had added "arty" and "artificial" he would have covered the field of invectives leveled at Adorno and his writings ever since. Loewith snipped out lists of themes from the book and packed them miscellaneously into paragraphs, quoting extensively. This was characteristic of the reviews. None of the reviewers considered why the book's style was so difficult or offputting, or if what they found interesting in it might have been an accomplishment of a style that they all considered a distraction. They all could, and did, deftly recite the problem of idealism, in Hegel, in Kierkegaard, in Adorno, but as a parody of the critique of idealism. Idealism foundered because of its inability to fulfill its claim of overcoming the division of form and content, of bringing its object to speech. All of Adorno's reviewers took their pose of masterful distance from the book as assurance that they could not possibly be implicated in such a difficult problem. It occurred to none of them to bring to bear on the form of the review a central insight of the book: that abstraction is the mark of the mythical. Bound to clearheadedness yet unable to organize a work that fragmented into a chaos of partial themes under the pressure of summarizing it, their vision drifted through the text with an archaic anxiety.

Chapter and Paragraph

It is hard to find other words than paragraph and chapter to describe the basic organization of *Kierkegaard*. Apparently, seven chapters are composed of a sequence of paragraphs. But these concepts are misleading, as any attempt to read straight from one paragraph to the next, even one sentence to the next, makes evident. The parts are not related to each other by way of the compulsion of argumentation, logic's instinctual life; while they are thoroughly logical, they do not develop by way of a subordinating logic of chapter and paragraph.[16] Adorno's ideal of form was that "every sentence should be equally near the center-point."[17] The parts refer to one another and complete one another by a principle of contrast. Topics develop without any schematized preparation and are taken up again at later points without any reference back to earlier discussions or any attempt to sum up the thoughts that have been developed. There is no "as we have seen," no "as we will see later," no introduction, summary, or conclusion.[18] There are no transitions other than those made by the material itself.[19] No more than New Music would settle for paraphrasing expression would the *Construction of the Aesthetic* settle for paraphrasing Kierkegaard. For Adorno the only solution to idealism is to fulfill it: to achieve the self-expression of the material. Each section of the book studies details and fragments of Kierkegaard's oeuvre as a microcosm of the whole. The image of an outdated travel guide, for example, studied at the beginning of chapter 2, shows the decay of a meaning that should be canonical. Adorno continues to pursue the figure of the separation of a canonical meaning from the text in other of Kierkegaard's images. This antinomy emerges as the figure of an objectless inwardness, one from which both meaning and the world of things are absolutely separate: "there is only an isolated subjectivity, surrounded by a dark otherness."[20] The construction pursues a compositional nominalism.[21] But because the particular element is itself a microcosm of the whole, every element is mediated by the whole. The construction obviates the distinction of thesis and argument.[22] Only to the extent that *Kierkegaard* fails could his early reviewers have succeeded at extracting the main points; every point succeeds at becoming the main point. To call the style mannered hedges: it is pretentious. Although this is galling, it follows from the demands of the material, not from Adorno's supposed high-handedness. If the material is to have full autonomy, if it is not to be subordinated to anything, a coyness is required: unerringly Adorno seems to take up something else whenever the text finally seems to settle into an issue. The result is hardly a harmonious flow, and it is not uncommon to find the jaggedness of Adorno's language censured in reviews as no longer German or any language at all. Adorno went so far as to displace the reflexive pronoun to the end of the sentence[23] to trip up its natural momentum. Related to his critique of the organic idiom of tonality, which achieves a gaplessness under a forward pressure that drives one note into the next with which it merges, the gesture of Adorno's language is an awkwardness to undo awkwardness: language that refuses to push— the idea of the human itself.[24]

From Kracauer to Benjamin: The Problem of Truth

When Adorno was fifteen he studied Kant on Sundays with Siegfried Kracauer, who was, if anyone, the origin of Adorno's idea of philosophy. Adorno wrote of these Sunday meetings: "I don't exaggerate in the slightest when I say that I owe more to this reading than to my academic teachers. Extraordinarily talented pedagogically, Kracauer brought Kant to life for me. From the beginning, with his guidance, I discovered that the work was not to be read as pure epistemology, as an analysis of the conditions of scientifically valid judgments, but as a sort of encipherment from which the historical situation of the mind could be read, with the vague expectation that with it something of the truth itself was to be won."[25] This "vague expectation" of truth directed the initial impulse of Adorno's study to decipher the social content of Kierkegaard's thought. But this expectation would never have sufficed for the writing of the *Construction of the Aesthetic*. With characteristic generosity devoid of any desire to claim Adorno as his student, it was Kracauer who pointed out in an affectionately careful and judicious review of the book that its methodology derived from the concept of truth developed by Benjamin in his studies of Goethe and the Baroque drama: "In the view of these studies [i.e. Benjamin's] the truth-content of a work reveals itself only in its collapse. . . . The work's claim to totality, its systematic structure, as well as its superficial intentions share the fate of everything transient, but as they pass away with time the work brings characteristics and configurations to the fore that are actually images of truth."[26] This process could be exemplified by a recurrent dream: throughout its recurrences its images age, if imperceptibly; its historical truth takes shape as its thematic content dissolves. It is the truth-content that gives the dream, the philosophical work, or the novel its resilience. This idea of historical truth is one of the most provocative rebuttals to historicism ever conceived: works are not studied in the interest of returning them to their own time and period, documents of "how it really was," but rather according to the truth they release in their own process of disintegration. Thus Adorno writes in *Kierkegaard*: "the innermost (and hence from Kierkegaard hidden) dialectical truth could only be disclosed in the posthumous history of his work."[27] Interpretation therefore depends on the historical configuration of the material.[28] The presentation of truth-content proceeds as a critique of the semblance of the organic, the claim to totality. The first step of Adorno's work is therefore to challenge the purported living autonomy of Kierkegaard's pseudonyms through a critique of his poetic claim: "By rejecting his claim to be a poet . . . his pseudonyms are excluded as the constitutive element of his philosophy. . . . They are not living bodies in whose incomparable existence intention is densely embedded."[29] Adorno shows the pseudonyms to be illustrations of philosophemes and thus breaks the shell of the philosophy; the imagery, however, rather than being reduced to the intention of these philosophemes, distances itself from it: "What the pseudonyms then turn out to say that is more than what the philosophical schematism had intended, their secret and concrete essence, falls, in the literalness of the disclosure, into the hands of interpretation."[30] This is not a matter of subtracting philosophical intention from imagery. Once interpretation has rejected the compulsion of identity,[31] the relation of the philosophemes to the imagery that illustrates them is reversed. The philosophemes become metaphors of the imagery that, taken literally, hold the keys to the philosophy. In *Construction of the Aesthetic* the bourgeois *intérieur* of the nineteenth century emerges as the central image of Kierkegaard's philosophy: this image is a peculiar interweaving of nature and history, and it pulls all of his thought into its perspective.

Between Neo-Kantianism and Marxism

Studies of Adorno's early writings have stuck to the facts and thus distorted them. They characteristically embrace Adorno's stated allegiance to neo-Kantian idealism in his dissertation and find a break from this position midway through his Kant/Freud study. This break is said to mark a transition from Kant to Marx; the first mature work of this Marxist was *Kierkegaard*.[32] But Adorno no more started off as a neo-Kantian—as is clear from his reminiscences of Kracauer—than he matured in any simple sense as a Marxist. *Kierkegaard*, in fact, itself places Marx in the idealist tradition by taking cognizance of Marx's effort in *Capital* to deduce society from the principle of exchange (a critique Adorno reiterated throughout his life). Adorno's positions in his early works did indeed become increasingly Marxist, but once Marx is recognized as part of the idealist tradition it is no longer possible to suppose that, as Adorno became a Marxist, a complete break from idealism was made. While there are points of complete opposition, philosophies are not mutually exclusive; it is possible, even necessary, to have Marxian thoughts as a neo-Kantian, and the reverse. When Adorno's works are not simply sorted according to the old saw of pre-and post-Marxist, a more concrete figure emerges. In his dissertation, *The Transcendent Thing and Noema in Husserl's Phenomenology,* Adorno criticizes the claim of phenomenology to having secured the mind as a sphere of directly experiential, absolute origins. This sphere of immediacy—Adorno shows—is predicated on a subterfuge. Husserl excluded the structural aspect of the object—which would have introduced synthetic, mediating mental functions—by positing a transcendental object, which was then placed by methodological caveat beyond the bounds of investigation.[33] This critique of a spurious immediacy is fundamental to all critique of ideology. In Adorno's work, however, this critique becomes more emphatic by drawing on the cognate critique of a false nature, as becomes more apparent in the Kant/Freud study. In this work Adorno employed neo-Kantian transcendental psychology to justify the psychoanalytic concept of the unconscious in opposition to the organic ideal of vitalism. An unconscious that is rationally investigable is defended against one conceived as incommensurable with reason and available only to intuition. Adorno then gives a social analysis of the motivation of the vitalist doctrine: it is an effort to establish "islands ... for the individual to which the person need only withdraw from the flood of the economic struggle in order, in contemplation or pleasure, to rest from the pressure of economic forces as at a summer camp for consciousness." But the separateness of these islands is illusory: "Freedom from the economy is nothing else than economic freedom and remains restricted to a small circle of people as a luxury."[34] The island beyond is dead center. Neither this Marxian analysis nor the psychoanalytic unconscious could finally be justified in neo-Kantian terms: both ultimately spring the unity of transcendental apperception; both reject the claim of consciousness that all its contents are "mine." It is not a surprise, then, that Adorno's neo-Kantian examiner, Cornelius, rejected the study. But however antagonistic these positions may be, Adorno was carrying out a related reflection as a neo-Kantian and as a Marxist: a realm of immediacy is shown to be established on the basis of a sort of dualism, which is itself shown to be merely tactical; once criticized, the claim to immediacy collapses. A great deal is implied here, much of which becomes apparent only in Adorno's later writings: the critique of a false immediacy, a false nature, has as its intention a true immediacy, a new nature, but dialectically through the greatest distance from it. The idea of the reversal of mediation into a second immediacy, a second nature, has its source in the romantic rejection of the antithesis of nature and technique and can be traced from Rousseau and Kant through Schiller, Hegel, and Marx, alternately functioning—as throughout Adorno's work—in sociopolitical and aesthetic contexts. In his aesthetics Adorno pursues this idea in every possible direction. In an early critique of the sound motion picture he writes that its effort to achieve a perfect organicity composed of image and voice actually tends toward stiltedness: "There is every reason to believe that the more closely pictures and words are coordinated, the more emphatically their intrinsic contradiction and the actual muteness of those who seem to be speaking are felt by the spectators." Although the effort to mimetically achieve organicity ultimately leads to stiltedness, which it is the role of film music to obscure, a true organicity can be achieved only by way of a principle of dissonant composition: "The relation between music and picture is antithetic at the very moment when the deepest unity is achieved."[35] Adorno pursues this same dialectic throughout his later writings, here characteristically: "Only the aesthetically completely articulated art work offers an image of an unmutilated reality, and thus of freedom. The art work that has been completely articulated through the most extreme mastery of the material, a work that by means of that mastery escapes most completely from simple organic existence, is once again closest to the organic."[36]

Idealism Versus Idealism

Kierkegaard's critique of idealism, particularly in the *Concluding Unscientific Postscript,* was devastating, to the point that subsequently the major works of objective idealism were hardly read.[37] Benjamin's unfamiliarity with most of these works, for example, was probably part of Kierkegaard's legacy. What is so important then, in Adorno's critique of Kierkegaard, is that it situates Kierkegaard within the idealist tradition, while taking the side of idealism against Kierkegaard. For Adorno, Enlightenment is bound to the problem of the recuperation of idealism because idealism holds the fate of the principle of identity. If reason is to be rescued from the vitalist critique, or the Kierkegaardian—in which thought attempts to repent for its claim to absoluteness by sacrificing itself in the paradox—then identity must become the force of nonidentity in such a way as to fulfill the claim to knowledge. It is therefore relevant to notice that the *Construction of the Aesthetic* is itself in the first place a "construction," a concept with a long tradition in objective idealism. Although Adorno's work does not deduce the object from the principle of identity, it remains allied with idealism in the ambiguity of its title as to whether the book is a presentation of Kierkegaard's construction or is itself the construction of the aesthetic; this ambiguity, it must be noted, amounts to a claim to know the object from within, the most emphatic concept of experience. Central to Adorno's construction is a reappropriation of Hegelian mediation. Mediation is usually understood as a going between, a third element that reconciles opposites, conceived on the model of communication and compromise. In Hegel's philosophy, however, mediation is the dialectical—that is, antagonistic—process of the object itself in its inadvertent yet constitutive dependency on what it resists; the object comes to have its other in itself in differentiating itself from its other, so that the more it is itself, the more it is finally not itself. What is excluded prevails, and this transpires most intensely and is best seen as the object's essence in the extremes of the object under consideration. In these terms, any effort to discover the truth of a matter by seeking the average or the mean of its reality sets up a smoke screen. Truth appears in the dialectical extreme; exaggeration is not just a rhetorical gesture, but reality's own route to the truth to which dialectical thinking relentlessly devotes itself. Thus, where the distinguished Helmut Kuhn felt that the failure of Adorno's work was that no fixed concepts emerged, he would have done well to have emphasized the difference between vagueness and a conceptual acuity that seeks reality at just that point where the concept itself is no longer absolute. Had he done so, Kuhn would have put his finger on the book's achievement, which is its capacity to immerse itself in the realia of Kierkegaard. In Adorno's study every fragment of Kierkegaard's work can be treated micrologically because each includes in itself its opposite as its own essence, and this opposite is the whole. This whole, however, is not the totality of thought but a self-antagonistic reality whose comprehension has been chastened of any last claim to organic oneness. There is a systematic aspect to this reasoning, certainly, and to the structure of Adorno's philosophy as well, but only insofar as that power is the capacity of the system militated in opposition to itself. Just as in Adorno's aesthetics, then, the art work is socially interpretable not because it represents society but because it acquires its social content through resistance to society and is thus the unconscious writing of history, so Kierkegaardian inwardness, the spiritual *intérieur*, gains its determinations through negation. In opposition to the privations of early high capitalism, the Kierkegaardian *intérieur* was to encompass "a lost 'immediacy'"[38] and function "as a romantic island where the individual undertakes to shelter his 'meaning' from the historical flood."[39] But precisely "by denying the social question Kierkegaard falls to the mercy of his own historical situation, that of the *rentier* in the first half of the nineteenth century."[40] The imagery of the *intérieur* reveals social contents: a class-based asceticism is sedimented in it. By the effort to overcome the body, this sociological spiritualism turns back on itself. Kierkegaard's imagery uses the living body exclusively as an allegory of truth and untruth: "This, to be sure, indicates the crucial reversal. If the body only appears under the sign of the 'meaning' of the truth and untruth of spirit, then in return spirit remains bound to the body as its expression."[41] The more spirit eviscerates the body, the more it depends on what it excludes: ultimately, "nature takes possession of it [spirit] where it occurs most historically in objectless interiority."[42] In the spirit's will to autonomy, it falls to the mercy of nature: "My soul is so heavy that thought can no more sustain it, no wingbeat lift it up into the ether."[43] Autonomous spirit is necessarily melancholic: "Bodiless spirit for him [Kierkegaard] becomes a burden that drags him into despair."[44]

Allegory

In the setting of the sun, the Baroque allegorists pictured the fall of the king. This allegorical image bears "the seal of the all too earthly": history, the king, "has physically merged into the setting," nature.[45] The unpuzzling of such natural-historical figures is the primary interest of Benjamin's study of the Baroque, *The Origin of the German Play of*

Lamentation. In his study of Kierkegaard's imagery, Adorno explicitly followed Benjamin's lead. Since Benjamin's theory of allegory stands at the center of *Kierkegaard*, as it does at the center of Adorno's philosophy altogether, its introduction would be useful here. This, however, would be made more difficult by drawing directly on Benjamin's work rather than on the work he was translating while he was preparing his study of the Baroque, and that may have given him his own critical insight into allegory, Proust's *À la recherche du temps perdu*. In *Combray* Marcel tries to understand the allegorical character of a servant girl, "a sickly creature far 'gone' in pregnancy."[46] What strikes Marcel about her is that her face shows no spiritual trace of the symbol born by her body: "The figure of this girl had been enlarged by the additional symbol that she carried in her body, without appearing to understand what it meant, without any rendering in her facial expression of all its beauty and spiritual significance, but carried as if it were an ordinary and rather heavy burden."[47] Here significance is not meaningful but a physical burden, and in this transformation of meaning into nature Marcel recognizes the servant girl's relation to other allegorical characters. Like the pregnancy of the servant, a portrait of "Envy" bears a serpent on her tongue. But, rather than the serpent being expressed in her face as "envy," Envy herself looked like "a plate in some medical book, illustrating the compression of the glottis or uvula by a tumour in the tongue."[48] Marcel sums up his observations and the entire fascination of allegory in a single parenthesis that distinguishes it from symbol: allegories are not symbols "(for the thought symbolised was nowhere expressed)."[49] This, however, does not mean that the allegories are inexpressive; their expression, rather, is by way of nonexpression; the collapse of meaning into nature. In a talk Adorno gave just before the final revisions of *Kierkegaard*, "The Idea of Natural-History," he presented the methodological idea of Kierkegaard (though not by name) as that of allegory: "Whenever 'second nature' appears, when the world of convention approaches, it can be deciphered in that its meaning is shown to be precisely its transience."[50] Paraphrasing Adorno, nature appears at the greatest extreme of second nature.[51] Although this thought is drawn from Benjamin, its form is Hegelian. The Hegelian dialectic, passed through Benjamin's idea of allegory, became in Adorno's work the form for the interpretation of all culture. No longer a dialectic of progress, shorn of any last trace of organicism, the Hegelian dialectic, as the critique of any first, continually transforms meaning into the expression of transience. For Adorno, as he once said in a lecture, "the aim of philosophy is to say by way of concepts precisely what it is that cannot be said, to say the unsayable."[52] He clarified this at another point: "One could almost say that the aim of philosophy is to translate pain into the concept."[53] This would be the aim of a Hegelian dialectic that has become the presentation of allegory.

Revisions

In a letter of September 20, 1932, written from the home of his fiancée, Adorno apologized to the composer Ernst Krenek for having been unable to respond sooner:

> I have been here for two months and living under the most extreme pressure. November 1st I must deliver the final manuscript for my book on Kierkegaard to Mohr, the publisher. Initially the revisions were only to trim the manuscript for publication; once I got into it, however, I found that I had to rewrite it altogether; certainly every stone of the original has been maintained, but not one remains where it once stood, every sentence has been reformulated, the whole has now for the first time been truly worked-through . . . and large and precisely central sections have been completely rethought. And all this has been compressed into the period between September 8th and November 1st. I must tell you, I am really in the harness: in three weeks I've dragged eighty pages out of myself, and I may say of the most rigorous sort.[54]

Adorno did not exaggerate the intensity with which the material was at once maintained and completely transformed. Here is a juxtaposition of the manuscript's first few lines followed by the corresponding lines of the revision:

> All attempts to comprehend the writings of philosophers as poetry have missed their truth-content. The object of philosophy is reality, which is interpreted by philosophy. Only by comprehending reality does the subjectivity of the philosopher stand the test. Neither the

communication of this subjectivity, however profound, nor the degree of the work's internal coherence, decide its philosophical quality, but only the claim and the justice of the claim to state the truth about the real.[55]

All attempts to comprehend the writings of philosophers as poetry have missed their truth-content. Philosophical form requires the interpretation of the real as a binding nexus of concepts. Neither the manifestation of the thinker's subjectivity nor the pure coherence of the work determines its character as philosophy. This is, rather, determined in the first place by the degree to which the real has entered into concepts, manifests itself in these concepts, and comprehensibly justifies them.[56]

Adorno's excitement in his letter was not only over his productivity but also over the unexpected emergence of what became his mature style. Characteristic of the revisions was that the language becomes more self-assuredly Hegelian; the most capable phrases—among which the first line of this passage—were maintained, while the rest (though this is not true of this passage) underwent extreme condensation. By the time Adorno delivered the manuscript to Mohr a month later, he had cut it by half. Structurally, the basic order of the chapters remained intact; Chapters 1, 4, and 6 were least revised, and many headings and subheadings were maintained throughout. Yet much was changed, most important: chapter 1 lost a section entitled "The Aesthetic as a Category of Knowledge"; the title of chapter 2 changed from "Subject and Ontology" to "Constitution of Inwardness"; the title of chapter 4 changed from "Analysis of the Existential" to "Concept of Existence"; chapter 5 lost three major sections—"Excursus on Constellation," "Excursus on Goethe," and "Abstraction and Concretion"; chapter 6 lost sections on the "Mythical Character of Kierkegaard's Christentum" and "Demythologization"; the title of chapter 7 changed from "Rescuing the Aesthetic" to the title of the book, "Construction of the Aesthetic," its first section from "Apology of Melancholy" to "Transformation of Melancholy," the second from "Semblance and Reconciliation" to "Disappearance of Existence," and the last from "Outline of the Ontological in the Fragment" to "Transcendence of Longing." Without trying to find the common denominator of all these revisions, what is evident is a trimming back of ontological efforts, though not to the point demanded by his later philosophy. In *Kierkegaard* Adorno is still concerned with the possibility of a rescue of ontology. Along with the reduction of passages on ontology, theological motifs are also dropped at many points. This, however, is more of a sublimation than excision, for theology is always moving right under the surface of all Adorno's writings. This theological context is so dense that one can easily fail to be struck by the peculiarity that, for example, Adorno dated the published notice of an edition of *Kierkegaard* "Easter 1963." The degree to which theology penetrates every word of his writings can be measured by the most misfired sentence he ever wrote, what is perhaps the lamest appreciation the philosopher of negation ever penned, one that points far beyond biographical attachments: in his introduction to Benjamin's writings he compared Benjamin's fascination to that of the reflected light of a Christmas tree.[57] Opaque ideas in Adorno (as in Benjamin) often become immediately comprehensible when grasped in this context of theological interests. The idea of "truth-content" for example, which has remained so obscure, is a work's content of hope. *Kierkegaard* itself is the research of hope in Kierkegaard's oeuvre. It is not hard to sympathize with this effort in any year, least of all 1933. Still, as the research of hope, *Kierkegaard* wants to take hope under its wing; when it does, it becomes ministerial and damages itself. On the last page of the book, Adorno writes of the "inconspicuous hope" sedimented in Kierkegaard's imagery; lists of similar passages could be given, including a passage in which he writes, "No truer image of hope can be imagined than that of ciphers, readable as traces, dissolving in history, disappearing in front of overflowing eyes, indeed confirmed in lamentation."[58] The passage is beautiful, but the mistakenness of this beauty is betrayed by its coziness, which brings it to the edge of rationalization.[59] Kafka's often quoted response to the question of whether there is hope, liberally translated, "Oh yes, great hope, but not for us," is soberly optimistic in comparison with these passages. The best that can be done for them is to translate them back into the helplessness that motivates them. In the revisions of *Kierkegaard,* particularly in the sublimation of the theological, the distance to his later works was already being covered. The author's notice to the 1966 edition of *Kierkegaard* drops "Easter." In *Aesthetic Theory* (1969), his last work, the idea of hope no longer sails in through the window on a silken pillow: rather the work hones itself rigorously to the idea of allegory's own jagged boundaries. In the sparseness of the late Adorno the air may be thin, but it is what can be breathed; it carries out the revision of the earlier image of the reading of the palimpsest: "Authentic art knows the expression of the expressionless, a crying from which the tears are missing."[60]

Second Salvage

Prolegomenon to a Reconstruction of *Current of Music*

Another way to say the search for reality is to say the desire for completion.

—Clifford Odets

The centenary of T. W. Adorno's birth was a lugubrious display internationally, but most of all in Germany. There the event was headed up by a brace of three heavily shod biographies trudging in decade-long synchronization toward the publishing occasion, as if the goal were to make sure that no detail of Adorno's life went untrampled. Even Adorno's writing table and chair were dragged into the Frankfurt ceremonies. Encased in a silicone cube, these mundane furnishings were established as a national treasure to be visited on Adornoplatz in hometown perpetuum. Suhrkamp Publishers and the Goethe Institute, working closely with a restaffed and now corporate-minded Adorno-Archiv, distributed so absolute a mass of memento, chronology, and photograph—the known antipodes to Adorno's philosophy itself—that even under scrutiny it was often hard to decide whether the topic was, for instance, the writing of *Dialectic of Enlightenment* or the framing of the Magna Carta. The jubilee successfully portrayed the life of the man as if a single stride carried him from birth to garlanded tomb. One result of these centenary achievements is that now every next mention of Adorno's life can only help steal away from the apprehension that "Life does not live" any sense this ever troubled the person who once set the apothegm to preside over

Minima Moralia.[1] The biographical focus, undermining the philosophy, finally undermined the biographical as well. This bears directly on the intention of this essay to provide a first, if provisional, introduction to *Current of Music*. For, as is to be explained, Adorno left the manuscripts of *Current of Music* in fragmentary condition; what is conceptually valuable in them now depends in part on reconstruction. An assumption of this reconstruction has been that, when a work is abandoned in fragments, reference to the life that left them behind can legitimately provide transitions to potentiate tensions of thought that, deprived of their law of form, would otherwise dissipate. Certainly this assumption might have been more naively pursued prior to the centenary year. The only alternative now—for this essay in any case—is to look the situation in the face and acknowledge that, in the transitions established here to provision a fragmentary work with a degree of tensed coherence, what is biographical in them has recently been woven into something milled out by the mile. Perhaps in this recognition what is now lifeless, with the feel of having never lived, will at least half speak of this situation rather than simply compound the recently achieved inertness.

New York City, 1938–1941

In 1937 T. W. Adorno had been living in England for three years, having fled National Socialism. Although he formerly had been a *Privatdozent* in philosophy—an independent lecturer—at the University of Frankfurt, the Nazis had deprived him of the right to teach, and the hardship of immigration had set him back to the status of a student at work on a dissertation, a critique of Husserlian phenomenology. He was obliged to hope that a D.Phil., taken at Oxford, in addition to his Ph.D., would provide the overqualification that an immigrant would minimally need to secure a position at a British university.[2] In October, however, a telegram from Max Horkheimer caused him to revise these plans. Horkheimer had for some time wanted to bring Adorno to New York City, and the telegram proposed the means if Adorno were interested in participating in the Princeton Radio Research Project, a study supported by a Rockefeller Foundation grant under the direction of the sociologist and Austrian émigré Paul Lazarsfeld.[3] The next day Adorno wired back his readiness to accept the position,[4] but hardly without ambivalence. On one hand, Adorno recognized that catastrophe was inevitable in Europe; he had no likely expectation of securing academic employment in prewar England; and his wife, Gretel, was ill. She found the English climate hard to tolerate, and it was hoped that she might recover in the United States. But once his plans to depart had become reality and, "contrary to all expectation," imminent, Adorno expressed in a letter of November 27 to Walter Benjamin what had all along weighed most against. "*Uppermost*"—Adorno wrote—were his thoughts on Benjamin himself, and in these few words he lodged his distress as poignantly as possible between two men who after a decade of close involvement still addressed one another formally, as *Sie*. If Benjamin would realize, he wrote—elucidating this *uppermost* by lending to the meaning of this friendship the attribute of what it exceeded—that *second* on his mind was that parting meant "the real possibility of never seeing my mother again," Benjamin would be able to "imagine how I feel about" the decision to leave.[5] But, Adorno explained, he could not refuse Horkheimer's proposal. He had been assured that fully half his time would be devoted to the Institute for Social Research, then affiliated with Columbia University, and collaboration on projects that he and Horkheimer had long envisioned, most of all a study of dialectical materialism. By early January, Adorno had met in Paris with Lazarsfeld and by late in that month had submitted to him a lengthy memorandum outlining his research plans.[6] On February 26, 1938, Adorno and his wife arrived on the steamship *Champlain* in New York City harbor. Adorno would remain in New York City until November 1941, when—without renewed funding for his position at the Princeton Radio Research Project—he would again be compelled to move in order to secure his proximity to Horkheimer, who had decided to go on to Los Angeles where his own fragile health, and the institute's finances as well, could be better maintained. Adorno would not return to Germany until 1949, having spent almost one quarter of his life as a refugee, a portion of that as an American citizen. He did not embrace German citizenship again until 1955.

Written in English

In his fifteen years as a refugee T. W. Adorno wrote several major works including *Dialectic of Enlightenment* (with Max Horkheimer,

1947), *Philosophy of New Music* (1949), and *Minima Moralia* (1951). Their dates of publication belie the years demanded by each of these seminal German texts, which no doubt received Adorno's most decisive conceptual energies. Yet, in addition to these and many other projects, Adorno in the same period also produced a substantial body of research written in English. The latter consists of distinctly secondary works from the perspective of the oeuvre as a whole, but these are nevertheless, in their own terms, of considerable interest. Among these writings in English are *The Psychological Technique of Martin Luther Thomas's Radio Addresses* (1943) and *Authoritarian Personality* (with Else Frenkel-Brunswik, Daniel Levinson, and R. Nevitt Sanford, 1950). "Current of Music" was the working title that Adorno proposed on various occasions for a volume that would have assembled the majority of the research that he completed during his first four years in the United States while affiliated with Lazarsfeld in New York City. The texts conceived under this title—approximately a thousand pages—constitute far and away Adorno's most extensive work in English.[7]

Yet Adorno did not succeed in his own lifetime at publishing this work whose topic and language were adopted under compulsion in the land to which its author fled. The study itself was rejected by a series of editors in the United States and ultimately left incomplete among the many materials housed at the Adorno-Archiv in Frankfurt. This essay intends to explain what Adorno meant to achieve in the book and why his efforts failed. It should be remarked at the outset, however, that this introduction in no way seeks pathos in defense of a work lost to history, as if deserving in reconstruction the rank of *texte maudit* or *Buergerschreck*, for it is neither. If passages of *Current of Music*—both published and unpublished—did once antagonize and have the capacity to do so again, it was not only ill will and happenstance that got in its way but just as much and more the work's own deficiencies. It is in full cognizance of the limits of these writings that *Current of Music* is now to be tentatively imagined into existence. This requires broad recognition and explanation of the complex situation in which this work—in its many parts—was written. In alliance with its own thinking, however, this reconstruction is certainly not undertaken here with the intention of setting the past back on its feet, like a golem conjured to walk the streets of another millennium, but rather by wanting to spark what is significant in that past when it is known self-consciously from the perspective of the present.

Music, Electricity, and Cultural Hunger

The current of *Current of Music* is electricity. Before the early 1920s and 1930s electricity had yet to be used on a vast scale for the reproduction of musical sound. The technology of radio transmission had been developed during World War I in the United States by a government that, in need of reliable means of communication with its European troops, seized by eminent domain the patents and work of private inventors. Only in the following decades was this technology exploited for the literal capacity evident in the electrical metaphor— the current that powers radio—to produce music in streams and even floods of sound across any quantity of space simultaneously.[8] The desire to receive this *current of music* produced the early momentum in radio sales: whereas only ten thousand families owned sets in 1922, twenty-seven million families—out of thirty-two million in the United States—owned sets by 1939.[9]

If it is easily imagined that the introduction of radio music would motivate the rapid distribution of the device, it is not so easily guessed that a large proportion of the music heard in the United States on those radios was art music of the European classical tradition. Many stations broadcast live classical music exclusively: In 1921, for instance, the Chicago station KYW broadcast "all performances of the Chicago Civic Opera, afternoon and evening, six days a week—and nothing else."[10] WQXR in New York City played classical music 80 percent of the time and in the other 20 percent talked primarily about it and the other arts. The more expensive radio sets were themselves advertised as having been built for distinguished music; they were fine "instruments" that the listener faced as they "played," and the listener was expected to be interested in their proper "tuning." No less than the conductor Leopold Stokowski gave instruction for bringing the equipment up to pitch: "In tuning-in on the wave length desired there is a central point of maximum clarity and truth of reception." The skill of "perfect tuning" was extolled as an optimal capacity, akin to having perfect pitch.[11] Radio stations that transmitted serious music portrayed themselves as conservatories: "A visit to station WMAQ [in Chicago] is like entering a music conservatory. You enter a reception room ... then on into the studio ... artistically furnished in brown tones ... here and there, a large fern ... and a Mason and Hamlin grand piano."[12]

This image of early radio devoted in significant proportion to European art music might prompt a now fading yet enduringly real resentment in contemporary American readers, as if that was a moment when *high* could still lord it over *low*. But in the early and genuinely class-conscious decades of American radio, when questions of the equitable redistribution of wealth and privilege were actually discussed—as they now rarely are—and an end was sought to much openly acknowledged resentment, the broadcast of European art music was a model of possible democratization. Contrary to what might be guessed at today, the distinction between *popular* and *classical* was loosely synonymous with what in those decades was discerned as the distinction between *light*—or *light popular*—and *serious* music. In the manuscripts of *Current of Music* Adorno himself regularly deals with these two sets of categories as being easily interchangeable in the assumptions of the age. The significance of this is in what the now mostly forgotten pair *light* and *serious* music contributed to the synonymity. The distinction it drew indicates that the idea of amusement had not yet subordinated music entirely. Although the exclusivity of music as amusement was ascendant, a contrary seriousness of listening was commonly acknowledged as legitimate and valued. When *high* and *low* were invoked, the thinking involved was complex in a way that is now unfamiliar, since in the minds of many what was *high* was often valued as what ought to become the possession of all.

The evidence for this goes far beyond what can be derived from juxtaposed sets of terms. For the idea of culture itself had not yet suffered the catastrophic implication of World War II; culture was still thought to be a human privilege marked by, but all the same distinguishable from, class privilege. When—for instance—Barnett Newman ran for mayor of New York in 1933, his manifesto was titled "On the Need for Political Action by Men of Culture." While his candidacy stood in minority and beleaguered opposition, he, all the same, had enough support to be able to write confidently of his candidacy that "culture is the foundation of not only our present society, but of all our hopes for all future societies to come."[13] This was characteristic of the expression of democratically minded individuals and institutions of various kinds and—in the "red decade"—especially those many on the wide spectrum of the left who readily encouraged and fought for the broad distribution of art music. In Manhattan, for instance, the City Center for Music and Drama was established by the

city government in alliance with trade union organizations to present
symphony, ballet, and opera inexpensively to working-class audiences. The center was vigorously capable of supporting its own ballet
and opera companies. In its own day, when the accomplishments of
the City Center were discussed, its success was generally acknowledged not in terms of bringing *high* to *low* but in the fact that unlike
the Metropolitan Opera, which was segregated, its opera house was
not.[14]

Radio was acknowledged above all other institutions in this period
as having the preeminent capacity to universalize performances of a
human culture that was previously restricted to the wealthy. Its diffu-
sion was civic policy. In 1937 New York City's Mayor Fiorello La
Guardia appeared on what was then the city's proudly owned municipal radio station, WNYC—then under the directorship of the former
head of the Socialist Worker's League Morris Novik, whom La
Guardia had appointed—to comment as a "music lover" on Beethoven. The mayor provided "little stories about all the composers represented on the program and the music being played. . . . He had the appearance of a man tackling an important job with great earnestness."[15]
It only makes the same point to note here, with the mention of Morris
Novik, that it was his office that two years later would engage Adorno
in plans to present a lecture series as a citywide educational introduction to modern music on Sunday afternoons, during the station's most
listened-to hours. Although those plans were only partly realized,
their existence is representative of a forward-looking orientation to
radio and music that could not now be conceived on a major American radio station.

In these first decades of radio, those who had hopes for it expected
it to wipe away the stigma of class privilege borne by art music, and
this expectation met with success. As one commentator in *Harper's
Monthly Magazine* observed, "Until the past few years such music was
the rather expensive privilege of the inhabitants of a few large
cities."[16] This observation was confirmed by statistics assembled in the
late thirties and reported in a 1938 article in *Harper's Monthly Magazine*: For though quantitatively all economic classes listened more
to *light music* than *serious music*, as a result of radio a majority of
Americans, black and white, came to like and listen to serious music.
Four-fifths of the homes in the nation heard at least one symphonic or
operatic broadcast a week.[17] Even in rural areas, where radio most

dramatically changed life but where interest in classical music was predictably less than in cities, there were stations like WOI in Ames, Iowa—much studied by the Princeton Radio Research Project—that combined farm news and market reports with its most popular program, *The Music Shop*, a daily broadcast of short symphonic pieces, chamber music, and music education.[18] These broadcasts were especially directed to "the farmer's wife," who, as Adorno mentions repeatedly in *Current of Music,* became a mythically invoked figure in discussions of radio's democratizing cultural potential. The invention of radio, it was said, would enable her to go about her household chores while attending Carnegie Hall and the Philharmonic gratis alongside the well healed and mink clad. And in some regions of the country this mythical intention found reality. A characteristic letter from a female listener to WOI reads: "The more I hear good music, such as you give us, the more I love it, and the more I hear that kind the more I dislike the other kind."[19]

What certainly rings of another age in this woman's comments is the, for us, apparently naive desire for self-improvement to be gained through familiarity with music held to be objectively superior. It is to be emphasized again that this woman was part of a movement. A now discredited idea of culture implicitly provided individuals with a critical stance toward their own perceptions and directed them with substantial expectation toward the promise of radio. Again, in the voice of *Harper's:*

> Millions are haunted by such feelings of hunger for learning, for acquiring new arts, for self-improvement. And radio today makes an earnest effort to satisfy that hunger.[20]

Radio Pedagogy

This statement evoking the power of radio to nourish an age urgently beset by the need for educational self-improvement could hardly be more emphatic. And to rid this hunger, radio institutions of several kinds were established, including "schools of the air" to which Adorno frequently refers in *Current of Music.* It was possible, for instance, to obtain a "broad though simplified education in the arts and sciences . . . by sitting in front of your loudspeaker" at WNYC's *School for Listeners* or by following programs at the University of the Air, broadcast by "The Voice of Labor," the Eugene Debs memorial station WEVD. The latter presented complete classes in history, philosophy, labor, literature, and economics.[21]

But the single most significant pedagogical effort by radio in those decades, and in fact the most substantial pedagogical undertaking ever in the history of American broadcast media, the *NBC Music Appreciation Hour*, was a result of the success of radio in making European art music available nationally. It was a program for the cultivation of musical knowledge and taste, and it is of specific interest here because in *Current of Music* Adorno devotes a lengthy essay to it and conceived the plan of his own educational broadcast in critical relation to it.[22] For better than a decade, from 1928 to 1942, the program was led by the conductor of the New York Symphony Philharmonic, Walter Damrosch. The program at its height was heard weekly as required curriculum throughout the academic year in more than seventy thousand schools nationwide, by more than seven million students.[23] Educational materials coordinated with the nationally broadcast concert season in New York City were printed in the hundreds of thousands and distributed to classrooms in yearly editions; teachers received accompanying pedagogical instructions and test blanks to administer. Even now, reviewing the achievements of Damrosch's program from statistics presented in the same 1938 *Harper's Monthly Magazine* article that reported the demographics of national listening habits, one might believe in the expectations it expressed, shared by many at the time, that the interest in serious music produced by radio had led the masses of Americans to the "threshold of cultural maturity":

> A sound and deep appreciation among the masses of our people is growing first in music and will draw after it, but more slowly, a love of the best in the other arts. . . . The American people, in the mass, are at the threshold of a cultural maturity.[24]

Statistical Inner Ear: Results

This passage was built out of the rhetoric of high hopes, certainly, but was founded, too, on developments in technology and an analysis of listenership in a major segment of American society. The reality it carried compellingly in its own moment heightens the acuity of the statistical riposte it receives in its encounter with how things in fact turned out. In 2003 there are 14,392 strictly "formatted" radio stations in the United States, of which 147 are classical stations, 34 of them commercial.[25] These statistics are not reported here as if they might reveal to anyone what has occurred in American music. The world as a whole is in all things more familiar with the United States than the reverse, but on the level of consciousness its commanding international presence is foremost in the music it exports, up until very recently by means of radio as its primary vehicle of distribution. Any number of American songs named here might ineluctably provoke their playing in an inner ear that is worldwide. Since music is the most binding and involuntary form of neurocultural memory, every mind reading this essay is obliged to acknowledge to itself that it is to some degree an artifact of what has transpired musically in the United States. If this seems provokingly self-evident, this is the feeling that the distinguished jazz historian, conductor, and composer Gunther Schuller touches on in his analysis of the situation of music as it had developed in the United States by the 1980s, a description that is equally relevant internationally: "We have here an essentially victimized American population whose freedom of choice in matters musical is virtually denied them."[26] From Schuller's perspective and the available statistics, then, the expectations of 1938 expressed in *Harper's Monthly Magazine* would seem to have been simply broadsided by the historical development. But this is not altogether the case, and, on second look, what that 1938 article presents turns out to have been more prescient than not as a harbinger of the situation Schuller portrays. For what carried the high hopes of 1938, the wave that can be felt buoying up these cultural anticipations, is perceptible as the statistical realities cited, themselves becoming statistics as reality. The early statistics not only reported a situation but increasingly became functional elements in the commercial manufacture of music, for they participated in the elimination of music that owed its quality to having been made on another basis. Given the significance of the rise of radio market research for the history of music in the United States, it is of central importance for understanding the conflicts that would shape *Current of Music* to note that a preeminent institution for the development of market research in radio in the thirties and early forties was the Princeton Radio Research Project, whose statistics, as it happens, the *Harper's Monthly Magazine* article relied on.

Third-Party Listening and Academic Tycoon

Lazarsfeld himself initially provided the offices for the Princeton Radio Research Project in vacant factory space in Newark, New Jersey. The rundown, haphazard location was an implication of the fact that this was a privately held research venture that solicited contracts from public, commercial, and philanthropic sources. A brilliant statistician, single-mindedly pragmatic and by his own statement prepared to be ruthlessly so, he developed a talent for transforming the practical problems of commerce and public interest into research projects undertaken in conjunction with university services, which he facilitated and supervised. Lazarsfeld's considerable significance in the history of sociology, beyond a group of skillfully conceived research projects, was for the invention in the late 1930s of an organizational structure that put the new science of sociology at the service of commercial interests. This innovation would complete his transformation from a young Austrian intellectual, passionately devoted as a Marxist activist to the implementation of "a psychology of imminent revolution," to the author of a valuable study of unemployment, to a professor at Columbia University in Manhattan who in later life would be an academic tycoon.[27]

While the Princeton Radio Research Project was situated at the turning point in Lazarsfeld's career, it was located at a significant moment as well in the history of the sociology of radio. Prior to its research there were few sources of information not only on the listenership of radio music but also on all aspects of radio audition, including attention span, listening preferences and habits, general program satisfaction and dissatisfaction, and local, regional, and national variables. According to the terms of its grant, under the title "The Essential Value of Radio to All Types of Listeners," the Princeton Radio Research Project established itself as a major undertaking for the collection and analysis of radio audience information. It was to develop the tools for audience measurement along many parameters and demonstrate the usefulness of these measurements for the improvement of radio. By learning more about what audiences wanted and how radio succeeded or failed to provide for these needs, it would help make radio as valuable and useful to its listeners as possible. The philanthropic nature of this project would have been unmistakable in decades when radio was not only looked to as a source of education and cultural good but lived in the national imagination as the voice of social cohesiveness itself as the one ready means of societywide communication and vigilance. In the iconography of the age, radio's high, beaming towers radiated a masterful charisma and, especially during the war years, were as much beacons of safety as thought to be key targets for enemy plots. The broadcast industry itself, having only recently won the privatization of the broadcast system and the right to advertise, in a series of much-disputed legislative struggles themselves still within living memory, was piously careful to emphasize radio's performance of social services and its contributions to national moral integrity.

This context certainly magnified the philanthropic claim of a project to research "The Essential Value of Radio for All Types of Listeners." But held up to the light and examined a second time, the title plainly also refracted other potentials. It might well have named an undertaking to provide information about what listeners most valued to some third party with heteronomous purposes for this "essential value." Once this is noticed, it is hard to decide what the title was about. It could, of course, have carried both meanings, as it seems to, but, if so, this ambiguity does not need to prevail in simple shapelessness. An otherwise rarely acknowledged hermeneutical device, a dinner party, solves the question. This particular supper, an award ceremony scheduled for the night of February 15, 1940, elucidates the definitive kinds of alliances at work at the Princeton Project: Frank Stanton, soon to be the president of Columbia Broadcasting System, wrote John Marshall, the grant supervisor at the Rockefeller Foundation, to announce with pleasure that on that February evening Paul Lazarsfeld would be honored by the advertising industry as the individual who had revealed "the educational significance of radio programs."[28] "Significance" could not, of course, mean that Lazarsfeld had discovered that radio had an educational significance, for which it was already so broadly admired. On the contrary, Lazarsfeld had been chosen advertising's man of the year in the area of research for having brought together people from commerce and academia and having thus succeeded in demonstrating the economic significance of radio education for advertisers. The award read:

> By integrating research efforts of individuals affiliated with both commercial and academic organizations, a significant beginning was made in 1939 to . . . interpret the social aspects of radio in terms of economic pertinence to the commercial user of the medium.[29]

The dates are coincidental, but it does represent a motivated convergence of realities that within days of this announcement further funding of Adorno's position at the Princeton Radio Research Project was denied by John Marshall at the Rockefeller Foundation, and Lazarsfeld himself learned that he had been hired as a professor of sociology at Columbia University.

Historical Accuracy

Deference to historical accuracy has required that the end of Adorno's employment at the Princeton Radio Research Program be indicated prior to a word being said about his part in the project, for in every regard the alliance was over before it started. Initially, however, the collaboration did have certain plausibilities. Lazarsfeld shared with Adorno an interest in experimentation in qualitative sociological research. This was relevant to the broad latitude of investigation granted Adorno when he was appointed director of the Music Study division that, on the basis of its research, was to provide proposals for the improvement of the reception of broadcast music. This responsibility was among the foremost to any success of the project since music comprised 50 percent of broadcast time and, as discussed, the programming of classical music in particular enjoyed indisputable national esteem. It must have seemed obvious to Lazarsfeld, given the expectations for what radio broadcast of serious music might contribute to masses at the "threshold of cultural maturity," that Adorno if anyone would have affiliated himself energetically with the cultural movement of the democratic left in the United States in seeking ways to ameliorate broadcast reception. As a cultural philosopher, as a distinguished music critic, as a composer and a musician, he apparently combined a devotion to serious music with the capacity for the technical musical discernments to address what was then the central problem of the reception of broadcast music: the divergence between the audition of live musical performance and its reproduction on radio.[30]

But it was a complete misunderstanding to suppose that Adorno would cast his lot with a movement to spread musical culture. He carried no torch for culture, and least of all for musical culture. When he arrived in the United States what was fresh to his mind was the thought of a *Bildungsbuergertum*—the culture-prizing bourgeoisie— then to be found in the streets of the "homeland of culture" carrying real torches. This capitulation of German culture had not been an utter surprise to him. On the contrary, German culture had failed to ward off the worst just because, as Adorno once wrote, it had long been the ally of the worst. Adorno had seen it coming in the deep perspectives of the opposition drawn by all radical art, since romanticism, to bogus culture. The music with which Adorno was most allied, the idiom of free atonality in which he composed, had inherited that jagged radical tradition. The concerts of the Second Viennese School had their own legitimacy confirmed, inadvertently, in the outrage, catcalls, and whistlings brought down on them by audiences sworn to higher things. Adorno's own account of trying to console Alban Berg after a concert premiere that had won direct public acclaim, walking him through the streets of Berlin much of an evening, may seem a charming tale of eccentricity until it is realized that, given what was on the horizon, Berg was right to be distraught. In the absence of a culture worthy of the name, culture for Adorno was what it was for Flaubert, namely, the power to resist it, and as such synonymous with art that is genuinely art. By the late 1930s, in "The Artwork in the Age of Its Mechanical Reproduction," Walter Benjamin forced this self-antagonistic struggle in the concept of culture to its limit. In utter opposition to the art religion of an elite whose eyelids shut tight under the magic that art spread over a foundering society, Benjamin sought to demolish that glow, to tear art away from its spellbinding semblance and, even at the price of art itself, achieve a stark power of critical observation. He would see art subjected to its industrial antagonist, the machinery of mechanical reproduction.[31]

Embodied in this thesis, Benjamin was indeed every bit as *uppermost* in the thinking of the new director of the Princeton Radio Research Projects Music Study as he had been for Adorno in Europe. Regardless whether Adorno had arrived in Japan or New Zealand, it was the logic of Benjamin's thesis that he was most urgently concerned to respond to. The questions it posed to him, in a catastrophic moment, could not have combined with the directions of his own thought in a more tense, austere view of culture. It is hardly worth trying to imagine anyone less ready than Adorno to be enthused by cultural boosterism of any kind. In the United States he perceived no masses prompted by a new familiarity with great music to the verge of cultural maturity, and, if he had, he would have judged it a specious achievement. Adorno would have been suspicious of—not thrilled by—the lady in Iowa who wrote to WOI enthused with her tale of self-improvement in a quest for the better things. For Adorno, music *appreciation*, inculcated by radio, could only instill the opposite of a capacity for musical experience. Alongside his later essays addressed to Stravinsky and Heidegger, his essay on Walter Damrosch's *NBC Music Appreciation Hour*[32] is the most sustained, vituperative attack in the whole of his oeuvre and, like those other essays, perhaps hobbled by the intensity of the siege. And if Adorno could not in any way value the most comprehensive effort of musical education in the history of the United States as a value of radio, Lazarsfeld had probably selected the person least likely to be of any plausible use to him in completing a study on improving radio reception. In the letter he would eventually write Adorno to bring his participation in the project to a close, Lazarsfeld would accuse Adorno of having given him what "is definitely a black eye for me."[33] Just months into their association, indeed, Lazarsfeld already sensed his misstep and that Adorno was a danger to the project. In December 1938 Lazarsfeld wrote Frank Stanton, perhaps to begin to register formally his coming disassociation from Adorno:

> I have to decide: whether W. A. [Wiesengrund Adorno] has just a queer way of behaving of which he might be cured or whether he has a basically wrong attitude which might disqualify him in spite of his other abilities.[34]

Mechanical Reproduction and Musical Abstraction

Lazarsfeld's emphatic normalcy would hardly have provided grounds for cooperation with Adorno's efforts to explicate musical experience

that disintegrates and shatters normalcy. Neither was Adorno's formulation of social problems to find substantial resonance among
many colleagues or readers in the United States. His detailed, outraged critique of Damrosch, for instance, was apposite to what such a
diluted, lowbrow program might have deserved in Germany more
than in a country where, except for Damrosch's program, schoolchild-
ren might never have heard the words *string quartet*. Adorno's critique
of culture, the kind of antagonism he felt toward evocations of "cultural treasure," was keyed to so different a society that it could not estimate the place in many lives of the serious music newly provided by
radio. The United States is, after all, a country that in its everyday
imaginings thinks of its origins in Bible and Constitution, not in a
poet, Homer; it has only intermittently granted artistic culture the status of being a vehicle of the highest things, and then almost exclusively
within the confines of the thinking and writing of artists themselves,
barely in a broader elite and not at all in the general population. In the
United States the phenomenon of a *Bildungsbuergertum* would be as
inconceivable as the word itself is stubbornly untranslatable; there
would never be an equivalent in the United States to a body of music
of such overwhelming dignity that its capture by a fascist party would
be requisite to legitimating the party's authority; and neither would
there exist in the United States—perhaps ever—a sustained and
deeply reasoned oppositional culture, buoyed by radical art, such as
Adorno himself represented.

All the same, Adorno pursued in his study at the Princeton Radio
Research Project an examination of radio that would serve as a way of
interrogating and developing the implications of Benjamin's formulation of the relation between music, industry, and culture. The actual
study undertaken is fascinating. Benjamin's thesis in "The Artwork in
the Age of Its Mechanical Reproduction"—that the reproduction of
art would deprive it of its magic spell and release its critical content to
a popular audience—had been conceived exclusively in terms of print
media and the visual arts, most of all cinema and photography. The
reproduction of music by means of radio in the United States put Benjamin's thesis to the test, as if a whole nation had decided to experiment with the questions he posed from an entirely different angle.
And the results of this experiment showed Benjamin's claims in an altogether different light, for what Adorno observed in listening to radio music was that the humanizing content of the music that he had

spent his life studying had vanished. Radio music, to Adorno's ears, was no longer *that* music.

Adorno wanted to address the disappearance of the aesthetic content of music in his study of radio broadcast, for the implications of this disappearance would completely transform Benjamin's thesis. It would no longer be able to claim to explain how the reproduction of art sloughs off its spell and emancipates a potentially valuable critical object. Rather, it would explain how the reproduction of art destroys that content and, Adorno would show, subjects the remaining husk of the art work, as a fetish, to a new spell; mechanical reproduction would not destroy the primacy of the original, as Benjamin asserted, but change music into nothing but the search for an original to be possessed. Most significantly, this critical metamorphosis of Benjamin's thesis would allow Adorno to import the model of the reproduction of art from the visual arts, as Benjamin had developed it, into the discussion of music on a compositional level, as distinct from Adorno's considerations of the reproduction of music in his earlier writings in which reproduction was examined exclusively as a technique of distribution.[35] This would provide Adorno with a framework in which the entire modernist debate over the questions of abstraction and representational and nonrepresentational forms could be developed in the analysis of music. Effectively, then, Adorno carried out an exchange of aesthetic motifs with Benjamin: Adorno was, as any review of the topics chosen in his *Collected Writings* demonstrates, least involved and responsive to the visual arts. But, by way of a study of radio, he would acquire for music the problematic of the visual arts while implicitly introducing into Benjamin's late aesthetics, which had the least to say about music, the ultimate imagelessness of music as a fundamental critique of a theory of reproduction that, in its messianic espousal of the reproduction of art, had itself failed to grasp aesthetic modernism in the visual arts.[36] This absorption of the key terms of the dynamic of modernism from the art form that had been the vanguard of aesthetic revolution since the nineteenth century would be decisive in the emergence of Adorno's mature aesthetics. Thus, although *Current of Music,* the work in which Adorno would carry out this thinking, would not be published, it did function as a kind of lens through which Adorno's early thinking was focused and, transformed, projected forward. Looking through this reassembled lens even now, it is possible to discern for the first time in

Adorno's writings the cardinal ideas of *Philosophy of New Music* and *Aesthetic Theory*.

Unmusical Music And Spatialization

Within several months of arriving in the United States, along with finishing his major study of Wagner, *In Search of Wagner*, Adorno had written a full-scale theoretical memorandum on radio broadcast music. In letters to colleagues and friends Adorno announced its completion. To Benjamin he wrote,

> My major report on radio research, in effect a small book, has also been completed in the meantime, and it has also been decided that the results of my work on music and radio should appear as an independent and probably substantial volume with Princeton University Press, and that means prominently too. In this connection I am also thinking of a shorter piece in German on the regression of listening and the fetish character in music.[37]

From the tone of this letter Adorno—whose prolificness was reputed—seems to have impressed even himself with the more than 160-page single-spaced, marginless study, finished so soon after his arrival and written in English. The pace of the writing, however, in combination with work on the Wagner study, indicated not only an intensity of labor but also that, at such an early date, this intensity would have precluded almost anything beyond the writing itself. The manuscript on radio could hardly have been based on substantial experience of the United States, about which the immigrant had not known much to begin with. What shaped the memorandum, rather, was a group of ideas that was long prepared to converge in an insight dealing with a problematic that was given substantially prior to immigration. The memorandum itself, "Music in Radio," would become the working manuscript for *Current of Music*.

As often happened in his work, Adorno began the study by completing a long draft that collected the material for the project. Much could happen to this draft: it could be drastically condensed, reorganized, and sometimes expanded again as a final text. In the case of "Music in Radio," however, the seminal and capacious manuscript was developed in several different directions, then broken up again and reworked in a group of overlapping variants. In the first stage of his plans for "Music in Radio," as Adorno had indicated to Benjamin in his letter, the text would be the primary source for the essay "On the Fetish Character in Music and the Regression of Listening."[38] That essay was written during the summer of 1938. Then, in response to a request from Lazarsfeld to summarize and clarify the long memorandum, Adorno presented its central ideas to his colleagues at the Princeton Project in a lecture-essay in January 1939 entitled "Music and Radio."[39] This essay also reoriented and refocused the material of "Music in Radio." The reconceived memorandum was then rewritten and much transformed during the following year in two drafts: first as "Radio Physiognomics"[40] and then as "Current of Music: Elements of a Radio Theory; Section 2: The Radio Voice,"[41] a text for which no other sections seem to exist. Adorno also prepared a much-transformed and abbreviated version of the latter text, titled "The Radio Voice: An Experiment in Theory," dated September 1, 1941.[42]

Although the initial draft took these several permutations, Adorno carried through the central thesis of "Music in Radio" with complete consistency. From the outset, and with increasing distinctness, the text is a physiognomic study that seeks to decipher general social tendencies in the phenomena of radio broadcast music. The tendency discerned in the phenomena is a mode of production that characteristically imitates nature rather than fulfills its own productive potential. The aim of the study is to demonstrate in detail the depredations that music undergoes when it is subjected to this mode of production: when broadcast artifice endeavors to appear as pristine nature, when sonic copy lays claim to origin, when music on the air acts as the reproduction of an original.

Radio music in its early decades offered itself to such an interpretation in a way that it no longer does, or at least not so obviously. Contemporary radio music is almost exclusively the broadcast of recorded sound, and in popular music that sound is itself predominantly electronically sampled sound to start with. It is increasingly the exception that radio music presents itself as the sound of an original, in the sense of the reproduction of live voices and acoustic instruments that are of a qualitatively different nature from the transmission itself. But, prior to the early 1940s, recorded music was only broadcast on avant-garde radio stations, and even then only as an exception. Virtually all radio music presented performances of live vocal and instrumental music either from the studio or concert hall. Radio, in other words, consistently claimed to reproduce live music as natural sound, every bit as live in the home and with the intention at least of a transparency of transmission, as if the radio itself played no part. But as Adorno would meticulously demonstrate, radio sets in the 1930s could achieve this illusion only very imperfectly: they received AM transmissions that excluded substantial parts of the upper and lower frequency ranges, they could not balance the instrumental sound that they did register, and monaural reproduction further diluted orchestral dynamics. This transmitted music seemed to have been projected against a broadly warped mirror of background noise that infiltrated it with the hissing electricals of signal drift and vacuum tube. Adorno ingeniously named this ever-present background surface of sound the audible "current" coursing through radio music and against which every performance seemed projected, the "hear-stripe"—a kind of sound that is now rarely heard except in the split second, for instance, when a TV set is turned on.

Adorno's own familiarity with the sound of vocal and acoustic instruments could not have been more acute or complete, and he, if anyone, could document with exactitude the divergence between live performance and radio-broadcast music. But while Adorno was as critical as possible of the reception, his approach was exactly the opposite of the finickiness of an audiophile. He had no doubt that the distortion impinged on the performance, and he demonstrated how it fragmented the work and distracted from concentration on the work as a whole. Yet he was not ultimately concerned to find ways to wipe out degrees of distortion any more than he would have wanted to set the eyes level in a Picasso portrait. He was, in other words, as much the ally of the distortion as he was of the music. And he did not think that any degree of technical improvement could exclude the distortion of broadcast radio music. The distortion was implicit in the fundamental problem, that of the structure of broadcast itself, and it was this structure, not the distortion, that Adorno argued was directly opposed to the form of music. Music, he claimed, in utter disagreement with the aesthetic assumptions of Benjamin's thesis, has no original. To exist, it must be performed. In the performance of music, origin truly is the goal.

Radio broadcast, by contrast, transforms music into a relation between original and reproduction. The original necessarily becomes a fetish that the reproduction seeks to achieve, but without possible success for the original that has been posited is an illusory origin whereas the object of the musical performance, what it makes, what is there conceivably to experience, has vanished. Adorno was able to explicate just what could no longer be experienced by showing, in an analysis of a Beethoven symphony, that the form of music is the process in which it consumes its own extension in time. This process, he argued, is what was no longer audible in the broadcast of a Beethoven symphony, and not only because of the distortion and interference that damages the dynamic conflicts of the music but because, ultimately, in radio broadcast music is spatialized. This spatialization is what is heard in the projection of the performance against the hear-stripe. The music obtains an image quality that puts in place of the consumption of its own musical time something more akin to watching a movie. In broadcast reproduction, then, the music gains an image quality that is antithetical to the inherent imagelessness of its temporal dynamic. While purporting to sound as natural as what listeners presumed to be occurring back of the microphone in the studio or concert hall, music necessarily surrendered its power over time and was no longer a Beethoven symphony. The depotentiated and fragmented object thus came to function as an item of exchange, a standardized commodity that served as a reservoir of secondary, infantile satisfactions and magical authority, those qualities that Adorno would show in other sections of his study to be those of a conformist popular music. This was ultimately Adorno's argument against the assumptions of the cultural and educative value of broadcast music. If the music could not be experienced, in what sense could it be said that "cultural treasures" had been brought to the masses? How could this music be educative and humanizing?

Adorno did not see any solution to this deficiency in radio reproduction. He even presumed and foresaw the possibility of improvements such as were later brought by FM and stereo, but he was all the same certain that improvements in one area would be paid in others. Contemporary experience confirms this: the superseding of the phonograph record by the compact disk intensified the clarity of sound but conspicuously simplified it; the compact disk circumvented the crackling background screen against which the phonograph performance was projected, but replaced it with a background screen that differs only by its total silence, without dispersing the image quality of the reproduced sound itself. But whether today the problem of musical reproduction has or has not been resolved, Adorno thought that the structure of the problem was insuperable and held, further, that since the knot of reproduction could not be untied, it must be severed. The performance of music on radio would no longer struggle against the unnatural quality of faulty reproduction or the image quality of the hear-stripe if it surrendered the claim to being an imitation of nature in the first place. Radio would succeed at this if, instead of broadcasting the reproduction of music, it played on the radio itself: "The idea is that we should no longer broadcast over the radio but play on the radio in the same sense that one plays on a violin."[43] This would transform every dimension of radio: Freed from a delusive goal, technique would no longer be preoccupied with finding ways to consolidate the illusion that radio music is the broadcast of the pristine nature of an original performance; radio studios would not aspire to the conjuration of phantasmagorical conservatories filled with potted ferns; radio design would not have reason to imitate chassis in the likeness of acoustic instruments. Radio would become a modern musical instrument. Its technique would engage the full productive range of the instrument's electrical phenomena. Distortion would not vie with normalcy of sound and the hear-stripe itself would become a compositional source. Instead of struggling to present itself as a transparent device of exchange and functioning to transform art into neutralized cultural goods, radio would explode the commodity relation and its shallow spells and present the human object of experience itself. Emancipated from the reproduction of an illusion of nature, radio music would potentially achieve the sound of a veridical second nature. Adorno cited the theremin as an instance of a productive power that, when utterly emancipated from imitation, becomes the expression of a new nature: "A feature which should be remarked . . . is that the more the theremin instrument emancipates itself from any instrumental models, the more it approaches the sound of the singing voice—certainly without trying to come to any *vox humana effect*."[44]

The thesis of playing on radio rather than broadcasting over it is intriguing for itself, for its many implications, and not least of all because it would not turn out even if the whole world set to work on it.

And then too, if it did somehow work, it would have the nightmarish quality of kitchen appliances swaying and singing to themselves. It is important to know, however, that, while Adorno pursued the logic of this speculation, he had no illusion that such music existed and was openly skeptical that such radio music could exist. Neither was he averse to the contradiction. He freely stated the need for such radio music even while debunking its possibility. For instance, in the lecture "Music and Radio" of January 1939, after condensing the central ideas of "Music in Radio," and restating the thesis that radio must emancipate itself from the reproduction of sound, he went on to say that even the greatest optimist could not be optimistic about the attempts that had so far been made to compose specifically for radio; the whole idea, in fact, of producing music to suit the construction of a tool was, in his words, "funny and paradoxical": "We confess our utmost skepticism as far as the creation of so-called positive contents out of the tool is concerned."[45]

But why would Adorno be both the proponent and so severe a skeptic of the thesis? If he did not think that music specific to the tool could be composed, if he was prepared to distinguish tool from spiritualized musical instrument, why did he assert the thesis in "Music in Radio," restate it in his lecture even while denying it, and return to assert the idea of "playing on radio" in the last complete draft that that text would take, "Radio Physiognomics"? The contradiction is not an oversight. It is a summary formulation of what Adorno undertook to demonstrate in the Princeton Radio Research Project but stated as radio's antinomy. It expresses what radio must be and cannot be: the self-manifestation of its own content. No doubt the thesis coupled with its own denial bewildered his colleagues. To Lazarsfeld, Adorno himself would have seemed ridiculous for presenting a plan the goal of which was in the same breath said to be foolish. Perhaps Adorno would have helped his colleagues make more sense of it had he provided the reasoning of the conundrum. But throughout his work in the Princeton Project he hesitated to do so. This hesitation was not emotional but structural and conceptual. As he wrote Ernst Krenek right at the beginning of the project,

In the last few days I finished my large memorandum for the Radio Project (a small book), in which the *concept of new music*—in our sense—plays a substantial role, without of course my having been able in the framework of this memorandum to define exactly what I mean by that.[46]

The concept of new music itself, free atonal music, defined the perspective of the memorandum in general and the antinomy of radio in particular. And this concept of new music was not included in the memorandum for the Princeton Project because it took shape in opposition to radio music. It is not only—as Adorno wrote years later—that the work for the Princeton project "*contained the core of the Philosophy of New Music* that was completed only in 1948";[47] *Current of Music* and *Philosophy of New Music* developed in inverse relation to each other. Presented in their actual antagonistic juxtaposition, the limit of the former is seen to carve out the boundary that defined what the latter sought to fulfill: The limit of radio music—its inability to be the self-manifestation of its own content—is in the latter work seen to be the achievement of new music. As Adorno wrote in *Philosophy of New Music*, what made new music new, its revolution, was that it no longer reproduced human emotion but became the immediate deposition of emotion in corporeal shocks and traumas:

> The genuinely revolutionary element in his [Schoenberg's] music is the transformation of the function of expression. Passions are no longer faked; on the contrary, undisguised, corporeal impulses of the unconscious, shocks and traumas are registered in the medium of music.[48]

The pure atonal revolution in new music, then, is fundamentally the critique of reproduction. And though an enormous body of thought is condensed here, it is evident that the rejection of the replicative function in music is based on a comparison with what transpired in the visual arts. Just as painting was driven to nonrepresentational forms under the pressure of photography, Adorno explains, so music is here said to have been compelled to defend itself against commercial intrusion under the pressure of mechanically reproduced music:

> That aversion of modern painting to figurative representation, which in art marks the same breach as does atonality in music, was an act of defense against mechanized art merchandise, primarily photography. In its origins, radical music reacted no differently to

the commercial debasement of the traditional idiom. It was the antithesis to the spreading of the culture industry into its own domain.[49]

This insight has incorporated the critique of radio music to provide the basis for every aspect of Adorno's critique of neoclassicism. In *Philosophy of New Music* Stravinsky is shown to compose "music about music," a duplicative and spatialized music that seeks authenticity by aspiring to the sound of the original, the first, the primordial, as the fetish of possession rather than as the object of emphatic experience. Thus the critique of Benjamin's "The Artwork in the Age of Its Mechanical Reproduction'" came to fruition in Adorno's work by way of a study of radio music in which the problem of reproduction was drawn into questions of compositional technique analogous to the revolution in the visual arts.

Aesthetic Critique of Radio Music

Current of Music is an aesthetic critique of radio music and, by that measure, it is most of all an aesthetics. The study deserves to be recognized for the distinctness this grants it from much of what now travels under the name media studies. Because *Current of Music* is keyed to aesthetic experience, it has something other to do than rake the loamy soils of industrial entertainment for traces of an oppositional culture that are scarcely to be found there. On the contrary, communication studies, film studies programs, and popular culture studies are what universities primarily have to contribute to a situation, well characterized by Gunther Schuller, that hardly lets anyone catch even a moment's breath away from it. *Current of Music,* however, has a great deal to contribute by providing clues to finding some way out. Its best clue, in fact, may be in what Adorno thought was "'funny" about the idea of composing music for radio itself. This introduction itself is in alliance with that approach in recommending the study of *Current of Music,* a volume that, if completed, would be of substantial girth, for the indications it might provide for losing interest in the topics it presents. That is certainly the point of the texts that might be assembled here. In them, Adorno listened in critical alertness for what was not to be found in radio music and industrial entertainment. This listening was motivated on behalf of music in which Adorno thought there was a great deal to be found. The problem, then, was to conceptualize the distinction. That Adorno sought to draw this distinction is the most provocative aspect of his thinking. This distinction ultimately concerns the question of the relation between knowledge and aesthetic experience.

"Our desire lacks knowledgeable music."

—RIMBAUD

It is worth momentarily putting the question of this distinction in the context of Adorno's philosophy as a whole in order to be able to approach it again more closely. The larger context makes it possible to see that reproduction, identity, mechanism, and spatialization are not single motifs but rather cohere in a single problematic. One way of stating the dialectic of enlightenment—approaching it specifically from the perspective of mechanism—is to say that it poses the question of how it is possible to restore to nature a qualitative dimension that it surrendered in its spatialization. It was the development of mechanism that translated nature into space by excluding as real any but quantitative determinations, faced by a dimensionless thinking self. It is simplistic, but nevertheless revealing—especially with regard to what was at stake in Adorno's struggle with Benjamin's evocation of mechanism—to see that Adorno's philosophy has nothing to do but seek to translate space back into nature. And it can only do this by somehow recovering the temporal dimension that mechanism excludes in the establishment of causal explanation. That form of explanation excludes time by formulating identity between origin as the cause and all subsequent phenomena as reproductions of that origin. The assertion of this origin is the false authenticity that Adorno was concerned to criticize in radio music under Damrosch's baton as much as in Stravinsky's primordiality.[50] Aesthetics becomes key in Adorno's thinking, as throughout twentieth-century philosophy, because it is understood as condensing the temporal dimension as *import* itself, which is otherwise held out of mind in the mechanical mastery of

space. Adorno's approach is conceived as *physiognomic* precisely in opposition to mechanism—in just the sense that "Radio Physiognomics"
is a dynamic rather than a descriptive title—and this physiognomy is
ultimately directed to art as the unconscious transcription of historical
suffering. This unconscious transcription of history potentially medi-
ates the translation of mechanical space into nature. The actuality of
this history—whether, in a sense, meaning is or is not transmuted into
import—determines the difference between having and not having
the qualitative object of experience.[51]

With this larger context in mind, the aesthetic question, as the
qualitative differential itself, is seen to depend ultimately on the possibility of making qualitative distinctions between art works: how they
do or do not consume the time that is or is not stored up in them. This
establishes, as Adorno understood it, the affinity between art and
knowledge: it is what art works know about us better than we are able
to know for ourselves. If this seems intellectualist, it is also the only alternative to it. For it is just what anyone means in saying "I love that
song," which at its extreme asserts a sense of having been understood
better than could ever have been imagined and predicates an object
that can be entered as nothing else can be. In Schoenberg's later music,
Adorno thought, this is an experience of being recognized by what no
longer resembles the self.[52] The critical question then, the one that
makes it possible to research aesthetic quality without any kind of
dogma or conceit, is research into the extent to which that understanding is feigned or real. This is the qualitative distinction that can
be made in music between one work and another, and it is the distinction as well that defined the direction of Adorno's thinking as it left
Current of Music behind for *Philosophy of New Music*. In this sense
Current of Music is itself a prolegomenon to being interested in a great
deal other than its own topics.

Exact Listening

After losing his job with the Princeton Radio Research Project,
Adorno wrote proportionately little specifically about industrial musical entertainment. It did not interest him compared to objects that significantly engage the question of composition and the truth-content of
music. But Adorno had other reasons as well for leaving *Current of*

Music behind. He realized that the work was faulty in various regards. Not only had transformations in radio reception made several of its theses obsolete, but it fundamentally lacked any adequate theory of listening. Adorno wrote,

> The reason for this shortcoming may well have been that I did not succeed in making the transition to listener research. That transition would be absolutely necessary, above all else in order to differentiate and correct the theorems. . . . It would be simply naive to presume an equivalence between the societal implications of the stimuli and the "responses," though, no less naive to regard the two as independent of each other.[53]

This is a fundamental criticism. It is apparent, for instance, that however intriguing his claim that a Beethoven symphony could not be adequately heard on the radio, many did hear it and with some kind of comprehension. While limitations of radio reproduction were commonly acknowledged, and Adorno was after all brought onto the staff of the Princeton project to help find ways to improve reception, still a vast population heard more in radio music than Adorno heard, even if, in important regards, they also heard less than a composer who would have been able to distinguish separately twelve notes sounded simultaneously. And while there is no doubt that Adorno's study of the degradation of acoustic musical experience through its electronic reproduction has much to teach and urgently deserves further study, it can not be claimed that those who were awestruck by symphonic music on the radio were all naive or duped with cultural goods and electronic fetish. One does not, for instance, have to go far in the memoirs of the age to come across the likes of sophisticated listeners, such as Clifford Odets, who rushed home on a Saturday afternoon March 9, 1940, to hear a broadcast of *Figaro*—on just the kind of radio Adorno studied—and, later that afternoon, was glad to be able to turn on the NBC Symphony.[54] Of the millions of others who were also listening to these broadcasts that afternoon, many were probably edified by the heroic sound of "cultural treasure," but they would not have kept listening if that was all they heard.[55]

Adorno's failure to understand the place of the listener in his work of this period was a motivated failure. It is in fact reciprocal with every strength of *Current of Music* as an aesthetics of radio whose immanent measure was conceived as the most advanced music of the age. When held to the measure of music that longed for an "illusionless self-declaration,"[56] radio became the object of a radically modernist listening. The quality of this listening is illuminated by comparison with Kandinsky's seminal experience of nonobjective painting in seeing one of Monet's haystacks turned upside-down and being unable to recognize the motif; it is a kind of listening matched by Giacometti's sketching of fruit seen in the distance as if it were as tiny as things literally are when deprived of the illusion of perspectival compensation. This radical aesthetic comportment, in its hostility to an illusion of meaning, seeks an object that is as illusionless as the thing in itself; it is a cultivated stance that was once bewildering to everyday perceptions.

It was as an object of this kind of attention that the Beethoven symphony vanished from the audible in Adorno's study of radio sound. Adorno extended his auditory analysis of radio phenomena to the listener on the basis of his thesis of the primacy of the object: "We are dwelling on the phenomenon because it is actually the phenomenon that determines the reaction of the listeners, and it is our ultimate aim to study the listener," Adorno wrote in *Current of Music*. While this logic can be followed, it is also a non sequitur. It is a formulation of the primacy of the object that functions to dismiss any real interest in the listener and, in its literalism, verges on a kind of behaviorism of the mind. Its own will to abstraction misconceives the primacy of the object by narrowing it to factual radio phenomena, much of which is in any case indistinguishable to untrained ears and not necessarily significant compared with the importance, for instance, of what was actually in the experience of the listeners' ears. Auditory experience itself shapes sound and compensates as much for its limitations in reproduction in radio as it does, for instance, in the sound of a telephone voice. It is just this experience of actual listeners that is missing, virtually on principle, from *Current of Music*. There is no mention, for instance, of what institutions such as the City Center for Music and Drama provided to the listening experience of large segments of the radio audience in New York City. Neither is there any consideration of the kind of question that a historian would think to ask, for instance, about the proportion of American radio listeners for whom the listening tradition of European music might well have been a familiar presupposition of radio perception since they were themselves of that origin. Instead of this audience research, and on the basis of little familiarity with the country to start with, Adorno effectively isolated himself with the radio, as if every aesthetic, psychological, and sociological dimension could be learned from its immediate sound.

First Salvage

A year before his death, thinking back on his radio studies in a lecture—one that has been drawn on frequently here—Adorno concluded that the absence of any adequate theory of the listener struck fault lines that irremediably fragmented his research. For this reason, he said: "I did not succeed in presenting a systematically executed sociology and social psychology of music on radio."[57] Adorno felt obliged to revert from German to English to capture his sense of regret that, instead of a completed theoretical statement, the best he could make of it was "*a salvaging action*." From the substantial work he had accomplished, only individual sections could be rescued. In this effort, during his years in the United States, he published three essays: "On Popular Music" (in *Studies in Philosophy and Social Science*, 1941), "The Radio Symphony: An Experiment in Theory" (in *Radio Research*, 1941), and "A Social Critique of Radio Music" (in *Kenyon Review*, Spring 1945).[58]

But while Adorno was critical of his work, there is no doubt that he valued it. From his first year in New York City he sought publishers for it through the Princeton Project. Later, living in Los Angeles, he was gratified that his radio essays had begun to make a reputation for themselves, though it also pained him that it had taken almost ten years for interest in them to develop.[59] Right up to the months before his repatriation he sought contact with an American editor in renewed efforts to see the volume in print as a whole.[60] On his return to Germany this philosopher—whose primary trait may well have been his faithfulness to whatever his life, intellectual or otherwise, had once touched on—did not forget about his radio studies. He succeeded, for instance, in incorporating sections from the "Analytical Study of the NBC Music Appreciation Hour" into "Die gewuerdigte Musik" (Appreciated Music),[61] and parts of the "The Radio Symphony" were adapted in the essay "Ueber die musicalische Verwendung des Radios" (On the Musical Utilization of Radio).[62] These essays became the first and last chapters of *Der getreue Korrepetitur* (The Faithful Repetiteur). The essay "On Popular Music" was edited into his *Introduction to the Sociology of Music*.[63]

Second Salvage

Adorno did not have occasion to reconceptualize his New York writings as a whole or even to collect them, but there is every reason to suppose that, if these writings were available, contemporary scholars would find much to pursue in them. The more one becomes familiar with these writings, the more one's conviction grows that much is at stake in them that deserves contemporary attention, both for their many achievements and for what can be learned from their stark limitations. And it would be possible to return to the substantial and diverse collection of his research for the Princeton Project and reconstruct something along the lines that the manuscript of *Current of Music* might have taken. Such a work would be a second salvage. As a reconstruction, it might be guided less by the intention of returning the pieces to where they might once have belonged—as an act of historical safekeeping, as if history were safekeeping for anything—than by the aim of collecting what Adorno himself prepared for publication and supplementing this body of work with writings and drafts that were abandoned in the convergence of many pressures. The resulting volume would certainly be a cumbersome surrogate for what Adorno might have written. Still, this second salvage would wrest these angular, misfitting parts back to shore and set them out for study. Readers of such a work would have to come prepared for the same halting labor that was responsible here in this essay for transporting Adorno's *Current of Music* one step farther in its perduring inexistence.[64]

Title Essay

Baroque Allegory and "The Essay as Form"

Antinomy of the Title

From *Minima Moralia* to *Metacritique of Epistemology* (*Metakritik der Erkenntnistheorie*)[1] the titles of Adorno's works are intentionally concrete forms. They seek to title emphatically, as names: "A title must hit home like a name."[2] For Adorno the title becomes a name in the mediation of art and concept, presentation and concept: *Aesthetic Theory* is a theory of aesthetics, a theory that is itself aesthetic. *Philosophy of New Music* (subjective and objective genitive) is a philosophy of music, one that is itself somehow musical. These titles claim that the work they contain is the presentation of the object itself. *Aesthetic Theory* is the aesthetic's own theory just as *Philosophy of New Music* is new music's own philosophy. In the title, then, as in the work, the mediation of concept and presentation establishes a unity of thought and object. Rather than functioning denotatively, the title as name is to be a microcosm of the work. To the extent that the title embodies what occurs beneath it, it closes itself off to the marketplace. Paradoxically, however, the aesthetic element through which this occurs, by permitting the essay's concepts to enter into a relation in which they may achieve their cognitive aim, at the same time makes the essay vulnera-

ble to the boutique, to an abstract autonomy that, in its empty difference, signals its conformity. The title *Prisms*, for example, as Adorno
recognized, fails on just this account. Thinking back on it regretfully,
Adorno sensed that *Prisms* could be a shop just next-door to *Le Motif*.[3]

Doctrine of the Name

"The Essay as Form"[4] was written over five years and finally published in 1958 as the lead essay of Adorno's collected literary studies,
Notes to Literature (*Noten zur Literatur*). Adorno counted it among his
most successful works. As the title insists, it is not a study on the essay
but the presentation of its form. As a self-conscious act of naming, the
essay per se "wants to help language in its relation to concepts, to grasp
these concepts reflectively in the way they are already unconsciously
named in language."

Aiding language to name consciously what it otherwise names unconsciously originates in and develops a psychoanalytic reflection. It is
of pressing importance to understand fully what Adorno meant by
this and how he carried out this translation of psychoanalysis in his
theory of language. But this concern must be set aside as secondary
since any comprehension of how Adorno sought to translate a psychological dimension into an objectively social concept of truth would
have to be predicated on an understanding of the other major source
of Adorno's theory of the essay as name, Walter Benjamin's study of
the Baroque *play of lamentation*, the *Trauerspiel*. Benjamin's *Trauerspiel* study itself developed in relation to the idealist struggle to recover
the possibility of objective truth from its nominalist-empiricist critique.[5] Inextricable from the ingenuity of Kant's work was precisely
that it incorporated its nominalist opponent by turning the nominalist
claim that the idea is strictly a function of subjective reason against
nominalism by taking its own thesis to the limit. Kant reestablished a
doctrine of ideas as the basis of thought's claim to objective truth by
showing that objectivity itself issues from thought.[6] This subjective recuperation of theological contents, ultimately the possibility of identity, was a Protestant, radically inward recovery of Greek philosophy.
The objectivity of the idea was formulated subjectively. A peculiar
part of this history is that it was a Pietist Protestant movement—
whose own tradition had origins in nominalism and itself potentiated

nominalism by the doctrinal exclusion of Greek philosophy from the-ology—that developed by reappropriating Greek philosophy. Ben-jamin, working after the collapse of the idealist synthesis, was related to this movement in that he also attempted to recuperate theological contents through a reappropriation of Greek thought. But rather than a Protestant-Greek synthesis, Benjamin produced a Jewish-Greek synthesis: "In philosophical contemplation, the idea is released from the beauty of reality as the word, reclaiming its name-giving rights. Ultimately, however, this is not the attitude of Plato, but the attitude of Adam, the father of the human race and the father of philosophy."[7] The name is an idea in that it is a form. The idea is a name in that it is expressive. The idea as name is an expressive form. According to this doctrine, the presentation of the form releases the name. Like the idealist doctrines of the idea, Benjamin's work was also conceived in opposition to nominalism, although the focus of his critique was dis-tinct. It was concerned with nominalism's refutation of the expressive content of language. According to the nominalists, the concept ex-presses nothing of its object. Here nominalism and idealism are un-wittingly mediated in one another. Idealism's ultimately deductive form also vitiates expression, even where, as in Hegel, its effort is to let the concept speak; the Hegelian dialectic ultimately sublates expres-sion by the full self-presence of the spirit in absolute knowledge.[8] Crit-ical therefore of both nominalism and idealism, yet fundamentally al-lied with the latter, Benjamin developed a doctrine of ideas that attempts to recover the expressive content of language in a fashion that, with idealism, justifies thought as part of the recovery of meta-physical contents. It intended to rationally gain a content that is more than rational.

The prologue of the *Trauerspiel* study presents Benjamin's program for the construction of ideas and is itself a model of the process defined by the program. Although it has rarely been noticed, the preface is written in parallel with the larger study of the *Trauerspiel*. Just as the larger study attempts to recover the name *Trauerspiel*, the preface means to recover "idea" per se as a name. The prologue proceeds by using the force of identity to gain the immanent tension—or form—of the word. It intends to reenliven the idea by presenting the antino-mical contents of the word *idea* in the history of idealism beginning with Plato, a content that includes the opposition of truth and knowl-edge, truth and *doxa*, as well as that of truth and phenomena. The re-

sult of this presentation may be summarized in an image. The idea is
to phenomena as is an expression to a face. This relationship of the
former to the latter is not deductive. An expression must be presented,
not summarized or deduced. This presentation is possible only as that
of the object's features, its elements, as the tension within and among
the elements. Gaining this tension is the work of concepts that, insofar
as they are restricted to grasping the antinomical content of elements,
and are at the same time freed from any deductive hierarchy, permit
the object's expression to appear as the form of these antinomical extremes. The concepts mediate the expression by arranging the phenomena in itself while allowing the order of the material to be subject
to the work's objective form. For this reason there are no summaries
in Benjamin's work. Either the idea appears or it does not.

The idea is constructed in opposition to natural history. Once the
"idea is established, then the presence of the inauthentic—that is to
say *natural historical* past and subsequent history is virtual."[9] The construction of the idea, then, is the recovery of the expressive form from
extensive history. Benjamin's "Epistemo-Critical Prologue," however,
does not explain the form of this history, "natural history." Its comprehension requires going over to the larger study where—since Benjamin deals with literary forms as models of history—it is found to be
a central aspect of Baroque drama. This study of the Baroque follows
the history of literature from the supersession of a mythical context of
nature in Greek tragedy to the return to a natural context in the six-
teenth and seventeenth centuries. Benjamin demonstrates this return
of history to nature in every figure of the Baroque by tracing out its
antinomical content. Post-Reformation allegory itself—the form of
the *Trauerspiel*—is characterized by just this "peculiar mixture of nature and history." What Benjamin discerns in allegory is its double aspect. On one hand he finds in it the essential mechanism by which history regresses to a mythical state of nature: allegory dominates nature;
it represents "the triumph of subjectivity and the onset of an arbitrary
rule over things."[10] Yet allegory is also the critique of domination. In it
thésis (positing, convention) becomes the expression of *physis*: "It may
not accord with the authority of nature; but the voluptuousness with
which signification rules, like a stern sultan in the harem of objects, is
without equal in giving expression to nature."[11] In allegory the force
of the illusion of human autonomy, knowledge, is turned against itself
and presents the only form of transcendence possible in a radically sec-

ular condition, the collapse of illusion. In this moment of collapse, nature gains a moment of expression and is referred beyond secular immanence. The allegorical *play of lamentation* expresses the moment of transience in which the semblance of human autonomy dissolves. It is the form that—just as does the idea in general—transforms history, specifically Baroque history, into truth. The presentation of the form of this collapse is the idea of the *play of lamentation* and at the same time the recovery of the expressive content of *Trauerspiel* as a name. *Trauerspiel*, then, is the critique of natural history by way of radical natural history. The prologue and the literary study of the *play of lamentation* converge on many levels, but most importantly in the problem of the opposition of idea and natural history. The prologue seeks to restore *idea*—as the form in which the word is expressive—from natural history, that is, from the extensive philosophical history of idealism, just as the larger literary study wants to recover the expressive content of *Trauerspiel* from literary history. Both words, *idea* and *Trauerspiel,* had been obscured by secular history qua significative language. The presentation of the form of transcendence in the word recovers the word itself. Just as Adam's names are inseparable from what is named by referring nature to creation, so the research of ideas as names restores the relation of culture to the divine by gaining the expression of nature. This process is the recovery of *origin* (*Ursprung*), the symbolic name: the revivification of the Adamic language in which sign and image are unitary.

Critique of the Name as Symbol

From the perspective of the *Trauerspiel* study, Adorno's "The Essay as Form" would need to be the presentation of an idea, an expressive form, as the memory of *essay* as a name, and this is largely what transpires in Adorno's study. Just as Benjamin reenlivens the "idea" by developing the relation of concept and presentation, so the "Essay as Form" makes the idea of the essay dynamic, with similar results. The essay is distinguished from art in that the medium of its attempt to be the full experience of its object is conceptual and it is distinguished from science in that it produces knowledge that is more than subjective definition. As these aspects of the essay are differentiated, a tension in the concept develops: the essay is not only opposed to science, as immanent criticism it shares a conceptual medium with science. But because the essay refuses to produce a conceptual hierarchy, it must arrange and fit together the elements of its object that it immanently develops; the essay therefore shares with art its aspect of presentation. Further, just as Benjamin presented allegory as the singular form of transcendence available to the Baroque, Adorno presents the essay as the singularly adequate form of social criticism. And, again, just as the study of the *play of lamentation* moves from an original mythic context to a second mythical natural embeddedness, so does Adorno's philosophy of history in which he locates the essay form. In opposition to Benjamin, however, Adorno does not conceive of the presentation of the essay form as a recuperation of *origin* (*Ursprung*), of the symbolic name. By the radical critique of any first principle, all *origin* is criticized as ideology. In "The Essay as Form" words directed against Heidegger also implicitly touch Benjamin: "For the essay, culture is not some epiphenomenon superimposed on being that must be eliminated, but rather what lies underneath is itself artifical (*thései*), false society. Thus, for the essay, origins have no priority over the superstructure."

This central conflict between Adorno and Benjamin—explicit ever since Adorno's "The Idea of Natural-History" (1933)—was most fully developed in *Dialectic of Enlightenment,* which was written partially as a history of the name per se. In this work Adorno refuses to conceive of the name as a pristine symbol, whose recovery would be that of God's creative language in which image and sign, word and object are unitary. The name, rather, is itself positioned within the dialectic of enlightenment: "The cry of terror with which the extraordinary is met, becomes its name."[12] The name fixates the unknown vis-à-vis the known and at the same time establishes the first dualization of nature necessary to its domination. The name is not just obscured by significative language, as Benjamin held; it already has a significative aspect that challenges its own unity with its object. Like all knowledge, the name is phobic. As the model of reflection, it wants to vanquish fear by proscribing the fearful; it itself bears the principle of immanence. The terror frozen in the name becomes the fetish symbol of the privilege that enforces the division of labor. This division of labor progressively separates image from sign as the division of science and art. Philosophy, hypostatizing domination, raises the concepts in which this division of labor is sedimented to the level of universal ideas; it

formalizes the division of sign and image, giving it a secondary position because of the mimetic element by which it is bound to nature.
The universal concepts of philosophy themselves, however, eventually
fall to the same criticism that philosophy once leveled at art. Ultimately "there is said to be no difference between the totemic animal,
the dreams of the ghost seer, and the absolute idea."[13] Operational
statements—language fully separated from its object—substitute the
neutral sign and formula for the concept. This completes the mechanism necessary to the domination of nature but regresses by the same
token to a bare state of nature. Unable to reflect on its course of domination, having excised the universal contents of language as superstition, thought is stranded in the position of mythic terror in which it
has no alternative but to affirm the status quo of measureless domination. The course of enlightenment—the progress in domination of the
name—is therefore the transformation of first nature into second nature, the establishment of a second mythical context.

Through the lens of Adorno's philosophy of history, sparkling
clearheadedness turns out to be depersonalized fear, though it is not to
be supposed that this fear would be assuaged by confusion. A new
unity of image and sign, as conceived by Benjamin, would not escape
the dialectic of enlightenment. The name as symbol is not an alternative. Yet this critique did not intend a complete break from Benjamin.
The possibility of solving the dialectic of enlightenment required the
recovery of the expressive content of language from the nominalist
process of secularization in a form that would make good on idealism;
that is, in a form that would justify thought as something other than
a power of domination, the only alternative to which would be irrationality. The recuperation of reason demanded a form of thought
that could claim to gain its object's expression in concepts; or, as
Adorno would put it, make the object's expression binding in its concepts. This had been the project of Benjamin's doctrine of ideas.
Adorno transformed this doctrine by criticizing its ontological claims,
which had unwittingly located itself in the dialectic of enlightenment.
Adorno carried out this criticism by pursuing a relationship between
allegory and Hegel's logic, which emerged in consequence of the rejection of *prima philosophia.* By the critique of *first philosophy,* the critique of any first principle, determinate negation can no longer be
conceived as the positive result of the negation of the negation. It becomes instead the form in which every concept, by its own claim to

identity, cancels its self-identity. Identity thus becomes the force of allegory: by its claim to self-identity, the illusion of self-identity—that is, autonomy—is destroyed. Where Hegel's dialectic gains identity through difference, Adorno—utterly at odds with any espoused philosophy of difference—hopes to break open the immanence of identity through the recuperation of sameness. This is difference through identity. The move away from Benjamin to Hegel therefore returns to a transformed Benjamin. Hegelian logic becomes a form of the *play of lamentation* while Benjamin's doctrine of the name surrenders the research of *origin*. Immanent critique, Adorno explains in the "Essay as Form," becomes the self-conscious critique of natural history, of society's embeddedness in mythical nature. Adorno writes:

> [The essay's] proper theme is the interrelation of nature and culture. It is not by coincidence that . . . the essay immerses itself in cultural phenomena as in a second nature, a second immediacy, in order through persistence to remove the illusion of immediacy. . . . The essay's impulse . . . is critical: through confrontation of texts with their own emphatic concept, with the truth that each one intends, even in spite of itself, to shatter (*erschuettern*) the claim of culture and move it to remember its own untruth—the untruth of its ideological facade which reveals culture's bondage to nature. Under the glance of the essay, second nature becomes conscious of itself as first nature.

Like post-Reformation allegory, this is a program of criticism that turns knowledge against itself. *Thésis* becomes the expression of *physis*, allowing Adorno to both effectively quote Hegel and yet mean a seventeenth-century allegorical form: "Thought holds true to the idea of immediacy only by way of the mediated." Radical determinate negation becomes the self-consciousness of natural history. Through the concept's self-criticism it destroys its own facade and becomes the memory of nature.[14] In Adorno's philosophy of history the recovery of this expressive content—the expression of natural history—establishes the single possibility for the *ratio* to become reasonable. Thought recovers the goal of domination—freedom from fear—that was expressed in the initial terror of an overpowering nature but was excised in the development of technical control over nature. The name in Adorno's work is allegory in the form of immanent critique.

Autonomy of the Name

"The Essay as Form" presents the essay as a form for demonstrating the collapse of culture into nature by the shattering of any semblance of meaning. This closely parallels the central idea of Adorno's *Aesthetic Theory,* which likewise presents a logic of the shattering of meaning.[15] For Adorno, the experience of important art, of art that is actually art, is a reversal of the Kantian sublime.[16] Rather than being an experience of the autonomy of the self, such as Kant conceived, the experience of emphatically modern art is that of the self's collapse, a *frisson* that destroys the self-preservative ego's semblance of culture and reveals history as nature. This direct parallel of Adorno's study of the essay as form and his aesthetics is implied by the location of the essay between concept and art. As has been seen, Benjamin also developed the relation between critical form and art. Yet the mediation of concept and the aesthetic differs for Adorno and Benjamin as follows from their contradictory formulations of the aesthetic. Adorno's rejection of the research of *origin* was of a piece with his valuation—in opposition to Benjamin—of autonomous art. There are therefore further formal consequences to Adorno's critique of the research of *origin* in "The Essay as Form." For Adorno the element of presentation is covalent with that of the autonomy of form and thus the "idea" itself is transformed. Adorno writes that the essay is an idea "in that it does not capitulate, does not bow down before what merely is." It gains this autonomy paradoxically. Through the immanent rational mimesis of its object, in making the object's expression binding in its concepts, the essay becomes self-mimetic. The self-reflective somersault of "The Essay as Form" is paradigmatic: the essay as form is itself an essay; it develops the content of the essay by immanent criticism as immanent criticism. The criterion of the essay's interpretive form is therefore "the compatibility of the interpretation with the text and with itself and its power to release the object's expression in the unity of its elements. The essay thereby acquires an aesthetic autonomy." The essay's critical force develops its autonomy: "The demand for the primacy of consciousness over being is dishonored. That does not mean that primacy is surrendered to existence."[17] This establishes the critical relation of the essay as form to metaphysical contents. As Adorno repeatedly put it, the question of metaphysics is: "Can that really be all?" In alliance with Kant and the whole of modern idealism, "The Essay as

Form" remains in the tradition of metaphysics by canceling it. Its critical force qua its autonomy makes it more than the status quo. By contravening the claim to the absolute autonomy of thought, the essay becomes mimetic of its object and, by the same account, critical in that it presents the object's self-criticism. Where metaphysics, by its claim to otherness, obscurely presents the given once removed, the essay as form, by critical mimesis, becomes actually other. In this sense the essay as form, as Adorno writes, "attempts to make reparation" for the loss of metaphysical content.

The second way in which presentation and autonomy are mediated in Adorno's "The Essay as Form" is in the introduction of modern compositional techniques.[18] Just as Schoenberg in "Erwartung" discovered a new principle of composition in density, which the equalization of every element in chromatic space allowed him to achieve in that it dissolved the abstraction of melody and harmony, the horizontal and vertical aspects of music,[19] so Adorno developed density as a principle of writing by criticizing the rigid distinction of horizontal and vertical aspects of thought, its discursive and associational aspects, through the equivalence of every element in the essay. It is not surprising that techniques of modem composition should be found in "The Essay as Form." Musical composition and discursive thought had the same problem to solve: composition according to the hierarchical tonic chord resulted in the collapse of tonality and the increasing irrationality, uncomposability, of music, a loss of the adequacy of the large form to the detail. Likewise thought dominated by the hierarchical, subordinating concept, for which material is always reduced to examples of concepts, became increasingly irrational in the loss of the adequacy of form and content. Density as form not only releases music from the obligation of completing every dissonance with a consonance and ultimately completing every work with the sound of ultimate repose, it allows the essay to refrain from completing a deductive context that is an image of harmony established over the head of its content. In free atonal music it replaces a form whose model is a repetitive and fateful nature with a compositional form whose idea of nature is one of plentitude while in the essay it allows immanent criticism to develop as a microcosm of the tension of its object by which the essay—like the title—becomes a name.

As a name, according to Adorno, the essay is a critical microcosm of society just as the title as name is a microcosm of the essay. The essay's critical force depends on its autonomy. To gain its object's tension it must close itself off to the marketplace. But this autonomy must be self-canceling. The essay only becomes expressive and points beyond itself in the tension-filled pause. The element of autonomy, however, is at the same time the temptation of the form to sacrifice its tension, to dig in its heels and demand a life exclusively of its own. Every sentence in the "Essay as Form" is full to the limit; the title itself, quietly enigmatic, is one of Adorno's best. Yet at the same time, certain phrases barely straddle the line between the trenchant and the sententious. In phrases like "the moment of irresponsibility, in itself an aspect of every truth that does not exhaust itself in responsibility towards the existent, makes itself responsible"[20] or "torn loose from the discipline of academic unfreedom, spiritual freedom itself becomes unfree"—important as they are—the defender of atonality seems to pound the tonic, however he might explain the rhetoric. One has a sense of having heard it before, even while reading it for the first time. The recognition of the putatively new as the archaic in these phrases indicates their relation to the boutique title. Adorno's critics, claiming to represent the social, chalk up such phrases to his high-handedness. In a substantially different context, criticizing contemporaries who claimed that Hegel's dialectic was marred by his political accommodation, Marx had better insight into what is involved in these lines: "Philosophy succumbs internally to the defects that it fights external to itself."[21] The critique of Adorno's high-handedness has been and will be that this aesthete blurred art and concept. The important critique of Adorno is, rather, that the more antagonistic and opaque society becomes, the more the attempt to name it will incline the essay toward metabasis. The essay will harden itself against what it fears will mythically engulf it. The boutique moments in Adorno's work, the points where it shines exorbitantly, are those where society prevails in refusing to allow itself to be seen for what it is.

What Is Mechanical Reproduction?

A GEOLOGICAL HAMMOCK architecturally tethered at one end by its own shopping mall—foot by foot the most profitable in the American West—and at the other by Hoover Tower, its own right-wing think tank, Stanford University is slung up against the last mountain range this side of the Pacific coastline, its glens and palm-studded courts crisscrossed by streams of pedaling students swathed in red sweat-shirts, some wearing red caps, all emblazoned with a primitivesque square-cut white capital "S." It needs a theory, I thought, the first time I saw it, these precious children on bike-back: Why must they wear the name of the place where they are at? Is it tragedy: a balmy clinic where prestige mercifully fronts for Alzheimer-stricken juveniles, precocious cohorts of the obliviously ambulatory? They ride and ride and at night, fallen and exhausted, known by their sweats and caps, are swept up by Hewlett Packard and Xerox trucks, by common citizens too, and nestled away with their bikes, their feet still in the stirrups, half kicking. Guards check the pressure on their tires and the next day set them all back out on their runs, staring out over their square-cut "S"s, as if they don't even know where they go to school.

This is a good theory, and much speaks for it. It may even cause us to comprehend with new kindness and heartbreak those often twinned Palo Alto infants in exercise perambulators, proleptically clad in their "S"-bedubbed red miniatures, their identically uniformed mothers jogging vacantly behind them. But even in these scenes the given theory does not make every detail equally transparent. Neither does it account for the campus shopping mall, or Hoover Tower, or explain why a dozen and a half piano practice rooms are dependably vacant, as is the elaborately appointed lithograph shop; it doesn't explain why a Rodin Sculpture Garden mid-campus jams together eight major works on a concrete slab and looks more like a Rodin parking lot. And how would the theory explain the university's own *pont japonais*—modeled of course directly on Monet's, but narrowly installed between three towering administration buildings and seemingly imported from a miniature golf course, or a Fred Flintstone cartoon, but definitely not from Giverny? Thus, however broadly explanatory the theory, confronted with the many details that won't stop nagging, a theory that explains less may ultimately explain more.[1]

On this score few theories of mass reproduction are better entitled to recommend themselves than Walter Benjamin's "The Work of Art in the Age of Mechanical Reproduction."[2] For this essay, virtually Benjamin's namesake, is a condensed weave of non sequitur and untruth. This should be obvious from any review of its much-cited central tenets: Benjamin's claim, for instance, that photography was the first revolutionary means of reproduction would have surprised pamphleteer Tom Paine. Benjamin's argument that in mechanically reproduced newsreels and illustrated magazines the masses are able to break imagery out of its peremptory auratic shell and learn to bring all things closer, both spatially and humanely, in recognition of their transience, strains dubiously against the fact, for instance, that the omnipresent reproductions of Hitler in films and magazines hardly helped the German masses of Benjamin's own time—people who to this day, along with their children and grandchildren, live under a quarantine on his image and paraphernalia—to clear their heads of their thralldom. This is of course not just a German matter. Worldwide hands fish lovingly into purses and wallets and fumble in bags hanging from walkers to extract ghostly smears of emulsion, those snapshots of whomever to provide the vision of a radiant individuality *hic et nunc*, distant at any degree of closeness. Clutch away the photo and tear it up, just to demonstrate Benjamin's thesis of the power of mass reproduction over fetish, and tears, not disenchantment, would be the result. Or, consider Benjamin's thesis that movies are a simultaneous collective experience. If so, why do two elbows converge with electric affront on a single armrest? And what then explains—when finally the celluloid loops out—that special display of dexterity as all succeed at piling untouched through the narrows of the flung double doors?

But if these many objections to Benjamin's essay teeter on the self-evident, why have they been remarked so rarely? The essay itself must benefit from a kind untouchability. It has been able to evade critical scrutiny, at any degree of closeness; lodged in its articulations is a force that goes beyond each particular assertion and assures that the false rings true however it may be threatened. The essay, in other words, is itself auratic. And—demonstrating both its power and the untruth of its theses—its own untouchability has not in any way been reduced by the essay's much-published and reproduced existence. Clearly, the essay is well protected on many fronts: its emphatic "Go to the movies, take snapshots, see the truth," warmly crowns the updraft of mass culture with ethical rationalization. And—in support of the essay's attack on art as art—these rationalizations fit tightly together with modernism's own anti-art tendency, which may turn out to be modernism's only enduring legacy. The literary journal *Granta*, for instance, extols its own challenging prose by asserting that "*Granta*, Britain's best-selling literary magazine, is edited by people who don't like literature." But these ideological resources, which pair up frequently, do not suffice to explain the essay's aura. Still, its inner workings—and those of that square-cut capital "S"—can be discerned: this aura has a form. And, though this form is manifest, point by point in Benjamin's essay, it is most convincingly accessible in Benjamin's idea of "mechanical reproduction."

American and French readers of the essay will be especially compelled to question the contents of this concept if they stop to check back to the original because, if they notice, Benjamin does not use the word *mechanical* at any point in the essay, not even in the renown title, which would literally read, "The Work of Art in the Age of Its Technical Reproducibility" (*technische Reproduzierbarkeit*). Throughout the essay each occurrence of *mechanical* can be replaced by *technical*. It is not that the English translator erred. The two concepts—mechanical and technical—broadly overlap; Benjamin's essay does assume a context of mechanical devices; and, by implying the current antagonism of the distractedness of mechanism versus presence of mind, "mechanical reproduction" invokes a commonplace that was certainly a source of the essay. And compellingly, as a translation of the original's many variations on the phrase *technische Reproduktion,* the self-evidence of "mechanical reproduction"—whatever it actually means—recommends itself over the literal "technical reproduction," whose weak semantic content dissolves unconvincingly.[3] French poses almost exactly the same problems of translation, and it can be assumed that Benjamin did not hesitate to approve Pierre Klossowski's translation of his essay as *L'oeuvre d'art à l'époque de sa reproduction mécanisée* for its inaugural publication in the *Zeitschrift fuer Sozialforschung* (1936).

Still, Benjamin might have regretted the compromise made in these translations. It is not only that film is the work of chemical, not just mechanical engineers, and cannot accurately be characterized as mechanical reproduction. More important, from title to epilogue, *technique* in its various agglomerations, including *technical reproduction,* threads an urgently avowed Leninism through an essay composed as an aesthetic pendant to Lenin's doctrine of the identity of industrial might and socialism. Benjamin chronicles, for instance, the rise of technical reproduction from the woodcut to lithography, moving in lock step with the rise of socialism as a variation on Lenin's thesis that "electricity plus Soviets equals socialism"; the essay's opposition to custom and craft in favor of standardization, automation, and the univocity of scientific solution are all ideals that Lenin himself espoused in the Taylorism that he disastrously imported from American managerial science and endorsed as Communism's only legitimate means. Benjamin exalts the ineluctability of the conveyor belt and ultimately a command economy when he praises the unrelenting gaplessness of film for dislodging the contemplative stance and private associations of the individual in front of a canvas; it is scientific precision that he extols in the surgical instrumentarium of the camera for its power to dissect life in contrast to the surface-bound magic of the painter's handicraft (233), and it is to "technique" per se that Benjamin looks for leadership when he deplores the fact that society is not "mature enough to incorporate technique as its organ" and that "technique has not been sufficiently developed to cope with the elemental forces of society" (242).

It is likewise to Leninist productivism that the essay owes a key aporia. For just as the insistence that technique is an absolute good prohibited Leninism from understanding why the forces of production, however ripe, did not compel society to take the necessary next step to a better world, so Leninism left Benjamin in the lurch when his theses came face to face with the reality of the movies of his own age, which he describes as "illusion-promoting spectacles" bearing a "phony spell" (231). The problem that arises from this confrontation is obvious: if technique automatically withers aura, why does a "phony spell" prevail in film as it exists? Benjamin solves this aporia programmatically, in fact, by situating the "phony spell" external to any investigation of the question of technique. He might as well blame foreign powers when he inculpates "the movie makers' capital" for producing this spell by "an artificial build-up of 'personality' outside of the studio" (231).

The "phony spell" is aura once removed, a residual technique-resistant ghost hopefully made unrecognizable as aura when lodged under other syllables. This ruse, however, maintains the purity of technique only at a price: it prohibits any investigation into the techniques of mass culture in film. Thus Benjamin cut himself off from such insights as are contained in his earlier study of aura, "A Short History of Photography," in which he distinguishes not between aura and the "phony spell" but between true and false aura, between the concentrated gaze of early photographic portraits and the *gommage* of pseudospirit instilled into faces and sunsets by the use of an erasure to "gum up" the negative in a prettifying manner. This technical critique of pseudo-aura could have become the source for a more profound aesthetics, and not just of film. Instead, however, Benjamin himself practices conceptual *gommage*: the exclusion of any technical investigation of the phony spell redounds to the untouchable aura of technique. Indeed the essay relies on the importation of a surplus indeterminateness to assert the self-evidence of the concept of technical reproduction. And it will be noticed that throughout the essay, however it extols technique, there is a minimum of genuinely technical analysis. It is a measure of the auratic power of the concept that it is possible to read this essay over decades without realizing that there is in fact no technical analysis of "technical reproduction" as an overarching process that includes photography and film. The broad power of technical reproduction is known only by its effects, which Benjamin presents as fourfold: 1. It results in many copies. 2. These copies are not dependent on the original to the same degree as are manual reproductions and therefore they can accent the original, regard it from various angles and magnify what otherwise escapes the senses. 3. It transports the original into places where it could not otherwise be brought, just as, to take Benjamin's example, a photo makes a cathedral portable. 4. And, by producing copies of this sort, it destroys aura. These powers are inimical to aura because the auratic art work bears the radiant authority of tradition, which it accumulates along the tether that it spans out from the moment of its unique inception. This uniqueness predicates its claim to authenticity, which is the evidence of all through which it has passed. By providing copies devoid of uniqueness, by contrast, technical reproduction snaps the art work free from this tether of tradition and thus deprives the work of the authority of time that constitutes and shines through its untouchable presence *hic et nunc*. Copying the art work, therefore, must compel it to surrender any claim to authenticity and any resistance to scrutiny (220–223).

Aura, then, is the aura of authenticity. And it is evident that Benjamin, the collector, conceived it on the model of the authenticity that antiques store up in the nicks and divots they acquire as they change hands over the centuries. On this model art works could be thought to forfeit their aura by being copied just as does a pressboard knockoff of a seventeenth-century armoire. But had Benjamin more concretely investigated technical reproduction in the arts, aura would have shown itself to be a more complex object and he would have been obliged to conceive its relation to reproduction differently. For even a tango, performed in the privacy of one's own bedroom, and only indistinctly executed, is not necessarily deprived of a degree of aura, an authoritative redolence of more than is there just because it is the umpteenth thousandth rendition and authorized by no writ of habeas corpus for the primordial movers. And if the tango seems all too manual in a discussion of technical reproduction, neither do hammers, strings, and escapements necessarily deprive a piano performance of the authority of its historical resonance *hic et nunc*. The piano is, in fact, an instrument of technical reproduction according to all of Benjamin's criteria: it in principle produces an unlimited number of copies; these copies are indifferent to the factually original manuscript; and the performances can slow, magnify, expand, distort, test, analyze any section, and more than meet the listener halfway. A Beethoven sonata can even be performed at different places and with overlapping simultaneity without surrendering its uniqueness. But if the presence of the pianist's fingertips once again threaten to corrupt even this event with the manual, musical recordings of Benjamin's own day—and even dance films of his own decades such as Mary Wigman's famous *Witch Dance*—were not and are not necessarily without the aura of their original, and this cannot simply be chalked up to the influence of foreign capital.

Perhaps it is unfair to Benjamin to cite these examples. In his correspondence he mentions a disdain for whatever made him tap his toes, an antipathy that also testifies to a limited interest in dance. And even challenging his arguments in the domain of painting might be foreign terrain because he could never have argued for photography as he does had he made himself familiar with modernism's critique of photography as the illusionary, trompe l'oeil medium par excellence. But if music, dance, and painting were not his *terre natale,* this does not account for a literary critic of the highest order urging that "from the perspective of world literature" the emergence of the printing press is "merely a special, though particularly important case" (219). Even limited to the modest perspective of European history, the mutually countervailing impulses of this clause can only he explained by the need to dispose of what is hard to get rid of. Benjamin jettisons any consideration of the relation of the aura of literary works to their reproduction because literature is so obviously the result of technical reproduction as he describes it: it exists in any number of copies; even if it is a disturbingly human act, it eludes every narrow reification-hungry debate over the difference between the manual and the technical; it is separate from its origins, etc. And, all the same, while meeting every condition of technical reproduction, the aura of *Absalom Absalom*, for instance, is not necessarily canceled.

On the contrary, the aura of the literary art work depends on technical reproduction. Had Benjamin pursued this thread, he might have realized that his own insight—that exhibition value is necessary to art—implies that reproduction is not added into art but is inherent to it.[4] This is apparent in the fact that, even before cathedrals became portable as photographs, masses of visitors were able to think back on what they had seen; and the inherency of reproduction to art is apparent again in the felt need to return in memory to a stanza to mumble through its syllables or to dredge up a song while the throat's own incapacity takes the sound elsewhere. Each art work says, "Be like me," without necessarily surrendering its uniqueness. Thus Benjamin's key thesis that "even the most perfect reproduction of a work of art is lacking in one element: its presence in time and space, its unique existence at the place where it happens to be" (220) is compelling only by the potentials of its negation; even the most imperfect reproduction of an art work is not necessarily lacking authoritative presence.

Benjamin requires that this implication be pursued when he writes that technical reproduction "enables the copy of the original" (220). In invoking the concept of the copy, he himself is implicitly obliged to admit that there is no true reproduction without the original: every copy is a copy of the original. But if the weave and pigment of a painting ultimately constituted the original, Kandinsky, for instance—on discovering that his new acquaintance Schoenberg was not only a composer but a painter—would not have requested photos of his works: "Actually, I can get along even without colors. Such a photo is a kind of piano reduction."[5] And if a musical composition were ultimately the material acoustic event, musicians—who often enough spurn the distortion free gold-coupled stereolab—would not be heard to say, provokingly, that they are not "really interested in how it sounds." Historically, and especially in modern times, to the horror of art dealers and stirring public incredulity, artists like Giacometti and Francis Bacon have destroyed more art works than they saved, effectively taking the side of what transpires in every art work. Each art work rejects its factuality, as the thing it is, by its form, which is the process by which it consumes its appearance and reveals what is more than this appearance. It is the reality revealed in this process—however difficult it is to say what this reality is—and not its material, that is its original. And it is because the reality of an art work is external to it that even in front of our eyes it is hard to locate the work precisely. Thus the most important art works, by the power and sometimes violence with which they shed their appearance, may make themselves seem irrelevant, as if they stand superfluously in the way of their content and no longer need to be seen, heard, or read. Deciding never again to play or listen to music may be a kind of devotion to it.

If the original is not ultimately the factual work, then the copy is not necessarily deprived of the work's authoritative aura and authenticity. It is important to realize, however, that while this criticism goes to the core of Benjamin's argument, the critique itself comes from Benjamin. In his study, *The Origin of the German Play of Lamentation*, he writes that "the function of artistic form is to make historical content, such as provides the basis of every important work of art, into a philosophical truth."[6] The "origin" of an art work is thus conceived as what wrests itself free by the power of form from the historical moment, though not in the sense of becoming timeless, but as a sedimentation of time that seeks fulfillment in a process that consumes its own appearance and ultimately transcends the work. "Origin" then—to cite Benjamin's favorite Karl Kraus maxim—is not the historical beginnings of an art work, but its goal; and what is original in the work goes beyond it.

These several ideas from Benjamin's own writings provide more than adequate resources to undermine the argument of the reproduction essay. Benjamin himself could have thought the contrary to each and every thesis of this essay, line by line. But, if so, his essay threatens to become substantially fishy. And, if it is not to be abandoned as such, it must be studied for its fishiness. Indeed the essay asks to be studied in this way, for it schools disbelief in itself. The essay is as a whole a *credo quia absurdum est,* though without making obvious what is to be believed. On one hand, the essay claims that film motivates the revolutionary transformation of the masses, adapting a proletarianized world to collective, critical experience and so forth. Yet, on the other hand, the essay at various junctures recognizes that this is not at all the reality of film. At one point Benjamin even writes, "As a rule no revolutionary merit can be accredited to today's film" (231). In context, this disclaimer is a critique of the films of Western Europe. This criticism, however, must be much more far ranging, for to the acetate stock of the West he counterposed films from no other cardinal direction. In fact, his accolade to the movies does not positively refer to, or discuss, a single movie and, completely contrary to the name-blabby genre of so-called film studies, hardly mentions a single film by title.

But if it is obvious that Benjamin's essay must be far more critical of film than the essay seems to state, where is the criticism lodged? An instance of what occurs throughout the essay is given by Benjamin's film audience. It attracts attention by its uneasy stirrings. For what Benjamin claimed to see in the movies through its eyes is not what the masses of that age or this one ever saw or would be willing to see. The identity of this audience is in fact puzzling because the fascinated moviegoer who marches out of the cinema feeling Bogart's trench coat dragging at his ankles cannot be recognized in Benjamin's figure of the distracted expert in the middle distance who presumably leaves the theater in cool self-possession. However, this paradoxically skimming—though erudite—gaze, in which Benjamin casts the model film viewer, is familiar as one incarnation of Benjamin's image of the Baudelairian *flaneur*, Benjamin's own self-ideal. This is the viewer who is so remote from the proceedings that he identifies not with the actors but with the camera; trained to works of the highest level of aesthetic density and tension, he perceives nothing of the enthrallment of those on either side of him; even the opportunistic quarantine of the "phony spell" external to film probably pivots on a complete and learned lack of recognition of the auratic claims raised by the stars as they stare down on him. The eye that translated Proust and habituated itself to the arcane *Trauerspiel* would not have needed to struggle to see through the magic of movieland to penetrate to the screen's bare factuality; his asceticism passes over the pornographic cornucopia without a twinge and instead admires the medium for its potential dimness.

With Benjamin's critical eye lodged in their otherwise diverse faces, his audience is an exotic hybrid population. It did not exist in his age, and not before or since. Yet it is exclusively this nonexistent audience that Benjamin esteems as an inescapable fact and automatic result of the movies themselves. But just how little Benjamin could have

believed in the actuality of this revolutionary audience is implied by
the fact that he only exalts film itself for what his essay perfectly well
acknowledges film was not: the proto-communist medium for the
cognitive transformation of the masses. This is why anyone may notice that Benjamin's applause for his topic echoes strangely throughout the essay. It is the form in which criticism is sedimented: film, in
all its aspects, audience included, is praised exclusively for what it is
not. And the eye that bestows admiration only where it finds nothing
to admire is utterly at odds with what it sees. This is not, however, to
say that the "'Work of Art in the Age of Its Technical Reproducibility" is a critique à *clef* of popular culture. It could not be a sly rhetoric
intending to stir critique under the mask of admiration, for Benjamin's critical gaze is too disembodied, too unconsciously fixed in admiration, to be the work of a beleaguered dinner guest furtively
mocking "a perfect evening."

But if the audience in Benjamin's essay is an elite critical eye masked
as the masses enjoying themselves in a vision gutted of aura, it may be
necessary for popular culture to revise its embrace of Benjamin. He is
not a man of the people but an elitist who in this essay—rather than
setting his critical gaze in self-conscious opposition to the status quo—
sought to inhabit the masses self-obliviously with his own elite con-
trarian gaze. When this is realized, the essay becomes more comprehensible in its complexity and its broad historical context emerges.
Benjamin intellectually made his way to the movie house in response
to the same forces that shaped a long tradition of German cultural
elites beginning with Lessing and Schiller and on through to Brecht.
They—contrary to the American image of German intellectual life—
have been far more isolated and culturally beleaguered than their
counterparts this side of the Atlantic. Pursuing a Lutheran sense of
the functionality of art, they hoped to overcome this isolation through
the fulfillment of cultural aims by means of aesthetic praxis. Their
various programs—for instance—for changing Germans into Greeks
anno 400 B.C. by exhorting them to aesthetic play, were naive and my-
opic. If anything, by constantly exaggerating the idea of art as social
praxis they made themselves the unwitting theorists of, and sometimes—as when Benjamin insists that Fascism fulfilled the aims of
l'art pour l'art (242)—the adamant participants in the destruction of a

hardwon cultural realm. At least Benjamin's perceptions of film combine into so unlikely a portrayal of its reality that they deprive the essay of any evidence that he saw many films or was interested in those he did see. He makes this plain when he asserts that the only merit that can be attributed to films as they exist is their "promotion of a revolutionary criticism of traditional concepts of art" (231). In other words, in the movies, this *flaneur* managed to sit still only by drubbing his wits into aesthetic reverie.

Benjamin sought to make himself Germany's preeminent literary critic. Yet in the reproduction essay he sloughs off literature as relatively trivial in comparison with film. He was reputed as a collector, a figure to which he attributed messianic status, and liked to bestow his closest friends with rare first editions. But in the reproduction essay an antiquarian concept of aesthetic authenticity is developed only so that technical reproduction can be admired for its annihilation of authenticity. In "The Work of Art in the Age of Its Technical Reproducibility" Benjamin rejects the magic of language, around which his early work was organized, in favor of the surgical powers of the filmmaker. As a scholar he acquired the most elite education and immersed himself so deeply in hermetic religious doctrines and his own secretiveness that his life's project, the *Passagenwerk*, remains largely unfathomable. Yet, in the reproduction essay, film is praised for obviating whatever distance an object may hold from its observer and exposing it to mass scrutiny. Though he was physically so standoffish that his closest acquaintances would never have hazarded a hand on his shoulder, nevertheless, in the reproduction essay, he extols film for its shoulder-to-shoulder togetherness.

To conclude that Benjamin betrayed himself in a politically opportunistic and apocryphal work seems an understatement. But something else is involved in this essay than self-betrayal, and invoking this moral optic obscures that in these pages the continuity of his thinking is so rigorously pursued that the idea of "technical reproduction" gives unparalleled insight into his entire oeuvre. This becomes especially apparent in sections 9 and 10 of his essay where Benjamin briefly discusses film technique. The importance of these passages must be emphasized because, insofar as the essay seeks to establish film as the art form to end all art, they effectively provide a quintessential statement—however meager—of how technical reproduction destroys aura, which, as mentioned, is missing from the rest of the essay. According to Benjamin, the key technical event is this: the camera severs the actors who appear in front of it from their own likeness. They step in front of the camera only to renounce their image, and ultimately its unity, to the editing table. Thus, Benjamin claims, a "feeling of strangeness . . . overcomes the actor before the camera" because the actors' "reflected image has become separable, transportable" (230–231). Having left the presence of the actor behind, aura—that is, presence—itself vanishes from the image.

Here Benjamin has provided a statement of the form of technical reproduction: it produces an image that is not a reflection of the self. This image was the object of Benjamin's interest throughout his life, and on more than an intellectual level. Indeed, in the reproduction essay he gives evidence that the fascination this image worked on him had preconceptual origins. For when he elucidates the actor's experience of strangeness in front of the camera he seeks to make this credible by speaking from his own experience: the actor's estrangement, he writes, is "the estrangement felt before one's own image in the mirror" (230). Though the experience of the self split off from its likeness and the beholding of this likeness as foreign is for most everyone a potential yet rare, late night, event, Benjamin asserts this depersonalization as normative. He insists that it is the constant condition of the reflection in the mirror and, by this exaggeration, he implies that the experience of depersonalization was his own norm. This implied claim, however, cannot be taken at face value. Though it is possible to assume from his reputed physical standoffishness that he knew the experience of depersonalization well, he was too productive and his emotional life too complex to have constantly lived in this state. Rather his exaggeration has the quality of being just that and as such indicates an effort to cultivate an experience that was a spontaneous potential for him. Benjamin, in other words, sought to produce an image of himself that was severed from himself. "Technical reproduction" was for him an ideal. This does not have to be deduced from his one exaggerating comment of his experience in the mirror. On the contrary, it is repeatedly evident as the forming ideal of his essay as a whole. At every point that Benjamin asserts theses that are so obviously opposed to himself that those familiar with his work must rub their eyes in disbelief at whether this was actually Benjamin's own thought, he is not betraying himself but rather demonstrating "technical reproduction."

Benjamin's taste, in other words, was for an image of himself to which he was not present. This was his *parti pris* for the dead and it endowed him with an unrivaled capacity to immerse himself in the antiquarian. Benjamin was revered for this power. Dolf Sternberger, the author of *Panorama of the Nineteenth Century,* voiced a generally acknowledged admiration for him when he thanked Benjamin for sharpening "my eye for the foreign and dead aspects" of historical documents.[7] Benjamin's affinity for the sepulchral made it possible for him to sift through the breathtakingly inert documents of German Baroque drama and rediscover and decipher allegory in its difference from the symbol. This distinction is complex, but it is initially glossable here as the difference between, on one hand, an image in which subjectivity withers away in the fragmentary form of a ruin, or a death's head, in the experience of time as painful duration; and on the other, a radiant image in which meaning is fulfilled in the mystical instant of the presence of spirit.[8] Benjamin developed this distinction in the *Trauerspiel* study in order to model a theological critique of subjective reflection on allegorical form.

If this distinction between symbol and allegory sounds familiar, it is because it is the same distinction made in the reproduction essay between the auratic presence of all time in the eternal moment *hic et nunc,* in which meaning appears as a totality, and the anti-auraric, cinematic image, in which the radiant presence of the face of the actor was constantly being stripped out of the image by the camera and deprived of wholeness by the ruin-making scissors at the editing bench, that is, in the experience of transience. The theological critique of subjective reflection in the earlier study, built on the allegorical image, later became a political critique built on the idea of technical reproduction. There is reason to be puzzled, therefore, when Benjamin writes in the later essay that "the technical reproduction of a work of art . . . represents something new" (218). How could it be something new if, after all, it was Benjamin's own research that dates the form of this image some four hundred years earlier and provided its seminal interpretation? But if no one knew better than Benjamin its antiquity and content, he least of all would have allowed that he was betraying

his claim to his previous insight into the Baroque. Rather he was reproducing this earlier insight technically: he states it in a form that fascinated him, one deprived of self-recognition.

Benjamin's powers depended on a guardianship of the boundary line
defined by depersonalization. And these powers were not only those
of incomparable insight into allegory, but powers of miscompre-
hension and distortion. For, if one's image existed in the mirror with
the independence that Benjamin asserts, then, staying up late, there
would be no double take in the mirror to check if one's face had really
lingered a split second overlong as one turned away. The double take
is the self seeking itself when it does not permit itself to know what it
is seeking. Depersonalization, therefore, is not the splitting off of one's
reflection as Benjamin stylizes it, but rather the form in which the self
is adored while unconsciously defending itself against the guilt of the
adoration. Certainly this is what is off-putting, to some, in the constantly reproduced image of the melancholic German critic, holding
his weary head; it is the James Dean effect in the same range of photos
for those who find that stance convincing. Likewise, if the movie camera did simply sever the actor's reflection from the actor, as Benjamin
claims, actors would view film rushes with indifference or morbid
dread. But actors go to screenings to witness the emergence of their
fame, which pivots on the exploitation of the separation of self and image, and the establishment of the primacy of the latter in the interest of
the self. The "dizzy rise to fame" is a description that has much in
common with the experience of depersonalization, and not least of all
insofar as it describes what is sought after as involuntary. And, likewise, on some level everyone is familiar with this ruse. Otherwise it
would not be possible to understand the insouciance with which people in groups pore over photographs of themselves when they would
never permit themselves to be caught beholding their own reflection
with comparable avidity. The snapshot, by its ostensible involuntariness, makes the defense of depersonalization available: the self is permitted to behold itself on the basis of an illusion of being on the other
side of its self-seeking.

Benjamin did not want to know the content of his reflection. And while his writings are magisterial and irreplaceable—just this one essay founded the entire contemporary discussion of the question of the transformation of art through its reproduction and formulated the set of questions in relation to which Adorno's *Aesthetic Theory* took shape—all the same, his work is sworn to rationalization. In the reproduction essay he decries Fascism for deceiving the masses with a "chance to express themselves" (241) without troubling to distinguish true from false expression. Likewise, in the Baroque study, he is drawn to and deciphers the absence of subjective expressiveness in allegory as a form of expression, but he never criticizes the actual inertness of the allegorical world he studied. He is rigorously antipsychological throughout his oeuvre and therefore only draws on psychoanalysis when it serves to avoid its insights, as when in the reproduction essay he insists that "the camera introduces us to unconscious optics as does psychoanalysis to unconscious impulses" (237). But this claim only holds if the preconscious—here the world of a range of gestures that are easily brought into consciousness when they are specially attended to—is substituted for the unconscious, whose contents are accessible only by interpretation under special circumstances. Had Benjamin been able to make better sense of psychoanalysis he would have had the critical means to avoid the rationalizing kitsch of the preface to the *Trauerspiel* study, where he epitomizes the Idea as the mother's face that lights up when the constellation of her children gather around her; he would not have made himself a spokesman of collective amnesia in his evocation of children as "messengers of paradise;" nor would he have won a place this year (1994) on a West Coast *Storyteller* calendar as one of a caste of New Age bards. It would likewise have deprived Benjamin of the boundary of depersonalization, and thus he would have been compelled to see that if he himself, looking into the mirror, is able to carry out the act of technical reproduction, then the camera is not all that austerely technical, nor all that opposed to the labor of manual craft. Rather, technique, as "technical reproduction," is a form of subjectivity that he relies on to defend himself from knowing who he is while he seeks himself in absentia. Isn't this, after all, the latent content of his argument in the reproduction essay? If the audience identifies with the camera—as he asserts—and if the audience can be recognized as Benjamin's eyes—then it is

Benjamin who is viewing the figure who seemingly struggles with the loss of self-recognition in the unreflexive mirror of the camera. This self-viewing is particular in that it is predicated on a taboo of self-recognition.

In the "Work of Art in the Age of Its Technical Reproducibility" Benjamin does not at any point investigate the aura of mass culture. On the contrary, he simply denies that it bears aura and explains why: technical reproduction makes presence wither by producing images that are not reflections of the self. But no investigation of mass culture is needed to know that Benjamin's assessment of mass culture is wrong: it glimmers with the presence of more than is factually there. For even if Benjamin's idea of technical reproduction balks at understanding what this aura is, his essay's urgently self-oblivious gestures inadvertently give some clue: "technical reproduction" produces aura in the form of fascination, that is, under the taboo of self-recognition. The essay lives from the same aura as does mass culture, which has the ability to glimmer only with what the audience can be enticed to put there without recognizing as its own. The tautology of this aura—which mass culture is constantly compelled to experience as its unsatisfying satisfactions—is a definition of its falseness.

It is well known that Benjamin aspired to the construction of a text composed strictly of quotations. Insofar as this project of a work devoid of any affirmative trace of its author was never realized, Benjamin's ideal of "technical reproduction" also remained unfulfilled. But this is not to say that the project and its ideal simply vanished. In Benjamin's own decades, Pound, Eliot, Joyce, and Musil worked on closely related efforts. And, on a much, much more mundane level, self-advancement through the manipulation of various forms of anonymity and depersonalization has historically been the rule, not the exception.[9] It is the ideal of the corporation, that *société anonyme*. And it is expressly shared by many when they speak of their lives as careers. The planned publication of the English translation of his *Passagenwerk* (*The Arcades Project*) will speak to this ideal by inspiring a manic professoriate in this country to disgorge volumes of assembled quotations in a mystery of selflessness and vita padding. It will make a comparable contribution to the enchantment worked by the historically arbitrary vicissitudes of Foucault's episteme and attract the self-styled priest class of deconstruction's self-seeking "Not I!" as it goes stale.

But while some faculty may still have to wait for the *Passagenwerk* translation, students turn out to be in advance of the learned. They have no need to study Benjamin to discover technical reproduction as a form. For what more ingeniously laconic presentation of the idea of a work composed purely of quotation than a primitivesque white capital "S" embossed on a red sweatshirt? In this subtly involuntary appeal to an anonymous power, their prestige, which they will have only so long as they are not it, they each head out over their handlebars, obliviously, pursuing their own better lives.

Adorno Without Quotation

Rolf Tiedemann gewidmet

WHEN SAMUEL BECKETT learned that he was to be awarded the
Nobel Prize in Literature, he disconnected the telephone, packed up,
and went south, to deepest elsewhere and foolproof incommunicado.
That story is known to many. By contrast a story known almost to
none—until this moment—is that, before the sun had glimmered on
the first full day of a yearlong schedule of official centennial celebra-
tions to mark the birth of Theodor W. Adorno, Rolf Tiedemann—the
founding director of the Theodor W. Adorno-Archiv, now emeritus,
and the editor of Adorno's *Collected Writings*—was already driving
south from Frankfurt for an extended stay, across borders, in the
Dolomiti. It is worth wondering how these stories may be related. If
readers could be encouraged to take sides here, some might insist—in
this year of intense Frankfurt biographical research (three new biographies of Adorno were published in 2003 with more of the same
forthcoming)—that these acts are so similar that causal influence must
be presumed. And evidence of this kind can be adduced: Adorno so
closely trusted Tiedemann that, in the late fifties and early sixties,
Adorno brought him along to afternoon meetings with Beckett. Certainly the formidable Irish émigré, who would insist on speaking German, must have communicated much, along with many impulses,

some perhaps unconsciously, to the still impressionable philosopher's assistant. Yet to seek to attribute Tiedemann's behavior on September 11th to these various afternoons, even speculatively, would logically be to presume that the origin of the human urge to flee was strictly Samuel Beckett's. Short shrift, then, for those who would find these stories genetically concatenated. On the other hand, there might be readers who would insist that these two stories have nothing whatever in common and should not be recounted in the same breath. After all, what Tiedemann would have seen disappearing in the rearview mirror on the morning of September 11th was a looming hundredth celebration conjuring Adorno's presence, not his own. For the stories to be truly akin, we would need to be juxtaposing Adorno with Beckett, and this is not the case. A debunking tactic determined to sunder story from story—and car from car—would only need to assert that Tiedemann is not Adorno. The force of pure tautology would take care of the rest.

I

There is no rush to establish here an early understanding of the relationship or disrelationship between these two events. On the contrary, even to be curious about it, much must be said especially for American readers of this essay, for whom—unlike its German readers[1]—Rolf Tiedemann has hardly been a familiar figure in intellectual life over the course of the last thirty years. For this reason, the best, though perhaps jarringly counterintuitive approach is to begin by rapidly sketching in the paradoxal recent development of substantial interest in Adorno's work in the United States. After all, this is hardly an elective affinity that could have been presumed. The whole of Adorno's thought concerns an idealist tradition to which, except for the peculiar moment of the St. Louis Hegelians in the mid-nineteenth century, there is nothing autochthonously comparable on the American side of the Atlantic. Up until the last two decades, in fact, even at major universities it was only possible by exception to seriously study the central works of this tradition. Likewise, the music and literature that constitute the topics of the majority of Adorno's writings are, with only several important exclusions, unfamiliar to Americans, even among the university educated. And where Adorno does touch on American

things most closely, in his critique of industrial entertainment, he an-
tagonizes virtually everyone in a nation where the ear is certainly the
most stupidified, rawly integrated and exploited of the senses. Add to
this that since the world wars the German language has become a
longstanding object of prejudice and generally shunned—again, even
by the educated—and the conclusion would seem self-evident that
Adorno's work would never be broadly studied in American universities, the only sphere of intellectual interest in the United States.

But in spite of the deep cultural antagonisms, the crackling foreignness of a philosophy that is foremost a critique of barbarism has
now become profoundly interesting to a nation whose most characteristic poet, Walt Whitman, espoused his barbaric "yawp" as a highest
dignity. Why this has happened must involve many sociohistorical
dimensions, including underlying continuities of thought that are
crudely betrayed by claiming to add their elements together suddenly,
as if they were ever ultimately estranged. English is, after all, in large
part some kind of German with many French words. But if the existing antagonisms, which have historically amounted to devastating opposition, are not to be denied, part of the reason for the recent interest
in Adorno's work may be in what historians recognize in the recurrently antitraditional basis of all tradition: that it is always established
in adoption from untraditional sources, and this occurs most of all in
moments of crisis. And it is in such a moment where all things now
stand; indeed, they now stand substantially beyond crisis and well into
catastrophe.

There are two levels of reasons for describing the situation in
such strong terms. The close reasons are that Americans during the
Bush presidency now find themselves in the midst of experiencing
what Germans themselves underwent more than half a century ago:
an episode of living in a country that has been seized by a minority
that has drawn it into desperate circumstances. This minority has
every intention of exploiting these events to assure that the transfer of
power it achieved in a dubious election can be made irreversible and
on every level. The administration's eye is especially on the judiciary
and means to achieve its aims by wearing away at the division between
church and state. A detail of this struggle, for instance—one completely familiar to American readers of this essay but not likely to be
known by its German readers—is the crowd that recently felt encour-

aged by the direction of national policy to occupy the steps of an Alabama state courthouse to blow rams horns and offer to "lay down their lives" to protect a stone engraved with the ten commandments installed in the vestibule by the chief justice. In such minor as well as in major confrontations the administration consistently encourages its partisans to strike at obliterating the opposition. This is not to say that this necessarily succeeds; in a complex sense, it did not in Alabama, though that success may come in the long run. But the intention itself of wiping out opposition is unusual in the country's long-standing bipartisanal concept of democracy and verges toward the unprecedented in intensity. One witnesses a country that has become broadly deluded. In the wake of the terrorist attacks, the nation as a whole has suffered a further attack on its sense of reality by the leadership's own drastically impoverished sense of the world. The situation now has the characteristic of the uncanny where the difference between daily life and what is actually transpiring has steeply intensified to the point that daily conversation has the feel of being unable to address, let alone comprehend, what all are now caught up in. The situations are as distinct as they are related, but to understand—as if in a laboratory—what it really meant for Germans during World War II to claim that they "did not know" it would be possible to study the United States right this moment, September 25, 2003, and find in a substantial majority the prevalence of ideas about the reasons for the invasion of Iraq that bear resemblances to the blindness in broad daylight and phantom reasonings of the earlier situation's murderous anti-Semitism.

These are some of the close reasons—which have in fact been developing since the mid-sixties—that have combined to cause a readjustment in the relationship of the intellectual contexts of the two countries and, specifically, for a sustained interest and examination of Adorno's writings. And though it hardly seems possible to imagine more comprising reasons than these, any discussion of the situation calls for a power of imagination that goes beyond imagination's own capacity. It would amount to hyperbole to go from such a statement to simply talking about it, as if it could be directly faced. It is obligatory, then, to first reject and avoid the matter, in alliance with the actual incapacity to think about it, and try it this way: anyone who might have spent time this past summer in a major art museum such as the Metropolitan Museum of Art in New York City, visiting any room of what can be called modern in the largest sense of post-Renaissance, perhaps the Pissaro room, could have noticed that the whole of what there is to regard on those canvases lives from the discovered sense of the cornucopia of nature, even when those canvases represent it in its variable abstract negation. This sense of the cornucopia of nature—if readers want momentarily to consult their own sensoria—is now gone. It has taken with it any implication of the utopic imaginings that accompanied what was once edifyingly called the modern rediscovery of nature. For the reality of the damage that has been done weighs too guiltily to tolerate these imaginings. It is extreme to think that in not many decades, if that, these paintings could themselves change from art to bare mementos of unfamiliar locale because the impulse that sustains them—the experience of natural beauty that the whole of Adorno's *Aesthetische Theorie* sought to comprehend—had long vanished. Still, however extreme this thought, what kind of extreme is there in the thought of the death of the eleven thousand people this past summer in France from the unprecedented heat? Or of the unprecedented flooding throughout Europe during the previous summer? There is a hole in the sky and 30 to 45 percent of all species are in jeopardy, a set of proportions that, even if the lower estimate is prudently preferred, necessarily deceives because it does not attempt to account for the condition of what really will be left after such vast subtraction. As every last person knows, there is nothing of this dimension in human history; nothing so irreparable could have previously occurred in human history. And for reasons that need to be understood we are not enough able to come to our wits in mutual acknowledgment of the situation even to be able to panic in its estimation as reason itself must need to. At the same time many may be finding themselves inadvertently recurring to the thought, and testing it repeatedly to see what real thinking it holds, that the disasters of the contemporary political situation—so willingly engaged by the Americans—and the antidemocratic transformation of society have begun to fill in a middle distance of one summer, or some number of summers, between where we now stand in time and cataclysmic natural events on a world scale that in fact are no longer to be avoided and may well implicate another form of society altogether.

II

An essay whose motive is its alliance with two cars traveling south—and especially with one of them—can itself move decisively in that direction by pointing out that there is only one reason to be all that interested in Adorno's work. This reason is generally recognized by those who are familiar with the work, but it is not always stated clearly: No other contemporary philosophy is able to set its finger with such precision, so unwaveringly, on the content of this historical moment. A question worth answering then is, how is it able to do this? There is more to say on this point than can be said here. But some approach to the question is gained if this philosophy's view of history, presented in *Dialectic of Enlightenment*, is considered. That work was itself conceived in a desperate effort in the 1940s to understand why history, instead of progressing, regresses. This speaks directly to our contemporary moment where Americans—certainly—sense themselves entering primitive times, socially, under the great velocity of that nation's weaponry.

But even a brief presentation of the thesis of *Dialectic of Enlightenment* must be prefaced with a heavy caveat. If this work especially deserves to draw the attention of students of Adorno in the United States, its study will at many turns demonstrate that it is faulty and limited in many ways: its analysis of the ultimate convergence of domination with fascism, for instance, is undiscerning in that fascism, whatever traces it has had in the United States, has never been a substantial threat because a country that knows itself to be made up exclusively of immigrants cannot participate in an institutionalized fantasy of the nation as a primordial family. Simply compare the rebarbative idea of "homeland" in "homeland security" with the German *heimat* or the French *patrie*. Likewise, Americans cannot guess at the strictures of formal paternal authoritarianism known directly to the generations of the Kaiserreich into which Adorno was born, a tradition of authority later usurped by Nazism. Just to discover what a handshake once meant in those contexts would require from most North Americans some amount of cultural-anthropological study. And regardless of comparative national perspectives and mores, *Dialectic of Enlightenment* was written under such desperate pressure to comprehend the regressive force of enlightenment that in the pages of that text—as the authors were aware—enlightenment itself becomes difficult to understand as a value.

With the expectation, then, that there is much to question in the work, the thesis of *Dialectic of Enlightenment*—by its nature only partially stateable at any one point—is that history regresses because progress, as the progress of domination, is sacrificial. Sacrifice is shown to be a logic of substitution that develops as the principle of identity—the impulse of self-preservation itself—in an ever broadening web of the exchange relation. The exchange relation generically consumes the particular while the principle of identity constantly hides from view the sacrificial mayhem at the interior of the process. Reality is thus mastered while the purpose of mastery, the possible satisfaction of the particular, is squandered. In the face of resources achieved at great price, and which society could well employ to satisfy its many wants and needs, progress is instead ever more blind to its purpose and ineluctably driven to become a demand for the sacrifice of the sacrificial whole. Thus images of the Great Depression return to American minds as puzzle-visions of farmers discreating surplus, putting an end to plenty, in order to survive scarcity: destroying produce and guttering tank-loads of milk into open fields. In crisis an unreasonable reason continues to call for sacrifice as if it, most of all, were the true need, still new and unmet. And thus anyone who glances through the *New York Times* finds that paper—a distinguished, moderate opponent of the current administration—consistently jousting in its editorial pages with the current Republican administration for who can urge the most willed sacrifice on a deeply distressed people.[2] Yet the United States now produces so much more than it did in 1950 that, if the country lived at the comfortable standards of that year, the entire population could take half the year off.[3] But instead, in spite of this prosperity, Americans work fourteen months for every twelve that Europeans put in. And what Americans have made of the country, as registered in American novels at least since the sixties in such works as Truman Capote's *In Cold Blood,* is notorious for its blandness, an "undifferentiated limbo of highways and drive-ins, garages and main streets, vandalized landscapes and faceless towns." As George Steiner wrote of this landscape, in the voice of sharp exaggeration that by that measure alone finally succeeds at hitting on a nerve, it is the "saddest place on the wide earth." Given what the country now tends toward, sadness may soon seem much the least of it.

III

To return then to the question: How does Adorno's philosophy of history seek to put its finger on reality, and how does it do so with an incomparable precision, and unwaveringly? The answer is deductively evident from the major thesis of *Dialectic of Enlightenment* as it has so far been considered: If domination sloughs off its own aim in a web of covertly sacrificial exchange relations, relations of ostensible equality in which nevertheless one side is always cheated, domination could only be brought to its senses, and what its achieved powers could serve, through a critique that is the ally of what is otherwise generically sacrificed—the *particular.* This philosophy, in other words, considered itself nothing if not a materialism, though plainly distinct from a long history of materialist thought that has characteristically amounted to the assertion that material is the sum of all, as if once this were acknowledged the ghosts would at last be driven out of the machine and with them, necessarily, all the demons as well. *Dialectic of Enlightenment* was not convinced by this logic, and its own materialism disputes it. For Adorno, materialism meant restoring to the material—nature, even as second nature—the comprehension of its content. The particular is just the material, its content restored in the sense of the comprehension of this content.

Though this materialism vies with Marx's own, it is distinctly a form of Marxism, and most of all in the sense that the restoration of the content relies on an insight that can be followed from antiquity's critique of *lex talionis*, to Rousseau, to Kant, to Fichte's critique of capital punishment, and most of all to Marx: that there is nothing that can be traded for life that is its equal. Wage does not compensate either in maximums or minimums; the internal structure of the wage relation is necessarily life robbed and sacrificed. This insight was a given for Adorno; pushed, it could be called the meaning of his thought. And while he was completely aware that Marx's theory of class struggle did not begin to comprehend the whole structure of domination and failed to carry through the critique of life as labor, still Adorno could not have imagined that anything could be hoped for socially that would not somehow make good on this fundamental insight into the inequality of exchange.

But in the never absolute partings between Marx and Adorno, the distinction between them that is most relevant to this essay (for understanding this essay's preoccupation with the direction that Rolf Tiedemann was going on the morning of September 11th) is also the distinction that most bewildered the students who attacked Adorno in his last years. The issue is this: Marx's materialism is the basis of one of the few philosophies in the history of Western thought that carries with it a program of action; it is, by that same measure, almost the only philosophy that can in this sense be directly joined. It is not surprising, then, that the students, who rightly understood Adorno's philosophy to stand inextricably in the Marxist tradition, would suppose that here too it would be possible to join up. The expectation of joining that this implied is still painfully obvious in the photographs of the faces of those students who crammed into the lecture halls just to have a seat.

But however large the amphitheaters in which this philosophy was heard, however voluminous in page count its forty some volumes are, the thinking itself is strictly a one-man boat. Even its wide gunwales provide no sitting space for visitors to occupy. This philosophy models a stance that can be held only by one person. The thinking itself insists it is able to put its finger on the historical moment just to the degree that it succeeds at shaping the experience of the particular as it suffers and is otherwise deprived of expression. That is why a negative dialectics is necessarily an aesthetics: for this is the only possible arena in which the fate of the particular can be perceived as a particular; the only dimension in which the elements of the world can be adequately formed in such a way that it becomes possible to shudder at what is, at its truth, as otherwise prohibited by the empirical obligation of self-preservation; and the only possibility for—in Wallace Stevens's words—turning the violence of what is against this violence, in a fashion that is potentially an act of consciousness distinct from retaliation, the tit for tat of the exchange relationship, and may even bespeak the "if it only were" of, for instance, Schumann's "Aufschwung." This necessity of aesthetics to materialism explains why the students who crowded Adorno's lecture hall, with the thrill of joining up in what anyone can join by wrestling one's way to a seat, would have had to wonder at, be bewildered by and finally hateful of, what to their minds they had been cheated into joining: what no one can march to. And while Adorno was flattered and delighted to have drawn vast audiences, the tenor of his work demonstrates that seeking them was not first on his mind. He evidently was not kidding as he repeated, throughout the whole of his writings, that to shape and comprehend the particular the artist and the social critic have no alternative but to work in isolation. Whatever the interdisciplinary claims of the institute, the message in the bottle—which is all that Adorno was ever at work on—cannot in any way be drawn up collectively and put in that bottle by many hands reaching at once. Measured by the philosophy itself, heard by the listening ear, the idea of an Adorno conference is a contradictio in adjektivum. Why else would Tiedemann have been driving south before dawn on the day of the inaugural jubilee?

IV

An essay that wanted to get lost for keeps might decide to take it on itself to elucidate Adorno's intellectual development. For it was not a process of development in the first place. If stages of a sort can be discerned in the writings, it cannot be said that one idea followed another in any kind of sequence. Adorno seems to have been so unimpeded in his intention toward the particular that, from early on, his thinking life was a process that pulled in what it needed to materialize its own characteristic shape. It is no surprise that his colleagues could be disquieted by this. Leo Lowenthal was obliged to discover Adorno making himself so abundantly free with his own best insights that they would disappear, one day to the next, into Adorno's own reflections and typescript without Adorno being at all concerned to write footnotes of citation. Certainly this felt predatory to Lowenthal as it did to Walter Benjamin and Siegfried Kracauer. Evidence of something like predation might indeed be apparent to anyone opening randomly to any page of the *Collected Writings* in search of quotation marks: they can be found, but the later the text, the more they are scarce, and an eye noticing this will begin to discern techniques Adorno developed for avoiding them. The most characteristic is his way of invoking large bodies of thought, or even a particular philosopheme, by means of a locution or imitated phrasal rhythm: no one needs to guess the who's who in any mention of the *retournons*, or what doctrine counterbalances those *starry heavens,* or how many changes can be rung on a thought *im Zeitalter seiner*—as "in the age of" mechanical reproduction—or where Adorno stood on the matter in the philosophy of language as to whether you should say it if you can't talk about it and also like to whistle. A philosophy that is—or is not—philosophy by its responsibility to the particular was, however, not in any sense too busy with itself to cite things properly: on the contrary, in its complete preoccupation with the particular it had nothing to do unless—rather than cite them—it could name them. Adorno worked around quotation marks and footnotes of citation because he experienced them as the ropes and posts of thought that thinks of itself as a wrestling ring where it will be decided who got there first and who owns what.

Thinking, for Adorno, as for Hegel, is how the mind is bound up in what it is at the same time separate from, and the being bound up is itself a determination of the separation as determinate negation. This is the contrary of the assertion of thinking as sitting on one's own property. The centralmost paradox of a philosophy that has exactly enough room for one person—that is just as standoffish as it is unguarded—is that this restriction is the actual source of its capaciousness as a critique of possessive individualism. It is what intelligence can possibly do that has not spent its years getting the latch on the front gate to click shut. The work as a whole, by a man who had no children, is ultimately a critique of the transcendental unity of apperception, the claim of the final mine-ness of each and every thought. That such an effort of thought is conceivable at all is apparent where line after line, sometimes for pages at a time, seems to make itself irresistible to the desire to quote it for what it has succeeded at putting its finger on. But succumb to the impulse, take it for aphorism, and in actual quotation the phrase or passage as soon changes to dust in one's hand and to nonsense on the wall for one's having failed to understand what everything about it said in the first place: there is nothing like this; reproduction prohibited, not by copyright but by reality.

V

Because the fate of the particular is the actual matter of this philosophy, the rigorous formulations have an exposed quality. Adorno was aware of this. The style is a self-consciously conceptual *sprechstimme* and hardly separable from the fragility of its plaintive voice even in so abstract a thought as "the whole is the false."[4] This is as good an expression as any to explain why this essay, however fixed its directional compass, cannot just turn south at any point. For it would be as complete a misunderstanding to suppose that Adorno's writings are a collection of aphoristically quotable lines as that the philosophy itself commends fragmentation. Such a philosophy would collude with what fractures the self in urging it to cooperate in all that means to invade it with commercial purposes of its own. To head off possible misunderstanding, the dialectical content of the idea that the whole is the false needs to be emphasized. For if the whole is indeed the false, driven to the point that it is aware that it is not the absolute, the whole becomes the capacity of the truth. This is the central idea of Adorno's philosophy. It is worth restating. The idea that the whole is the false is by its own measure, by its own insight, the idea that the false is known only by the power of the whole. In this dialectic— Adorno and Horkheimer speculated—enlightenment comes to term. For if the identity of the whole is the capacity to grasp what is opposite itself, then domination is conceivably the capacity to suspend itself in self-relinquishment in the object it has always sought: it would be domination that as real mastery would no longer have any need of violence. This is the process that is perceived in Adorno's writing at its most compelling, line by line. A picture made of this process would look like a one-man boat that is a critique of possessive individualism—a critique of possessive individualism by means of its own individuality, by its own wholeness, not by self-sacrifice. Such a philosophy does not intend to abrogate the transcendental unity of thought, but to complete it. By the measure of its own wholeness, the same measure by which it suspends its wholeness, it would win the ability to put its finger on what is most real. Wallace Stevens sketches some part of this same idea in his "Esthétique du Mal": "Except for us, Vesuvius might consume / In solid fire the utmost earth and know / No pain."[5]

VI

The best reason to quote Adorno is in the recognition that the most legitimate urge to do so is every reason not to quote him at all: For this philosophy's best capacity for insight is in its development of an enlightenment skepticism toward self-sacrifice. By contrast, the quotation of Adorno is itself so often a sacrificial gesture of imitation. Identity that fails to come to term in what is other than itself is inevitably imitation of what is greater than itself as a power of self-assertion. What it wins, it wins as property. The many essays clotted with quotation from Adorno consign a philosophy to a neoclassicism that is its most substantial critic; the quotations are the marks left behind where the tension of the struggle for truth capitulates, seeking someone stronger in which it hopes to acquire a voice for itself. By that measure it is denied its own voice, which is all it has by virtue of which something might be pronounced other than the self. Adorno certainly did not mean to be that someone stronger who would interfere with this voice. And, incidentally, in this regard it is worth commenting here—to keep things in perspective—that Adorno is not the only person who ever recognized some relation between maturity and a power of self-relinquishment. If we were to look for another example of this capacity, Rolf Tiedemann's edition of Adorno's *Collected Writings* would come directly to mind.

VII

Certainly the most interesting idea in the whole of Adorno's work is that identity, the power of tautology itself, can be cultivated as the capacity of its own critique. The point is one known to all musicians, and certainly it is as a musician that Adorno had occasion to consider it: the self is the only ability for differentiation by which self-relinquishment can occur. It is the capacity that an audience has every reason to envy in the human at the keyboard, even if nothing more comes of this feeling on the way home than making grimaces and gesturing large with the arms and hands held high in the air. The thesis that identity is the critique of identity works a wedge into the grip of the claim that what is mine is strictly mine. It uses the capacity of that grip to loosen the hold, but not disparagingly, as if that grip were the low contrary to brotherly love. In its awareness of the fruitlessness of sacrifice, it takes the side of the struggle for self-preservation more seriously than that struggle often can for itself. Adorno's philosophy ultimately wants to show that the weight of the burden of self-preservation is one we have long not needed to bear to the degree we have and certainly not in such a fashion as we have for almost a century so that we are now far past verging on annihilating ourselves and all that is around us. In the thesis of an emancipated tautology as the capacity of the self to immerse itself in what is other than itself, to follow the material where it wants to go, Adorno conceived his version of the ontological proof of god, which in his lectures on philosophical terminology (*Philosophische Terminologie*) he named the most interesting problem in the history of philosophy. In the context of Adorno's thinking, Anselm's proof would become something like the proof of possibility itself. There are many ways to misconstrue this idea, but if in this essay there is now some readiness to make sense of it then a kind of progress has in fact been made here. It is what Adorno would have thought progress might be. This essay has in any case been an experiment in tautology, in wanting to be anything but tautology. From its first page it is a critique of the most obvious sorts of property relations. And by the same measure, without the same capacity of identity that would have wrenched completely apart the two stories with which we began, this essay would now be unable to find the direction that it is instead easily able to take.

South as Such

For a negative dialectics the unpardonable sin would neither be unpardonable nor a sin, but the philosophy does share in the ancient recognition that every degree of despair is failed self-assertion evinced in the claim to being beyond any kind of help, as beyond possibility. Adorno's thinking as a whole is a materialist critique of historical despair. The puzzle it confronts is why the way out looks sealed when every door swings wide on broken hinges. It owes to its particular solution of this puzzle its many limitations of historical and aesthetic differentiation, and specifically its often remarked feeling of narrowness—a narrowness in the closely muffled clowning of the syntax and a narrowness in every dialectical reversal that limits itself to bare shifts between black and white when the frank voilà of the gesture would rather transform these many colored handkerchiefs into those many colored birds. Adorno is right that possibility wins nothing by our astounding ourselves with numbers on the relative productivity of nations decade to decade. It depends, instead, on a kind of direction, in the movement of what is certainly a paradoxical one-man boat, as of various kinds of cars and allied essays going south. For if it were possible to flee on another's behalf, to take that person along in absentia, so to speak, as if Darwin had arranged that for us as a real potential, working perhaps in alliance with all that Lévy-Bruhl knew of selves that are more than punctually themselves, who would not seize this moment to go back to what the terrors of mid-century have left in our minds and, in instants of a contemporary *Aeneid*, step through the rubbled walls, the blown-apart ovens, chambers, and human kilns, to take up burden after burden on our backs and head toward an ultimate south, anywhere to escape, in lines stretching forth from all directions, in every latitude and longitude?

Popular Music and
"The Aging of the New Music"

We may smile at the bombastic way in which Adorno categorically condemns the music situation today.
—David A. Sheldon, "The Philosophy of T. W. Adorno"

A WORD AGAINST POPULAR MUSIC sets most everyone on edge because of the urgency of the functions it must fulfill and because it cannot actually fulfill them. Popular music must libidinize dead space: on highways and through airport corridors; it must manufacture a busyness and direction to time that is in fact stagnant or anxiously, dully swirling; it must take up the slack of empty—usually wordless—waiting in stores, at home, in subways, at social events, and while waiting on telephone lines. In countless situations its role is to make time pass. Popular music is music that seeks to master time by its rigid exclusion, generally by means of rote repetition. This form of mastery is the point of convergence between amusement and labor and explains the laboring quality of the rhythms of popular music. In contrast to the music of the Sirens, which promised an end to labor, popular music complements labor since its arbitrary forward pressure is labor's own sounding ideal.

By contrast, music that would be music—what Adorno called emphatic music—volatilizes time. Whether this occurs depends on the actuality of memory: the expression of the musical material in the new.[1] This cannot, however, occur in popular music because its function is to mask anxiety. However loud or rambunctious, it is not capable of pursuing the tensions of the material it engages and has limited interest in doing so. It must deflect memory and expression while providing their surrogates. This poses one of the central formal concerns that make popular music popular: the deflection must present itself as the immediate manifestation of subjectivity, popular music's primary ideological posture. It has one solution to this problem, and this solution is apparently inexhaustible: subjectivity is excluded through its dogged simulation by the use of clichés, not only harmonically and rhythmically, but most obviously in the lyrics, from down home wisdom, to weary reflexion, to my girl, and so on. Wherever language has hardened from the exclusion of subjectivity, it becomes material for popular music; each song needs to quote no more than one cliché to feign a subjectivity that is no longer subjective, however tear-drenched, torn, or flamboyant the appearances.

Obviously, nothing guarantees that, where music fails to volatilize time, new music succeeds—if it does—on the basis of being called new music, not anymore than its success or failure turns out to be a matter of the size of the audience it commands. But anyone wondering for a moment what might be involved in understanding why music fails or why it succeeds, emphatically, as music itself, will, by drawing a total blank, find reason to be interested in Adorno's musicology. And one of his most interesting and controversial statements on the problematic of new music is his "The Aging of the New Music." An aspect of this essay that will in particular interest American readers because of the generally unchallengeable place of commercial music in the United States is that one implication of the history of new music, as Adorno presents it in this study of the aporia of emphatic music, is that the separation of popular and new music involves the latter succumbing to the same limitations as the former.

"The Aging of the New Music"

Against "New Music"

Adorno's "The Aging of the New Music" was first delivered as a lecture in 1954 during the Stuttgart Week of New Music and was repeated on several occasions before it was published in *Der Monat* in May 1955 and in an expanded form in 1956 in *Dissonances* (*Dissonanzen*), a collection of Adorno's essays.[2] The essay confounds the stereotype of Adorno as an apologist at any price for new music. Here he upbraids serious composition of the postwar generation as "Music Festival music." He does not criticize the exclusion of new music but its mindless toleration: "It [new music] is tolerated as the private activity of specialists, a cultural necessity in some not quite clear fashion" (p. 100). In words that may seem to parallel those of any conservative detractor of modern music, the philosopher best known for his defense of the autonomy of art lambastes modern music for having lost touch with the world: "No one is actually challenged [by this music], no one recognizes himself in it, or senses in it any binding claim to truth" (p. 100). When these lines were first heard, they brought conservative music critics to the brink of ecstasy; immediately they were quoted in defense of restorative music. It is not surprising that younger composers felt betrayed. They were outraged that Adorno had played into the hands of reaction and that he had needlessly rubbed salt on the wound by repeatedly presenting the essay and publishing it so widely.[3]

The essay, however, did not mark any shift in Adorno's understanding of modern music. He had always been its critic and he had no other way of proceeding. One of his most important books on music, *Philosophy of New Music,* far from being blind adulation of the composer who most importantly broke with musical tradition and gave birth to New Music—Schoenberg—is concerned with the immanent tendency of his music toward meaninglessness. While Adorno completely understood the necessity of the introduction of serialism, and held that Schoenberg could not have continued to compose in his first expressionist idiom, he nevertheless found that Schoenberg's free atonal, expressionist works were in certain regards superior to the later serial compositions.

His explanation of Schoenberg's development is important for understanding "The Aging of the New Music" and basic to his understanding of Schoenberg's work is a concept of musical material that Adorno developed most succinctly in *Philosophy of New Music.* Musical material has usually been conceived as an inventory of physical resources, somewhat along the lines of conceiving the material of social history as a list of those present in the period to be studied. Adorno, by contrast, conceived of musical material as sedimented history. Following a thought that he first presented in his early lecture, "The Idea of Natural-History," he described this sedimentation as occurring in such a way that the more the material *appears* as nature the more intensively historical it is. As he wrote, the elements of music "bear historical necessity within themselves the more perfectly, the less they are immediately readable as historical characters."[4] To the extent that composition is successful, it transforms second nature back into history as first nature; it releases—gives expression to—the history sedimented in the material for "second nature is in truth first nature."[5] Schoenberg's discovery was that the more that composition is carried out without recourse to any pregiven form, the more rigorously a polyphonic nominalism is pursued, the more the material can be rationally dominated because the material itself is nominalistic. Compositional nominalism subordinates the material to the composer altogether, but with the result that the composer can potentially follow the material "where it wants to go" to an altogether greater degree than in tonal music. Form becomes the voice of the material in a new way: expression is transformed from the narration of emotions, whose arch figure is the Baroque *Affektenlehre*, to a deposition [*Protokol*] of expressive contents. New music no longer wants to be the image of expression but the expression itself. Whereas romantic expression hovers over the work and gives the work a reflection of the infinite, the expression of new music is that of the collapse of the self: here the extremes of expression and nonexpression touch.[6] The intention of the introduction of serialism was to bind together the horizontal and vertical dimensions of music. However, the total control that was achieved did not succeed in the unification of the dimensions of succession and simultaneity, but instead hardened into a mathematical system of rules that predetermined all intervals, making them in essence equivalent. Composition became the quotation of prearranged material, giving it a legalistic quality. Insofar as serial composition is as a whole derived from the theme, theme became the totality of the work and as such, having abolished any contrast to itself, necessarily disappeared, dissolving the differentiation of the composition. To compensate for the resulting diffuseness, Adorno saw that rhythm in Schoenberg's serial works takes over the role of establishing unity, which was once the expressive achievement of the theme. The course of new music, then, developed as a movement in which control separates from the material and becomes irrational, progressively, to the exclusion of the new.

Theory of Aging

Adorno finished *Philosophy of New Music* in Los Angeles, the year before he returned to Germany. After his return he became a professor at the Darmstadt school of composition, the focal point of musical development in Europe at the time. There Adorno came into contact with the composers he would criticize—though generally not by name—in "The Aging of the New Music": Luigi Nono, Karel Groeyvaens, Karl Heinz Stockhausen, and Pierre Boulez. They—and most of all Boulez—were in that period the key figures of total serialism, "totally organized music," which was at its height in Europe between 1947 and 1953.[7] Adorno could not have been surprised by the direction these composers took. They followed the trajectory of automatism, which Adorno had recognized as a potential in Schoenberg's later work, by pursuing serial technique beyond pitch to every parameter of music rhythm, intensities, and timbre. The music that resulted was effectively a collage of prefabricated organizations, which gives it a "pointillistic" quality.[8] Just as total serialization was an extension of Schoenberg's work, Adorno's criticism of the movement was itself a further formulation of his own critique of the aporias of Schoenberg's music.

As in *Philosophy of New Music*, the focus of Adorno's criticism in the "Aging" is the fate of the musical material: "In the leveling and neutralization of its material, the aging of the new music becomes tangible" (p. 100). This was the result of total serialism's replacement of composition by mathematical devices of organization. Adorno was not alone in this criticism.[9] In the same years Milton Babbit criticized total serialism for confusing the preparation of materials with composition: "Mathematics—or, more correctly, arithmetic—is used, not as a means of characterizing or discovering general systematic, pre-compositional relationships, but as a compositional devise."[10] Adorno's critique, however, went beyond Babbit's for he showed that what is fundamental to the subreption of mathematics for composition—to the estrangement of technique from the material—is the result of the fetishization of the material. This is a surprising idea, first because obtuseness to the material and infatuation with it appear contradictory and, second, because it might be thought that, given Adorno's own concept of musical material, his theory of composition would itself be based on its fetishization and unlikely to raise such an objection. How this all fits together is clarified by Adorno's theory of the aging of the new music.

According to Adorno, this aging did not befall new music by bad luck, accidently spoiling a good thing. Rather the senescence of the movement was implicit in its birth, which was its separation from popular music: "The more the market debased music into a childish game, the more emphatically true music pressed toward maturity through spiritualization [*Vergeistigung*]" (p. 104). A great deal would need to be said about Adorno's idea of spiritualization to fully elucidate it, but in brief it is art's movement toward autonomy. And, in this progress toward autonomy, Adorno recognized an antimony. Spiritualization is an effort to rescue art from trivialization by mass culture, yet the autonomy of art immanently destroys it. The decline of autonomous art was predicated on its initial success. In the course of spiritualization art rejected all predetermined forms at the same time that there was an intensification of the expression of art works. This intensification itself was attributed to the material, as if it were meaningful in itself: "this misleads a composer to sacrifice the ability, insofar as he has it, to form constellations and encourages him to believe that the preparation of primitive musical materials is equivalent to music itself" (p. 105). This fetishization of the material is of a piece with its abstract organization because form itself is a subjective act, a capacity that fetishization paralyzes: "confidence in the meaningfulness of abstract material" leads the subject to fail "to recognize that it, itself, releases the meaning from the material." Only "the power of the subject . . . brings an object entirely to itself" (p. 114). In other words—and this is the central idea—only subjectivity can mediate the self-expression of the musical material, yet just this requisite subjectivity is paralyzed in total serialism by the fetishization of the material. Thus the history of modern music that Adorno sketches in "The Aging of the New Music" comes to this: the loss of expression in total serialism, which is Adorno's fundamental criticism of the movement, originates in the separation of serious music from popular music, and this loss is the point at which new music again converges with popular music.

Boulez and Benjamin

Adorno's theory of the aging of new music plainly refuses to envision any propitious unity of serious and popular music as a solution to the current situation. Both sides are damaged; they are driven in different though related ways toward parallel rigidifications, central to which is the separation of subjectivity from its material. This thesis is not only the nexus of Adorno's critique of new music from Schoenberg on; it is central to every sentence Adorno ever wrote. One reason for quoting extensively from the "Aging of the New Music" is that in Adorno's comments on the "sacrifice" of the "ability to form constellations," and the role of subjectivity in the release of meaning from material, the relation of Adorno's critique of total serialism to the rest of his work, far beyond his musicological studies, becomes vivid. This will be particularly evident to those who have Adorno's critique of Benjamin's writings on Baudelaire in mind. Just as Adorno criticized the serialists in 1954 for the fetishization of material and the failure to actually release this material, in his often-cited correspondence of 1938 with Benjamin he criticized Benjamin for depending on the unrealizable hope that the material would speak for itself: "You superstitiously attribute to material enumeration a power of illumination that is never kept."[11] Parallel to his critique of serialism, Adorno claimed that Benjamin's study had fallen under the spell of the material; its organization, though seeming to conjure a cosmic historical context, was "located at the crossroads of magic and positivism."[12] Adorno's critique of Benjamin's montage of quotations, his ideal of a work composed strictly of quotations, later became Adorno's critique of serialism's compositions as montages of quotations of prefabricated material.

As is well known, Adorno's criticism of Benjamin's essay was of what Adorno held to be a failure of theory. Clearly, the remark in which Adorno drew together what was at stake in this criticism must have been painful for Benjamin, though the significance of Adorno's comment beyond this is somewhat obscure: "This . . . brings me to the center of my criticism. The impression that your entire study conveys . . . is that you have done violence to yourself."[13] The sting of the comment, which any close reader of this correspondence has no choice but to suffer, has generally been understood as a psychological barb gratuitously added to a harsh criticism to make it sting for keeps. Sympathy for the recipient of the letter has made it difficult to perceive why Adorno called this remark "the center of my criticism." Why it is the focal point of Adorno's criticism, however, becomes clear—and in a fashion that helps advance the discussion of the dispute between Benjamin and Adorno in its popular comprehension—

when the same form of criticism is understood in "The Aging of the New Music." Here it will be noticed that it is exactly in the same terms of his dispute with Benjamin that Adorno explains why the serialists failed to do justice to musical material: "As if objectivity were the result of a kind of subtraction, the exclusion of an ornament, and were nothing other than a residue, it is supposed that through an absence of subjectivity one would be empowered with an objectively binding force, the destruction of which is blamed on the preponderance of a subjectiveness that in fact no longer exists" (p. 114). The failure of total serialism to release the material, to gain objectivity, was the result of the exclusion of subjectivity, just as it was the failure of theory in Benjamin's work. Both the serialists and Benjamin hoped to assure transcendence by the exclusion of subjectivity. The damage Benjamin did to himself was damage done to the material, which is the most significant criticism that Adorno had to level at the failure of theory, whether a theory of musical composition or a theory of modern poetry.

For Benjamin and the total serialists of the fifties, subjectivity had become anathema just as it is in every popular critique of the enlightenment, beginning with the Old Testament: what went wrong was the rise of subjectivity; its domination of nature separated humanity from nature; the recovery of nature requires the exclusion of reprobate, sinful subjectivity. This is the key theoretical position that Adorno was concerned to counter not only in his arguments with Benjamin and the serialists, but throughout his writings. It is clear that Adorno was working on this criticism from the time of his first published philosophical work, *Kierkegaard: Construction of the Aesthetic*. In this work Adorno showed that Kierkegaard's philosophy is an effort to achieve transcendence, to escape fallen nature, by the sacrifice of the intellect in Kierkegaard's doctrine of the paradox and ultimately in his idea of the leap of faith. Yet this sacrifice only results in a subordination to that nature from which Kierkegaard's philosophy wanted to escape.[14] Kierkegaard's doctrine turns out to be a ruse of self-assertion: "through sacrifice he [Kierkegaard] asserts himself."[15] In *Dialectic of Enlightenment* Adorno developed this critique of Kierkegaard—of self-assertion through self-sacrifice—as the form of history altogether. The enlightenment resulted in the subordination to that nature from which enlightenment was to free humanity because, out of the terror of primitive scarcity, history became a process of self-assertion through self-renunciation. Knowledge thus separates from its material and loses its telos.

The counterfigure to this dialectic, which Adorno developed first in his book on Kierkegaard and later in his criticism of Benjamin and total serialism, is the idea of objectivity by way of the radicalization of subjectivity. The substantial interest of Adorno's work is that his critique of enlightenment is an effort to fulfill enlightenment. He fully takes the side of the dialectical autonomy of subjectivity and the self's attainment of real control over nature. Real autonomy, however, would be the liberation of nature. Any effort to escape subjectivity, any damage to it, results in the assertion of the subject as an absolute subject. The sacrifice of subjectivity, of which Adorno accuses Boulez and Benjamin, is actually a ruse of self-assertion, the establishment of pseudo-objectivity.

True subjectivity—Adorno held—transcends subjectivity. As identity, it is the principle of domination, but it is only subjectivity that raises the critique of the domination of nature. In Hegelian terms—an origin of Adorno's position—true subjectivity extinguishes itself in the object as memory of nature. In art subjectivity is the principle of form as the coherence of the work through which the work speaks. This is the concept of technique as the sum total of the forces of production understood as a capacity for liberation: "The result of artistic technique is, as true domination, always at the same time also the opposite of domination; it is the development of subjective sensibility for receptiveness to the impulses of what itself is not the subject."[16] A good gloss on this passage can be found in Adorno's book on film music, written jointly with Hans Eisler, *Composing for the Films*. In this work the dominating rule of the composer is held to be legitimate "only if it goes beyond itself entirely; only if it gains an expressive element. It is this expressive element that makes the work 'something more than just having been made.'"[17]

Only subjectivity, then, can follow the material "where it wants to go" and achieve what is more than what the self posits. This is not guaranteed by a willing eye for the cosmos or an openness to being. On the contrary, the inner form of cosmic posturing is sacrificial and the compositions that result (as is the case in much of Cage's music) do not go beyond a kind of bureaucratic file shuffling. To follow the material where it wants to go requires all possible subjective resistance and spontaneity, as Adorno wrote in constant reformulations: the material must be broken out of the nexuses in which it is organized; it is only possible to do justice to the material by its transformation. He expressed this same thought in a somewhat different context, but in a way that applies to art when it is kept in mind that Adorno conceived of art as the memory of the history of suffering, when he insisted that tradition can only be maintained through resistance to it. This dialectic contains the whole complexity of Adorno's musicological insight that the division between the composer and the material is potentially overcome only through resistance to the material. This proposition is, of course, allied with Benjamm's dictum that history must "be rubbed against the grain." But precisely here, where Benjamin and Adorno converge, what distinguishes them becomes starkly evident in a way that can be understood and estimated in a fashion that goes beyond wanting to identify with one or the other of these critics. For where light is cast directly onto Benjamin's *parti pris* for mass culture his conformism appears. There is clearly a deeper link between Benjamin's work and mass culture than his political confession: the radio tune's "helpless, helpless, helpless" bears the strongest affinity for the ideal of a work composed entirely out of quotations. The appeal of Benjamin's theory of culture to radical politics may be what is least radical about it: selflessness that has always been the form of sacrificial self-assertion. Benjamin's popularity is an element in an ancient history of martyrdom that far preceded the tragedy of his suicide. It was against this in Benjamin that Adorno had dearly struggled in his criticism of Benjamin's work on Baudelaire, criticism for which mass culture could not possibly forgive Adorno in its pathos for the ripped jeans at the knees, the tattoo on the ankle, the pin through the nose, or for the weary thrill of being a member of the team that always loses.

Whereas Benjamin's attachment to popular culture automatically won for his writings the seal of "praxis," Adorno's writings are said to be without any reflection on the issue of what is to be done. This deserves reconsideration. As Adorno wrote, "Correctly understood, praxis is . . . what the object wants: it follows its neediness."[18] In *Philosophy of New Music* Adorno came to the conclusion that the construction of the material resulted in the loss of expression; what he suggested was more radical construction. Construction is both the ability to manipulate the material and to break it out of the forms in which it has rigidified. What Adorno has to recommend, then, is— more subjectivity. This is not a demand for arbitrariness, but for the freeing of the social forces of production, which in art are forces of expression. This recommendation holds equally good for popular music. Though, if popular music followed this recommendation, if subjectivity in it could achieve a capacity of maturity in which it became the match of its own contemporary powers for rhythmically drowning itself out, that music would no longer be popular. The music would volatilize every element that popular music otherwise uses to keep time at a remove and every single social function of the music would vanish. In the adequate composition of the social antagonism condensed in the musical material, successfully following it where it most wants to go, in opposition to every pretense of subjectivity, there would be little left to discuss in such questions as "Who's to say what music is truly 'emphatic'?" and "Isn't musical taste all relative anyway?"

The Impossibility of Music

THE SPHINX has in every age been proud of keeping up with the day and—his or her—latest riddle has once again hit square on the bull's eye: "What are increasingly alike but have ever less in common?" The humorless beast has never once troubled to change the answer to any one of these puzzles, not when it can gloat that once in the hot seat no one ever gets the answer right, however notoriously invariant the answer. Yet the sphinx makes sure that the punishments inflicted keep up with the trends. Currently, the stumped, puzzled, and confounded are directly returned to doing whatever they were previously at—watching movies, listening to any form of portable sound, attending music festivals, visiting symphony hall or the newest MoMA, any city. These punishments are no dilution of the sphinx's classical punitive prerogatives. Its life depends so exclusively on wrong answers; it is so devoted to obfuscation, that it hardly distinguishes mauling its opponents from befogging them mentally. This explains why the sphinx has always been an effusive art lover, treats its own questions as art works and considers itself an artist—though without pretension or need to publish or rent a recording studio. Chronicling daily the entwinement of mythical and cultural history, the sphinx would insist that its original question to Oedipus counts as the first document of

mass culture. Because they produce semblance, the sphinx uncondi-
tionally supports the arts, high and low, but most of all music.

Very Popular Music

By any pragmatic measure music, as *popular music*, has the greatest social significance of the arts. No attempt, however, will be made here to
defend this thesis and neither will popular music be engaged as ideology, whether experientially or in compositional terms. For popular
music is a mouse guarded by a lion and demands to be treated accordingly. Disregard it in order to save attention for considering other music and a roar sets up: "You didn't even listen to my favorite song!"
The complaint has its legitimacy. But if a composer demonstrated in
detail that, for instance, a much heard song like "Hey Jude" stays
trapped in a particular way in the proverbial ear because the song itself is trapped in its own compositional inability to develop its harmonic implications, there is hand wringing and keening: "But, poor
mouse! that's how I like my song. I'll never forget it! And why are you
so serious now when the song only wanted to make us happy? I'll bet
you love it just as much as I do, because you remember every word
and note of it too!" This is the voice of the third largest export item of
the United States. It so succeeds that it cannot even be named without
reaffirming the status that it presumes. Thus, if ignoring it is no more
likely to be productive than studying it in detail, the genuine single alternative is to assume in this essay that twenty generally fruitless pages
have just been presented on the topic. All that those pages in any case
might have won, for all their trouble, would be an agreement to refer
to commercial music in the future henceforth exclusively as *very popular music*. And not even that could be hoped for.

If there is anything, then, for this discussion to depend on, it must
be an assumed dissatisfaction already felt for the given musical landscape and an allied interest in Adorno's musicology. On this basis it is
possible to return—with some unavoidable review and overlap—to
the discussion of this musicology begun in "Popular Music and 'The
Aging of the New Music.'"[1] And while the very popular impulse—
always the social defender—might greet this transition with a sense
that it represents an intention to leave society behind for a more clos-
eted study of pure music, the opposite is the case. Adorno held that so-

ciety can only be experienced in emphatic art. The point of all his writings on art, in fact, is that aesthetic importance is defined by the binding perspicaciousness of its social content. In his musicological writings Adorno developed this idea on the basis of a transformed concept of musical material, which is otherwise commonly understood in technocratic terms as a completely fungible raw material. Vincent Persichetti, for example, opens his valuable and well-known study of twentieth-century harmony with a characteristically administrative idea of musical material that reflects the power over musical material that was achieved in this century: "Any tone can succeed any other tone, any tone can sound simultaneously with any other tone or tones, and any group of tones can be followed by any other group of tones just as any degree of tension or nuance can occur in any medium under any kind of stress or duration."[2]

In contrast to this enlightenment concept of musical material as raw material, Adorno wanted to show that the material itself as a whole expands and contracts and has a historical tendency; every element of a musical composition is social and has a telos; form itself is the sedimentation of techniques originating in social life, and the social consciousness that historically organized sound cannot be subtracted from any particular chord. If composition is to succeed, then, it must compose history from the perspective of the present. This is not to say that composition is a conscious struggle with historical themes. Within the sphere of autonomous music the material asserts its historical impulse most insistently the more it has lost any direct reference to society and appears virtually as Persichetti described it. This aesthetic sublimation of the explicitly historical quality of sound is a transformation of history into nature, a second nature. As Adorno explains, following the idea of natural history that is central to all his writings,[3] at the moment a chord no longer permits its historical reference to be heard, it demands that the music with which it is being fitted together do justice to its historical implications. Therefore, the more autonomous the construction of music, the more blindly it proceeds with regard to history, the more composition potentially becomes the unconscious writing of history. This transformation of history into the immanent demands of sound is the Hegelian ruse of reason in composition; it is the restriction of composition to the nonintentional.

The ability to proceed blindly, however, and get things right, meaningfully to form what transpires historically, depends on the adequacy of technique. There are several ways of paraphrasing the idea of technique that make what is at stake in the concept apparent: technique is subjectivity, the active principle of identity, as well as the possibility of responding adequately to something or distorting it. Whereas in the empirical struggle for self-preservation technique subordinates its object to a false identity of subject and object, in the autonomous sphere of art, potentially beyond self-preservation, the principle of identity in technique becomes the immanent capacity to follow the demands of the material according to its own dialectic. This dialectic is the antagonistic movement of society. The adequacy of technique, therefore, is the capacity of the compositional subject to act as the total social subject and, rather than dominate the material, give voice to the antagonistic social whole.

This act of expression is more than a factual rendering of the social for it follows the social material where it goes beyond the object by its own force. The measure of a composition's social spontaneity is just its ability to go beyond society by way of the process that makes the social essence appear. The aesthetic *frisson* is a shudder at the socially implicit disaster that otherwise transpires unperceived. However, this shudder is not an experience of terror but (insofar as it results exclusively from the adequacy of composition) a form of historiography in which the presence of the forgotten and the feeling of "if it only were" are unitary.[4] This is the moment that Benjamin describes as the kairos of dialectic at a standstill.

Semblance at the Top

As has been promised, this introduction to the potential sociality of emphatic music will not take any opportunity to veer into a discussion of how, for instance, popular music might be pronounced an ideological semblance while classical music is proven to be truth revealed. On the contrary, the sphinx is right that all art—all music—is semblance, right into its smallest molecule. All pianists are acutely aware of the role illusion plays in each legato and most contemporary performers come to resent the murky spirit instilled by the sustain pedal. Every performer must contend not only with the technical difficulties of varying the character of repeated phrases but also with a degree of disgust for music that coheres only through the simulation of individuality. And, even if one has never laid a finger on the piano, real suspicion must mingle somewhere with the act of setting the needle back to the beginning of a record that a second earlier claimed to be in the process of transforming the universe.

These elements of semblance in so-called classical music are not a haphazard agglomeration of illusions, but, on the contrary, have a common origin in the development of music as semblance—a semblance that Adorno criticized in ways similar to his critique of popular music. Adorno traces the development of musical semblance from the rise of *musica ficta* in the fourteenth century and the introduction of unwritten chromatic accidentals. This was the mark of incipient freedom in the control of the musical material at the same time that it achieved an early simulation of subjectivity. Throughout its succeeding history the development of musical forces of production served this simulation of subjectivity as the composition of an image of expression.[5] A comparable example of this process of growing control over the material, subjectivization, and semblance was the subordination of the church modes to the major/minor system. This event made modulation possible, the manipulation of whole sections of dissonance, and, thereby, for the first time, expression became an element of the total musical structure and with a wholly new force.[6] From the eighteenth century on this expressive resource was especially utilized for the purpose of the heightening of development, which became the primary device for the objectification of subjectivity in music. But, insofar as modulation and development were subordinate to the structure of the cadence, music remained conventional and an image of expression. Beethoven, as Adorno points out, was bound to semblance just because he could do no more than imitate individual expression through the manipulation of the robotic conventions sedimented in the history of Western music in the process of reason's growing control over the musical material.[7] This semblance was the limit of classical music's compositional power. And, whatever its achievements, Adorno was still intensely critical of it as semblance, going so far as to say that both as music and expression it was questionable. Like the psychological literature of nineteenth-century realism, only a fictive, stylized subject is expressed.[8]

This is, however, not all there is to say about so-called classical music and semblance. Like popular music, it is semblance to the degree that it is conventional rather than composed, but it is also semblance to the degree that it is truly composed. And this is the real introduction to the dialectic in which the whole of Adorno's musicology is immersed, which is hardly that of popular music—but the impossibility of music. To the extent that music is composed it lays claim to being an organization of sound existing wholly within its own internal relations. It thereby gains an illusion of autonomy from the social world out of which it is at every point constructed. Art's autonomy is its real yet illusory distance from the struggle for self-preservation. This is music's—and all art's—constitutive semblance and the source of its free radiance as beauty: the substance of its impossibility in the sense of "if it only were." But just this break of art from any social function, which depends on its compositional integrity, once again subordinates art to social functions and to ideology, that is, to socially necessary semblance. Just by its distance from self-preservation, aesthetic autonomy offers a glow of reconciliation, a claim to universality that makes it the ideal and ready representative of all particular interests. As beauty, art is always ready to bestow the crown of spirit's presence. Here, again, the details are too obvious to mention: corporations invest in opera to obscure their rapaciousness, the grand piano in the corner says that money is everything and nothing, as well as blessed, and there is not a line of Beethoven played correctly that does not somehow say "I have been chosen not to get my hands dirty." All art, but most of all classical music, is the spiritualized world of privilege. The American recording industry only continues to produce money-losing classical recordings for the status it accrues even in the eyes of people who would never listen to the recordings.[9] Even as a tax write-off, classical music is no less for sale than popular music, and in this regard more ideological because, unlike popular music, it claims to be beyond all that.

Sphinx and Art Hatred

It is the sphinx's unqualified love of art that reveals its alienness to it. For, in that art's potential to shatter the social facade depends on its constitutive semblance, art is involuntarily allied at every point with ideology. As a result of this antinomy of aesthetic semblance, the more one is interested in art, and hopes from it, the more it is necessary to hate it. This hostility toward aesthetic semblance has been potentiated as the social web has tightened and art's tendency to betray itself has become inescapable. All modern artists have had, as a result, to struggle against the impulse to destroy their work.[10] Francis Bacon, for one, tended to destroy all paintings that were not removed from his studio, and particularly the best ones.[11] And modern art's antipathy toward itself not only aims at the destruction of what has been made. Rather, every molecule of semblance is bound to an element antithetically critical of semblance. As a result, in each of the arts, the antinomy of semblance resulted in a crisis of form and the development of art works that attempted to go beyond semblance altogether, from the abstractionist refusal of representation to Strindberg's rejection of the suspense drama, to the dissolution of narrative distance in Faulkner and Kafka.[12]

Anti-Illusionistic Semblance

In music the anti-art, anti-illusion impulse has been an element of its entire history, but most especially in the period of the rise of its greatest powers of semblance. This complex, dialectical history needs to be presented here if the form of the crisis of semblance in modern music is to be understood as well as how the music that developed out of this crisis in the first part of this century was able to become music that was no longer the semblance of subjectivity.

The rise of semblance in serious music itself involved the critique of semblance because, unlike semblance in popular music, here semblance was a technique for the intensification of compositional self-adequacy. The power of semblance was opposed to semblance because the musical aim was the potentiation of the individual subjectivity of the composition. This antisemblance element in the rise of musical semblance is demonstrated by the fact that, as the power of semblance increased, semblance itself dissolved. This is apparent in the history of the development section of the sonata. In the sonata, development models subjectivity as the thematic material unfolds into its possibilities and oppositions and then rebuilds itself in an act of confirmation.[13] In the classical sonata this process was restricted to the center section. But, according to its own logic of particularization, development began in the late Beethoven and especially in Brahms to spread through the whole of the sonata form. This anti-illusionistic intention of development, however, persistently undermined both the process of development and its power of illusion. For development is such only so long as there is a theme that is distinct from the process of development that it undergoes. Once the work was fully dynamic, however, once it had raised its power of semblance to a maximum, this distinction of theme and development was dissolved along with the possibility of development.

In related ways the whole integrative force of tonality brought about its own destruction through the progressive mastery and disintegration of the potentials of contrast from which tonality derived its semblance of subjectivity. The movement of tonal cadences increasingly sounded merely conventional, arbitrary, and subjectively posited. The further dialectical irony of this history is that, while the dissolution of semblance was the result of the anti-illusory impulse in tonality's development, the more that compositional semblance dissolved, the more illusory composition threatened to become. This is because there was no other way than tonality to establish musical meaning. "All that was left to add to this language was the abortive gesture, the deliberate slackening of discipline, the willingness, in fact, to do for an expressive reason the wrong thing."[14] The process of tonal integration destroyed the conventionality of tonality but at the same time made composition arbitrary.[15] This was the impossibility of music in the first decade of the twentieth century.

Expression Without a Glow

The most anti-art composer of the first part of this century—Arnold Schoenberg—is the composer who to popular ears once seemed the most rebarbative and isolated of any. But it was Schoenberg who developed a radically social form of composition in which expression is no longer a semblance of subjectivity. At the point that musical enlightenment had dissolved all the conventions of tonality as subjectively posited and seemed to be on the brink of uncomposability, Schoenberg responded to the freedom of the material that had implicitly been gained. He mastered the material by virtue of the tendency inherent in it. In musical-historical terms he did this by unifying the horizontal and vertical dimensions of music, the polyphony of the fugue and the homophony of the sonata. Schoenberg composed a simultaneity of sounds that was not based on subordination to a tonal center, but rather resulted from the independence of the voices and was therefore at the same time the composition of music's sequentiality. This musical construction, then, is built on a principle of contrast, and this principle is at the same time that of the release of the dissonant, expressive force of the material. Musical construction became that of completely individual expression and thereby went beyond the simulation of expression that had been the limit of the whole of traditional music, which to this moment remains the boundary of all popular music. In Adorno's words: "The truly revolutionary element in Schoenberg's work is the changed function of musical expression. Passions are no longer simulated, but rather genuine emotions of the unconscious—of shock, of trauma—are registered without disguise."[16] This is not an illusionistic, but a depositional (*Protokol*)—police blotter—expression, and therefore the first music in which each note must truly be as it is. This transformed musical time. Whereas traditional and popular music remain indifferent to the passage of time because their form is based on repetition, the individuality of Schoenberg's music establishes its identity only as identity in difference. Musical time thus becomes meaningful as the transition to the nonidentical. This musical order fulfills the technical potential that society has within reach but denies itself: an order in which difference is free yet binding in its expressiveness.[17]

Impossible Solutions

This is a condensed introduction to the social content of Schoenberg's music. But, by way of conclusion, it should not be imagined that Adorno thought Schoenberg had brought music to its apex and a moment of perfection that musical history then lost from view. On the contrary, every impossibility of music is a social impossibility, and however music succeeds in solving any of its socially coded problems, the result must be new impossibilities so long as society itself is an antagonistic whole. As Adorno wrote of Schoenberg's critique of musical semblance, this act could still not overcome the limit imposed on every artist's power, which is that it is an aesthetic power and thus bound to semblance because it cannot carry out the social transformation it implies. Therefore, however anti-auratic its expressiveness, its social content, by which it goes beyond society, is once again aura and semblance, by which the composition is potentially neutralized. In all his musicological writings Adorno pursued the presentation of every such aporia that developed out of Schoenberg's achievement, wanting to demonstrate the social content of these aporia and to find ways in which a binding music could still be composed. He never, in any of this, thought of going back to Schoenberg. Just as in *Aesthetic Theory* he wrote that nature does not yet exist and that spirit itself (*Geist*) does not yet exist, in a late major essay he wrote: "That which the great composers of the Vienna School, from Haydn to Schubert wanted—a music that was wholly formed, completely correct, completely binding and yet at the same time in every moment completely subjective—has to this day still not been able to find its voice."[18]

This desideratum of a fully composed, binding expressive voice has become comic. No expression could be true if subjectivity is so overwhelmed that none is possible—an experience that North Americans may now be experiencing with a particular directness.[19] This aporia of expression has pulled the entire history of art into its vortex, and a great deal that not so long ago was of the greatest importance has come to sound absurd as a result. These works may be beyond any plausible defense. But at least it should be possible—even while promising not to mention it—to pull popular music into the same anti-illusionistic vortex by recognizing the social content of its compositional form: just as each note in it is subordinated to a whole that is indifferent to it, without recourse to expression and without any internal necessity other than the degree to which it is rudimentarily dominated, the society that it legitimates and cloaks is one in which everyone is asymptotically one too many.

Apple Criticizes Tree of Knowledge

A Review of One Sentence

SAMUEL BECKETT is conjured out of his cave more than is decent, and most often to decorate expressive deficiency. This reviewer, too, may be repeatedly guilty of this compensatory subterfuge, and who doesn't stand in hope of vivifying a foundering paragraph if all it takes to tag on a lightning bolt is the claim that something or other "is much like Beckett's *Endgame*"? For the ease, however, with which Beckett's work has lent itself to facile invocation Beckett himself deserves some blame. It is telling, for instance, that his writings never fell to the censor's bludgeon, were never decried a public menace, were never once docketed as fonts of adolescent despair and suicide, as were repeatedly Sartre's mediocre narrative and plays. In his later years Beckett was more than aware of the deficiency this pointed up in his work, and finally, finding that no provocation sufficed to alarm the authorities, he was driven to censor his work himself. Thus, in his famous staging of *Waiting for Godot* in Berlin in 1975, Pozzo—as ever—drags with a yank on the rope knotted around his slave's neck and exalts: "Think pig! . . . Think!" And Lucky—as ever—snaps upright, eyes bugging. But as Lucky's mouth chokes open to recite the most famous monologue of twentieth-century drama—the erudite, scatological "Qua-

quaquaqua"—the slave instead glares out at the audience in goggle-eyed silence.

Here Beckett had intervened to scotch the speech. Its cunning, un-punctuated hilarity had once deftly fitted thumbs to the collective jugular, as to insist: "Isn't collapsing cornered thought, the whole effort ever made to think, a hopeless riot?" But long anthologized with the best of the best, soliloquies from Augustine on, the *quaquaqua* had surrendered the tense grip in its fingers and become a sure thing. The crowd pleaser invariably brought down the house as the audience thrilled at the resiliency of its own historical immunities, unbreached by even forced doses of self-recognition: Lucky would stammer to a halt; the audience would cheer. Beckett understood that the speech had to go and if the guardians of the good and the true could not be shaken from their slumber, Beckett had demonstrated that his own alertness was unimpeded.

No doubt, from reports of the evening's stunned expectation, Beckett's ruse did the trick, and no doubt Beckett at least briefly savored some factor of pure audience disappointment. But if the censorial ruse was first rate, it was also too clever by half for its own good, for the device could hardly be repeated, and this brought the play to a stalemate. After that single performance, *Godot* fell into limbo; and with the death of Beckett—since the pivotal *quaquaqua* could neither be pronounced, omitted, nor recreated—it even came to seem that the play had been left behind in perpetuity, unperformably shattered. Until, that is, the publication of *Philosophical Interventions in the Unfinished Project of Enlightenment*. This book's appearance witnesses language itself, on world historical scale, struggling to come to the aid of Beckett's play. For in this book the distinguished philosopher, trusted cohort, and expounder of Habermas's communicative reasoning—Karl-Otto Apel—presents an essay every sentence of which is *the* sentence. Though it is not until the concluding passage that all messianic hopes are fulfilled, syllable by syllable:

> As a metaphysics-free, transcendental-reflexive confirmation of the in-escapable presuppositions of philosophical argumentation, the transcen-dental-pragmatic justification of the standpoint of reason also contains the standards able to unmask crypto-metaphysical theorizing, such as that already pointed out in variants of scientistic reductionism. (p. 351)

True, these numb words performed from under the proscenium arch would be met with so much coughing, noise in the aisles, roughhousing, and snoring that getting through to the last syllable would demand a robust *comedia erudite*. But Lucky and Pozzo are by origin helpful types and would want to pitch in with a ready prompt and a suggestion or two. In fact, if we listen in on Apel's sentence again, hear it from near the end of the line—and with improved enunciation—anyone can easily judge its potential for opening night:

APEL (*reading from a book open in his hands*): "*. . . to unmask cryptometaphysical theorizing, such as that already pointed out in variants of scientistic reductionism*" (p. 351).

LUCKY: Nice, but you forgot, "Please don't hit me."

APEL: Hmmm . . . hmmm . . . (*eyes search farther down the page*) . . . I see, I see . . . How about, "*Justification-free transcendental pragmatics as* even earlier *pointed out . . .*"? (p. 351).

POZZO: Approximately, approximately—*Pan! dans les gencives.* ("Bang! Right on the kisser!") Don't forget to be funny!

APEL: That's not fair, Pozzo, philosophy is not supposed to be funny. Let's see how the essay's last line will play. Why don't we? Ahem: "*The barbarity of reflection*" may still lead "*to a regression of human culture back to primitive conditions*" (p. 351).

LUCKY (*distracted, plucks an apple and gives it a bite*): It's a risk.

Right Listening and a
New Type of Human Being

ADORNO's *Aesthetic Theory* is currently the object of considerable interest in this country. This is a good thing, but puzzling too. And it is this puzzle that here deserves to be addressed. The book is more distant from us than might be indicated by the immediate response the new translation has found. It, and Adorno's philosophy as a whole, involve a way of making distinctions, types of distinctions, and experiences that are inimical to these shores; in our own heart of hearts, down home, they rub us the wrong way. If Adorno's pronouncements on jazz have notoriously aggravated many, and by the power of hearsay alone, without almost anyone having read the relevant essays or wondered what music exactly he was criticizing or what he might have been right about in his disparagement of big band jazz, this is only the barest indication of his capacity to bother us. Of the musical compositions that might spontaneously occur to the inner ear of the overwhelming majority of the American readers of this essay—themselves an educational elite—there might not be a single song that would have resounded in Adorno's own ear as other than "trash," and as so stereotypical and faulty in its construction that the puzzle for him would have been how anyone could distinguish one tune from another. To our minds this must represent some special grudge Adorno held against all things popular. Yet this was not at all the case. For neither did Adorno like Dvořák, Hindemith, Elgar, Debussy, Stravinsky, or Sibelius, among many, many others. And there was much he found wanting in Schoenberg, Berg, and Webern as well. Adorno may have been as dissatisfied with each and every composition—with music and indeed art altogether—as anyone has ever been. This dissatisfaction has an implication that is so remote from us that it verges on the unintuitable this side of the Atlantic: for if Adorno was dissatisfied with all existing art, it was because he was intent on finding the *one* right art work, the one that would be *the* art work. In other words—and this is the thought that more than any other in all of aesthetics has the ability to press the mind of our commercial tribe between thumb and forefinger: Adorno thought not just that one work of art may be liked better than another, but that this one work would be, in itself, better than another.

This was not momentary bad manners that slipped into an otherwise distinguished philosophy, any more than St. Augustine absentmindedly lost track of the main point of his theology when he admonished his readers that one can love the wrong thing. Adorno's philosophy conceived as a whole seeks the primacy of the object. His critique of the judgment of taste is inextricable from this central philosophical intention, not as one element compelled to conform to an overriding thesis but as the originating impulse of that thesis. His philosophy of the primacy of the object has its source in the experience of one art work as superior to another. It could not be otherwise. There is no other basis, one side or the other of the continental divide, on which to understand or sympathize with the intensity of his thought. Without an ear for emphatic music, for music that means to be *the* music, every line Adorno wrote echoes hollowly convoluted or blindly exaggerated. The philosophy of the primacy of the object itself derives from the audibly urgent primacy of one art work over another in a mind that is prepared to hear it. Not to be pugnacious, but blunt: our minds, in general, would rather not hear this primacy; even when we sense it, we do not feel right about it or know what to make of it. Though we insist on having our preferences, and consider the freedom to like and dislike inherent to democracy, these preferences are limited to the judgment itself. Whatever we find to like in an art gallery we want to assume someone else might with equal justification dislike it. And we suppose that what someone else likes, we might just as well, and with equal justification, dislike. In the morality of our everyday aesthetics, what is important to us is that one likes and dislikes and is at any moment ready to call a truce over the objective claim of the distinction rather than insisting that one has put hands on what all the world must acknowledge as the *one* right thing. We are sure that anyone who would argue that taste should subserve the object—that the object itself wants to be the one and only right thing, that if seen or heard "correctly" the correct object would be chosen and the "wrong" one dismissed—is streaked with authoritarianism.

In the everyday aesthetics of North Americans, the author of the *Authoritarian Personality* would be an autocrat, and when he lived in the United States he was experienced as that by many. This is so plausible to us—to those who are certain that many paintings are required to cover the many walls—that something must be said at the outset to make Adorno's position even momentarily worth considering. On this score, though Adorno will not find many allies among art consumers, he does have many among artists. Here is what Francis Bacon (the painter, not the philosopher) has to say on the topic of what one might have a taste for: "Of course what in a curious way one is always hoping to do is to paint the one picture which will annihilate all the other ones, to concentrate everything into one painting. . . . I've got an obsession with doing the one perfect image."[1] And, in fact, the Centre Pompidou prudently reserves one wall for each of Bacon's paintings, as if neighbors in any proximity, even framed and under glass, might otherwise be eaten alive. It should not, however, be supposed that such a claim to being the only art work is exclusive to art works with explicitly ferocious imagery. Even Wallace Stevens, who thought that modern poetry must "speak words that in the ear / In the delicatest ear of the mind, repeat, / Exactly, that which it wants to hear" had tolerance exclusively for one poem.[2] Thus in "Credences of Summer" he wrote that "One day enriches the year. One woman makes the rest look down" only because that poem tests itself,[3] as a credence of poetry, by its capacity to transmute these ultimate elements of natural beauty—one woman, one day—into the poem's own claim to being the one poem. But why then, if there is only to be one work, are there so many art works? From the perspective of art—from the perspective of a genuinely monstrous productive energy such as Picasso's—the answer is that there is a multiplicity of works only out of wanting the one art work.

If this momentarily suffices to grant Adorno's position a degree of tolerance, still we are hardly ready to accept it. It is not ours. And if, as claimed, Adorno's position is central to his aesthetics and to his philosophy as a whole, and if we are still prepared to have much to do with either, we must come to terms with the foreignness of his critique of taste. It will not, however, help this discussion to focus immediately on this question of a taste for the one right art work. This would involve us just as soon in a narrowly tangled dispute. The aim, rather, is to sketch the foreignness of Adorno's aesthetics to us in several dimensions, including national levels, and then come back to this specific problem. We cannot approach it meaningfully until we have collided as openly with Adorno's thought as we do implicitly. This antagonism is worth investigating. If the interest in Adorno's *Aesthetic Theory* is puzzling, it is just as certain that there is an urgency right now in understanding the work correctly, for what it really has to say. This would not be recognized by pretending that *Aesthetic Theory* is waiting to embrace us at the gate.

I

To begin, then, to discern the alienness of Adorno's work, the broadest reason for this is just that the book is an utterly speculative work, an aesthetics. Aesthetics is itself the most remote region of philosophy, and in that remote region, *Aesthetic Theory*, if one went to look for it, would be found at the vanishing point, the distant limit. In its complexity, in its sometimes hermetic, Pythian expression, the book stands at the philosophical maximum. In its very tone, as is reputed, the book portrays itself as a philosophy, which to be philosophy at all would need to be the only philosophy. And, while *Aesthetic Theory* is located at that limit, in absolute distance and tone, we are located at the other extreme, at the philosophical minimum. We would not only shy away from the warmonger aesthetics of a Francis Bacon, we would not even join in an arm wrestle over the difference between stoicism and skepticism. What would bother us, on the contrary, is if we learned that some contemporary of that seminal third-century Greek skeptic, Sextus Empiricus, had been denied "the right to say it," whatever it might have been. Then we are ready to go to war, and not with paint either. It is this mix of avoidances and proclivities that marks us, under the banner of civilization, as the least philosophical people that ever walked the earth. If this is not self-evident, if there is doubt, notice how right this second, in your own reading sensorium, just this mention of the word *civilization*—an irredeemably philosophical concept—may already have caused the inner hackles to stir. "What do you mean"—the inner voice of the inner hackles asks—"by 'civilization'"? Who is "civilized" and who is not? And who are you to say which is which? But, whatever the answer to this string of questions, whatever civilization may mean, the main point—that we are the unphilosophical—is hardly unprecedented. To Tocqueville, for instance, it was preeminently obvious: "Americans—he wrote—have no school of philosophy peculiar to themselves." And later he added, "Less attention is paid to philosophy in the United States than in any other country of the civilized world."[4]

Allow Tocqueville's pronouncement to antagonize us a bit so we can overhear the inner voices of the lurking national audience in us all get mad and, though basically disinterested in philosophy, demand: "Who is to say who is philosophical and who is not?" Tocqueville, who certainly considered himself a philosophical man, apparently felt prepared to make the distinction. And his answer is valuable because, as will be seen, it helps differentiate the tradition in which Adorno worked from anything North American. Thus, when Tocqueville distinguishes the philosophical from the unphilosophical, he shapes this as a distinction between the "philosophical ideal" and its opposite—the thought of an American. But how, we want to ask, does the philosophical ideal think? Tocqueville calmly answers: as does the deity. Then how does the deity think? There is reason to hesitate at this moment in acknowledgment of a general hesitation. The line of reasoning pursued does not produce a climate that the unspeculative are generally pleased to inhabit. But here, anyway, is Tocqueville's lucid response on the question of divine ideation: when the deity thinks, he does not, for instance, view the human race collectively. Rather, he sees individuals, each separately, each in the resemblances that make each like his fellows as well as in the differences that make him unlike his fellows.[5] The thinking of the deity, in other words, is the fully articulated perception of the one and the many. The deity is not ever obliged to make unlike like, or to subsume the particular to the general in order to know it, but thinks emphatically only, so that in place of concepts there would effectively be only proper names: in such a mind a painting perceived as a painting would have to be *the* painting as nothing else made of paint and canvas could be.

The deity, therefore, has no need of normative or general ideas. General ideas are, rather, the necessary instruments of the frail human mind; they are what the mind has recourse to when it has no other way to grasp reality. This frailty, Tocqueville points out, is the exaggerated characteristic of the unphilosophical American mind. It is the fate of the mind most exclusively shaped by the pressure of equality. For under this pressure every mind is necessarily suspicious of every other mind, since in this circumstance each mind is necessarily in competition with every other mind, and thus no mind can accept anyone else's judgment as its own. Rather, each intelligence seeks to control each of its judgments with the tenacity of a hermit. This narrow American type of intelligence, out of its weakness—says Tocqueville—is compelled to insist on wanting to answer every question on the basis of its own self. Deprived of any historical resonance by the democratic break from tradition, this mind has no alternative but to take itself to be a general self. Therefore the American has such a strong propensity for general ideas, those that—contrary to divine ideation—demonstrate little articulation of the one and the many.[6]

Without examining Tocqueville's speculations step by step, each of us in the privacy of our own isolated reading caves may recognize enough of ourselves in this foreign philosopher's social analysis to acknowledge that he discerned something of a national power of mind: it is the capacity of the principle of equality, demanding absolute competition, to isolate and compel each of us to want to answer any and every question autarchically. On the basis of what appears to be a ruthless individuality, however, we all the same produce ever more general ideas, deprived of the articulation of the one and the many in which particularity could be experienced. It is a function of this generality that what we most want to do when we think is to conclude that all things that confront us are the "same." In this affirmation is our affinity for a suburban Buddhism and an eagerly contorted yoga. It helps lay down the tracks for the perception that what the individual seeks to do in a market economy must be good and right for everyone else. It may even be perceived as a blessed surprise, as the form of our own most involuntary self-transcendence, which it is since it entirely fails its own desideratum of individuality. Thus, nothing is more obvious to us, for instance, than that all that sounds might as well be called music, that every ragged list of words might as well be called a poem, that wherever people accumulate is a civilization; we are obliged to insist, and are most proud of ourselves when we insist, and feel the power of a certain kind of nation when we insist, for instance, that everyone who thinks is already a philosopher, to the extent that anyone might want to bear that appellation. This power of the general is what we consider "transgressive" and the pursuit of "difference" when the Guggenheim Museum mashes together a display of Armani suits with Cézannes, flatwear and motorcycles.

II

The tradition of thought that Tocqueville expresses—in the choice between thinking like the deity and thinking like an unphilosophical American—is not shy in its preference. Even feeling partly revealed by it, Americans might suspect Tocqueville of being anti-American. Nonreligious Americans may themselves intuit something heretical in Tocqueville's supposition that he knows that and how the divine thinks. And precisely this suspiciousness of religious heresy in a philosophical undertaking is what is needed here to be able to study Adorno's work in the self-consciousness of our own national comprehension. In this frame of mind, consider, for instance, the most quoted passage from *Minima Moralia*:

> The only philosophy which can be responsibly practised in face of despair is the attempt to contemplate all things as they would present themselves from the standpoint of redemption. Knowledge has no light but that shed on the world by redemption. . . . Perspectives must be fashioned that displace and estrange the world, reveal it to be, with its rifts and crevices, as indigent and distorted as it will appear one day in the messianic light.[7]

The urgency of this passage, which can be felt to this moment by any voice willing to experiment with it, is the alarm that what has transpired may never be known for what has occurred. These lines have been much quoted only because one can hardly help but quote them. All the same, it is not sure that, this side of the Atlantic, we realize what we are dealing with in this passage. Notice in fact that, even though the passage doesn't seem complicated, it is not obvious how to understand it. Clearly, Adorno insists that the one, the only possible, philosophy, must aspire to a divine vantage as a surrogate for a messianic light to come. But if we take Adorno at his word—if, for instance, we begin to conclude that he held that philosophy must entrust itself to the light shed by some messianic plenipotentiary on the order of John the Baptist, the glare of misinterpretation becomes prohibitive. The passage is not a work of theological fervor. It does not want us to bend at the knee. On the contrary—and here we have arrived at a set of boundary lines that are not always so available to the eye— Adorno can invoke the messiah qua philosopher just because as a philosopher Adorno was not a religious man. Though he had the bearing of a priest back of the lectern, it was a philosopher's lectern he stood back of. Thus the passage cannot be interpreted to say that philosophy should take up the stance of John the Baptist, but as a demand that John the Baptist should be a philosopher. And Adorno was only able to urge this in the confidence that as a philosopher he would not invoke the magical contents of what he named. This prerogative was his as a capacity that he inherited, as did the whole of European philosophy—Tocqueville included—as it came into receipt of a theology shaped by the thought of antiquity and transmuted by the Enlightenment. The turning point in this secularization was, of course, romanticism, that profane mysticism, which, as we can now see in Adorno's passage, wanted to conjure the image of divine light not to behold the deity as its source above, but to illuminate a damaged nature below. The passage exhorts us to the secular act of a genuinely isolated, elite individual who without a doubt seeks another world, but not that recommended by any church.[8] Adorno's philosophy thus was able to be as full of theology as was Kierkegaard's, without his being any more a believer than Kierkegaard was—the single distinction being that Kierkegaard struggled to be a believer and Adorno did not.

III

Adorno was only able to write this much-quoted passage in *Minima Moralia* because he had no need to worry, as would an American, that at dawn on the day of publication a millenarian congregation would be there to greet him in his kitchen for prayers, cookies, and a march on the canyon—to view those aforementioned rifts and crevices—in expectation of the messianic light. It is noticeable, in fact, that any effort to situate Adorno's passage in an American context makes comic ironies fan out in every direction. For instance, a rigorously trained American philosopher in scrutinizing Adorno's passage might reject it out of hand, as hocus-pocus, and hardly philosophical. But the magical intensities presumed of Adorno might verily be the beam in the beholder's own eye. For it is here, this side of the Atlantic, that the magical claim of these theological concepts has remained undiminished, not on Adorno's side. And, to bring the American situation more into focus, this same philosopher-reader—who, on the job, back of the lectern, might look like a dentist—having made short shrift of Adorno on the grounds of symbolic logic, could well lock up his professional office for the week, looking forward to joining the chorus at church on Sunday. American philosophy, in contrast to European philosophy, is shaped by the ramifications of a national order that, in its primary desire to protect religious freedom, established religion as the truth of the private sphere, thus isolating religious thought from the process of enlightenment. This is why, statistically, by documented sightings alone, the Virgin Mary in any given year spends more time on American shores than in Italy or in the whole of western Europe.

IV

For North Americans, aesthetics is the most remote dimension of philosophy. As a preeminent American Kant scholar, Robert Paul Wolff, for instance, would proudly announce to his yearly Kant seminar that he had never read the third critique. It was dispensable—he said— and anyway, he preferred lying on the sofa watching James Bond movies. In the German tradition, by contrast, aesthetics inevitably becomes the keystone of any philosophical construction. Thus Adorno necessarily stood at the apex of his intellectual ecclesia as a priest of art. This is not a metaphor. And here, however much the problem is to make Adorno as foreign as possible, described as a priest of art he will necessarily become inscrutable to the point of nondescript. For without special study, the office—a priest of art—is unknown to us. These words are not combined in our language. In German thought, however, intimations of the office go back as far as Cusanus, and the institution emerges full blown in Wackenroder and Tieck's seminal romantic work, *Outpourings of an Art-Loving Friar*. Notice that the title of this book must catch the American ear entirely off guard. To read the book is to encounter the vision of art taking the place of divine mediation. Art, the good friar explains, "must come before love . . . for art is of heavenly provenance." Or again: "Art must become a sacred love or a loved religion. . . . Earthly love may then take its place after art."[9] Theologically, art has here taken the place of Christ, by whose sacrifice human love becomes possible.

It must be emphasized that in the whole of American thought there is nothing like this. In the first place, there are hardly any comparable philosophical speculations on the topic. And if one consulted the epochly correlative volumes of American romanticism one would discover that the American movement is in fact distinct from the European movement specifically by the hesitant, muted presence of any kind of art religion. Adorno illuminates this difference when he writes, in his *Beethoven*, that in the nineteenth century the European middle class prayed while listening to Beethoven.[10] In those concert halls the magical aspect of religion was preserved as a kind of aesthetic ecumenicalism that was one level on which a solution to the wars of religion was found. In its ideal of a person of taste, the middle class was united, beyond the bloody nation-mangling struggles of the reformation. For Europe, the greatest hopes became lodged in aesthetic hopes. By contrast, Americans simply pray when they pray, and that is often. Though they may sing in church, they have rarely experienced music as a secularization of the divine; in their historiographical imagination, because it postdates the division of art into high and low, art does not originate, as it does obviously for all Europeans, in religious imagery. Otherwise the United States would not have been so able to become the primary world purveyor of industrial literary and musical entertainment.[11] And neither would an Americanist, who sought an elite intellectual to compare directly with the aesthetical romantic elites of European romanticism find anyone closer than perhaps Thoreau, who would listen to Bach in ecstasy and then get drunk.

When Adorno informs us on European habits of aesthetic prayer, there is no doubt that he himself prayed in this fashion. As proof the whole of *Aesthetic Theory* might be cited. But, for something that comes more in a nutshell, note that he accounted for Hitlerism by a loss of the experience of emphatic art: "It is the lack of experience of the imagery of real art, partly substituted and parodied by the ready-made stereotypes of the amusement industry, which is at least one of the formative elements of that cynicism that has finally transformed the Germans, Beethoven's own people, into Hitler's own people."[12] However much one wishes the thesis were true, it is well known that some number of SS officers were as proud of their powers of Mozart on the pianoforte as of their cruelty in the bunker. But it is the starkness of a contrast that is at issue here: for Adorno, and out of a centurywide European development, the most profound human hopes, theological hopes, took shape as aesthetic hopes. Only in this context could Adorno's challenge to the possibility of "poetry after Auschwitz" hit so central and common a European nerve that ever since the whole of his philosophical writings—in newspapers, journals, and many books—have been known by that one maxim. *Aesthetic Theory* itself is nothing but an extended meditation on that question, and the implications of an envisioned, catastrophic end to art. In the United States, however, if one wanted to formulate an even vaguely compelling equivalent of that maxim, one that risked something comparable, it might read on a Holiday Inn marquee along a Georgia highway: "Is there Jesus after Auschwitz?"

V

If Adorno's thinking is recognizably alien to our own, it is worthwhile to turn attention to the obverse, and recognize our foreignness to him. When he came to the United States in 1938, about a century after Tocqueville and much in his tradition in the critique of equality as well as in his regard for the idealist concept of truth, Adorno found himself involved in a study of how music is transformed when it is mass-reproduced by radio transmission. In the early decades of radio's development, and most of all in the thirties and forties, the American democratic left hoped that radio would finally lift the stain of privilege from cultural treasure so that, along with the scions and chauffered arriving at a Carnegie Hall performance of Beethoven, so would—in the language of the times—the farmer's wife in Iowa, just by being at home next to her radio receiver.[13] Adorno, however, dissented from the democratic left's hopes. He perceived that subordinating music to the principle of equality would not universalize cultural treasure but neutralize it. For the mechanism of radio transmission, the vehicle of commercial equality, so damaged music that all it accomplished was to change cultural treasure into the fetish of cultural goods. In 1941, however, after he completed what he could of this study, *Current of Music*, Adorno turned his attention from the depredations of radio transmission to a consideration of the recent transformation of the recipients of radio broadcasts, the listening inhabitants of this country.[14] And in a study entitled "The Problem of a New Type of Human Being" he no longer argues that it is a major social concern what radio transmission does or does not do to the music itself. The issue is that the kind of person that had emerged in the United States is one that culture is no longer capable of cultivating. Given this new type of human being, the fiction could no longer be maintained that it was progressive and humanistic to encourage men and women to hear Beethoven symphonies, read Milton, or meditate appreciatively on Raphael's Madonnas. Culture itself had entered into such opposition to the real conditions of life that it could no longer fulfill its age-old hope of humanizing the individual.

Adorno was aware that these observations, though in some regard they took up where Tocqueville left off, were in their extremity of formulation unprecedented. No one had previously considered that the nature of the person could be so transformed historically that culture would become inadequate to humanity. Adorno went on to describe whom he thought we are, these people who are beyond culture's power to cultivate. Whereas culture presupposed an autonomous individual—Adorno observed—the contemporary American has been so overwhelmed by real and constant anxiety, has been so broken in on by heteronomous forces, that this autonomy and its capacity to breach subjectivity's own claustrum could no longer be presumed. Adorno thought that this incapacitation of the person began in earliest childhood, and he noted several aspects of what he believed had happened: First, the world no longer provides actual images to the American child, but only images that arrive with the insignia of their own untruth stamped on them; second, the objects of action have all become technical objects that primarily demand adaptation to their own instructions; third, the collapsed family no longer provides a buffer between society and person, which is part of why the American child is flooded with anxiety; fourth, the traditional language of people has been supplanted by a language of advertisement that no longer fulfills but instead leaves people speechless. Furthermore, and fifth, libido is directed toward tools, so that the world of things becomes a substitute for images. And sixth—which Adorno thought most important—is the transformed relation of people to their own nature, their own bodies. A society of sports had developed, he found, that had suspended the longstanding cultural taboo on naked physical power. This has been responsible for efforts to convert cultural objects into categories of physical performance. The translation of novels into films would, for instance, be a variant of this.

The discernment of these six aspects of a new type of human being is genuinely provocative and substantially advances Tocqueville's study of the dynamic in which identity obviates the capacity for anything but the general. Each element deserves lengthy consideration, as does the idea in general of persons who are no longer to be cultivated, in the sense of gaining a capacity to be involved in what is other than the self. But, just touching on several of Adorno's observations, it seems evident, for instance, that North Americans are at once swamped with images and bereft of image, that some part of the comfort found by adolescents in ostensibly destructive fantasies of exploding computer-envisioned missiles against electronically illustrated aliens is secured in masterful obedience to narrowly rule-driven, bureaucratic structures. It would, in further confirmation of Adorno's observations, be hard for many Americans to think of when the sight of rigorously exercised arms was not de rigueur even for concert musicians performing in décolleté. Certainly, as Adorno might have pointed out, it is the libidinization of portable devices that infuses them with such honored positions on restaurant tables as people sit down to meet, as if it is the devices who are getting together to chat. And, again, confirming Adorno's sixth point, the interactive museum machinery that now claims to make holdings accessible to visitors largely serves, instead, to surrogate experience with sports-modeled kinetic activity.

It might be worthwhile, here, in fact—even at the risk of a degree of awkwardly self-conscious essayism—to use something of this neo-museum style of infused, kinetic interest to concoct a kind of self-test on the exactitude of Adorno's third claim on the ontogeny of this new

type of human being: namely, that we are not to become cultured individuals because we have been broken in on too many times. Cor-
roboration is not hard to find, though the following miniature psychological test for regression—which would be the overarching
tendency of such a self—requires at least that each reader find some
equivalent to a phrase like *Lone Ranger* to experiment with. These
words themselves may suffice and will be used here for demonstration. But, if not, a swelteringly voiced *Hey Dude,* or some similar
phrase will work equally well. And at a loss there is no need to look
farther than, for instance, a fragment from that first popular song
that one heard and remembers having hated, until it was so consistently repeated that one started playing it oneself—an event that is
now a primordial phenomenon at the beginning of adolescence. Take
that rhythmical song fragment or the phrase *Dude* or *Lone Ranger*
and notice how it works back of the eyes, along the cheekbones,
stretch out in it, regard it with a bodily, sportive interest, and wonder
where it got its familiarity with you. This may take some time and is
not to be rushed. But wonder most of all: what of this sense of familiarity—as if it would serve as the basis of familiarity with most anyone—exists? For if in this observation the discovery is made that,
other than to repeat it, there is no actual familiarity in that fragment;
if there would be nothing to say to someone to follow up on the
prompt "remember the Lone Ranger" or how "Dude" was said or
how we remember "that song"; if the memory turns out to have
nothing particular to it, as to how life was one way rather than another way, then what is being perceived as familiarity is only the
memory trace of regression. What stands as a plenipotentiary of familiarity is a moment when the self could no longer hold out against
the pressure of what was forced on it. Much of what we have in our
heads at this point—regardless whether the reader is among the
group that in this country would make up an intellectual elite: pro-
fessors, deans, graduate students—has this quality rather than any
quality at all of being our memories. And, if the test is over now, we
can conclude that what might just have been felt—including the
crooked grin, maybe the sense of something yellow on the face, along
with whatever disappointment with the quiz itself—is how Adorno
thought that "new type of human being," who is not to become a cultured individual, would feel.

VI

Adorno would not have minded this way of making a sport of regression. He was not a rigorist. He did not conclude his reflections on a "new type of human being" by insisting that some way must be found to return miscreants to culture. Resentment's preoccupation with "high and low" culture was not ever Adorno's mentality. On the contrary, his approach to the postcultural human, as to any situation, was to try to discover what new powers the transformed moment might capably release. For Adorno, the only way out was through: even the expectably contented mid-American guffaw over Adorno's athletic disinclination would have been dialectically worthy. Thus Adorno concluded his essay by listing what powers this new type of human being might have, among which he mentions a cold readiness for sacrifice, a cleverness in the struggle with mega-organizations, and a speechless preparedness to do what is decisive.

Perhaps in the war years several of these powers were actualized. But, whatever came of that, and whatever of those powers may indeed be ours, this discussion has now come around to consider more closely Adorno's *Aesthetic Theory*. For his approach to the capacities of the "new type of human being" closely parallels what he considered to be the fundamental capacity of art: it is the possibility of turning the powers of the world against itself. This is a dialectical way of putting something that fits our—genuinely undialectical—ears better as Wallace Stevens would put it, speaking of poetry, when he wrote that it is a "violence from within that protects us from a violence without."[15] It could not be more obvious, but there are no other powers adequate to reality than those of reality itself. Again, as Stevens put it, "reality is the only genius."[16] Thus, just as in his study of the "new type of human being" Adorno tried to discern a way to militate its powers against those in which they originated, in his aesthetics he thought, similarly, that art itself must turn the violence against the violence, but in the realm of illusion. For it is only in the realm of illusion that the violence against the violence would itself be free of violence. Only there could it be shaped as the articulation of the one and the many, in which what is brewing in us all—which is for sure, if not only, a disaster—can possibly appear in such a way that, whoever is capable of concentrating on it, rightly exclaims, "if it only were." Art is the conceivable point at which the brewing disaster becomes inextricable from "if it only were," the image of reconciliation. Or to condense it again: art is the effort to shape the truth in the form in which it can rightly be longed for, in that moment when the body is covered with goosebumps. It is because there is a discernible difference between the false shudder and the true shudder that an aesthetics that is devoted to the primacy of the object claims that one art work can be, and absolutely must seek to be, better than any other art work. The process of each and every art work that emphatically undertakes to be art is the process by which the work destroys its own illusion.[17] In Benjamin's terms, certainly the origin of Adorno's aesthetics, every work ruins itself for the truth. Even the most stereotypical tune, by bringing itself to a close, however predictably, insists that there should only be one art work. Because art seeks the utterly real, no art work can tolerate any other work, let alone its illusion-bound self. To presuppose many works, a diversity of art works, is to assume that art is finally no more than an illusion, good at best for covering those many walls waiting for decoration. Thus Adorno's dissatisfaction with each and every art work was his alliance with each one as it seeks to be the only art work. If there is anything despotic in this intention, it is a despotism of the desire for the particular and real in opposition to what simulates it.

VII

It is worth thinking back to Adorno's list of the powers apposite to a new kind of person who is not to be cultured. Note that he did not enumerate probable powers of patient translation or a discernible eagerness to study *Aesthetic Theory*. But he might have seen this coming, had he thought about it. In his own genuinely haughty, uncompromising style, shaped by disdain for the philistine, he could have written, "Textbook dialectics—only the excluded can be needed." *Aesthetic Theory* could only have been written on the basis of Adorno's return to Germany from the United States. The book stands in utter opposition to what we are. This formed the potential for the book to become more important here than in Germany, a potential that is now urgent. This is not to say that we need *Aesthetic Theory* so we can pretend to be priests of art or speculative philosophers. Neither is in the offing. But, at this moment, *Aesthetic Theory* could provide the basis on which to experiment with ways that taste can be disputed and the correlative impulse to develop an exactitude in listening, what Adorno called "adequate listening." As he wrote, "It is more essential for the listener to please the Beethoven symphony than for the Beethoven symphony to please him."[18] Ears adequated to this level of differentiation, that would listen for what is emphatic in art and take its side, in opposition to all that is not—might tolerate for a moment such arch apothegms as "right listening means above all the overcoming of the current false listening"[19] and even discover Adorno to be correct that jazz as he knew it, then synonymous with sweet and swing, was the reggae of the thirties and forties. And that the howl today over Adorno's antipathy to that bland music obscures a wide-eyed contemporary aversion to advanced jazz, which is a genuinely marginal music that has internalized the entire development of twelve-tone music that Adorno once championed, that is itself hardly played on "all jazz" radio stations, and whose minuscule listenership is more restricted than that of so-called classical music. *Aesthetic Theory* could become a power of differentiation to let things drop; to dig in one's heels with a willful disinterest in amusement; to let the many movies spool silently elsewhere without worrying that one is being left behind by having missed them; to protect the museums from the Armani and motorscooters; to notice that what now makes our toes tap and our faces light up with miscellaneous recognition is no one's memory; to act on the impulse to protect ourselves—or our imagination anyway—as the power over possibility, from what otherwise uses that power to break in on us almost second by second to defeat that possibility.

Ethics, Aesthetics, and the
Recovery of the Public World

CLINGING TO THE SIDES OF ONE'S CHAIR in dread anticipation of a discussion of ethics, aesthetics, and the public world is not needed. There is no intention here to launch into these matters with any pretense that they are genuinely alive to us, however much discussion they receive. Readers will not once again be summoned to prop forward as if the various debates implicit in the topic are just waiting for troops to join battle. Though not so long ago people did vigorously discuss these issues without too terrible a sense of putting themselves on, the concepts themselves and their nexus now have a stale, remote, archaic quality. A team of archaeologists sent out on their behalf that somehow turned up their mummified remains in a cache of steel-gray army trunks and unraveled the shrouds would—under their very eyes—see these concepts change to dust. Such an expedition turns out to be neither fantastic nor rare: the contemporary glut of discussions of these concepts comes repeatedly to this very result, though they rarely admit it. Even the distinguished, sometimes heroic, work of Juergen Habermas has the feel of speculations on a phantom limb. To gain some perspective on the possible recovery of the public world it is necessary from the outset to consider these concepts' hollow resonance.[1]

I

As regards ethics, the whole cast of characters is missing: the generous, the dutiful, the beneficent, the noble and their dark counterimages, the miserly, the wicked, the unprincipled—all those figures who staffed bourgeois literature from Molière through Dickens and Balzac have vanished. Even if we sometimes seek to catch glimpses of them in occasional faces, we don't actually encounter them. Any one of them would now be an eccentric and, though there is currently no end to blasted and anomalous people, the figure of the eccentric shared their fate. From a contemporary vantage point, the tribe as a whole, frocked in what now seems medieval costume, is flickering out.

Why these figures and the ethical reflection that was their substance have become archaic is known to everyone in some fashion, and, because it touches a common nerve, one might just as well not hear about it. But, then again, whatever the reluctance to think about it, it cannot be passed up either. For ethics poses the question of individual universality; it seeks to define and test the necessity of the person in the relation of the one and the many. If ethical questions have been infiltrated by a pervasive sense of arbitrariness, then no less pervasive is the sense of having given up on what might make any person other than one too many.[2]

As a drama of the self-evident, what everyone knows of the reason for the passing of compelling ethical reflection will for now be left unstated. And there are precedents for hesitating on these matters. Reluctance on the topic burrows through the culture on many levels. This can be seen, for instance, in the fact that all Western languages freely assert the entwinement of morals and economy in a single word. That word is the good, which pedantically comprises both the good and the goods. Wealth has been the standard of goodness in all times and in every domain of thought, from the Greek *Kalokagathia* to the praise of a poem's rich textures.[3] But however pedantically the identity of wealth and goodness is insisted upon, this identity—such as the identity of the good and goods—is remarked upon with surprised obliviousness. The speaker of the poem's praise would feel antagonistically misunderstood if it were met by an irate "Are you saying that the rich are right?" Similarly, the revivalist minister can be expected to drive by the local Coca-Cola bottling plant's "redemption

center" without a twinge of recognition. Though economics and ethics completely overlap and speak the same phrases about free lunches
and fair share, though the languages of economic debt, culpability,
and guilt are completely homologous, in spite of this, the surprise, in-
comprehension, and anger that often greets reference to this common-
ality signal that a boundary exists between these spheres that is no less
real than their identity. This boundary line can be described, for it was
carved historically. It did not exist, for example, among the ancient
Greeks, for whom virtue (and that could only have been a manly
virtue) was identical with wealth and property and entirely defined
public status, a status that could only have been public since characteristically opposed to any kind of social standing was the *idiotes*—not an
individual of limited mental dexterity, but the epitome of the private
sphere itself, a person with no interest in public life and as such an exile from it, the basest form of life and of no conceivable utility.[4] By utter contrast, Christianity for the first time in Western thought set
goodness at odds with utility. Christians resolved to store up goods in
heaven, at a cost to themselves, on the same model that the mundane
store up goods in warehouses at a cost to everyone else. But this goodness was spiritualized as a private quality opposed to public values.
This boundary is necessarily a complex, layered, and hardly schemati-
zable one that more struck a fissure through every social element than
it established a simple dividing line. But in all instances of this division
the private aspect was deemed the more real and the public aspect was
conceived as secondary and a facade for the private. Modern ethics
thus emerged as the internalization of exchange relations that became
spiritualized through the power of opposition to, and in alliance with,
the same relations external to itself.

II

Yet this inner calculus is decreasingly relevant and to get at why this is
the case, and present it in a way that is more illuminating than the banal reasons generally familiar, is difficult not least of all because there is
no part of this event that is not genuinely banal. The topic here is in fact
the powers of the banal. In order to avoid being swamped by these
powers, some of their energy must be siphoned off. A test might, then,
be recommended that will touch the competitive nerve. If this test is be-

ing announced suddenly, that is just how tests are. This quiz is of the "What is wrong with the following?" variety and requires some concentration. The question is, What is wrong with the following sentence? *"You are free not to think as I do; your life, your property, everything shall remain yours, but from this day on you are a stranger among us."*[5]

The sentence is from Tocqueville's *Democracy in America*, written in Jacksonian times, the 1830s, when America emerged as an entrepreneurial power of international importance. Tocqueville, in the sentence quoted, speaks for this entrepreneurial world; he gives it his voice to pronounce its judgment on each and every person. In the form of all ethics, Tocqueville absorbs an economic principle and heightens it to the point that it becomes a potential source of criticism. And there is no doubt that even today this maxim of universal banishment packs something of a wallop. But this critical force could hardly be what it once was. And skilled linguistic sensoriums will immediately perceive what goes wrong with the phrase; they will sense where the maxim becomes a logical conundrum, falters, and its critical force expires.

For those however who sense nothing of this, what those sharper sensoriums are compelled to wonder is, Who is this *us* in the latter part of the phrase "from this day on you are a stranger *among us*"? If, as Tocqueville insists, each person is free to think and live as each cares to think or live—if the maxim states that each has become a stranger to the other—who is the *us*? Either the *us* exists and the criticism is false—because then Tocqueville is hiding that each is not a stranger—or the *us* is an illusion and there are no conceivable grounds for the complaint since strangers can only be strangers with reference to some us. Thus, carefully regarded, Tocqueville's sentence is faulty. Even if its criticism is recognized as true and one wants its toxin to take hold and administer its sting subcutaneously, the sentence itself dilutes the sting. It is worth noticing, incidentally, that for Tocqueville this *us* was not ironic or a placeholder. The fact of the sentence, that it was coherent for him, makes evident that in its own time it drew on a content that has now become illusory and threatens the critical content of his thought altogether.

What was tested, then, in this brief quiz, was a power that few may realize they possess: a historical sensorium that has the ability to perceive an emergently illusory aspect in the construction of a sentence. And this example is useful for understanding the dynamic of the decay of ethics in its relation to economics. For the ability to sense how this

sentence tends toward disintegration—for it is the sentence itself that
has aged and been transformed and even gained a new expressive force
in the yawning abyss it now pronounces at the same time that it is
washed over by its potential neutralization—is itself an act of the market. Those acute sensoriums that spontaneously picked out the problem in Tocqueville's maxim, who were not fooled for a second, owe the
cultivation of their involuntary historical perspicacity to the market.

However condensed, some explanation of this capacity is needed.
The market on which society as a whole began to admit its complete
dependency in the seventeenth century was the first social order not
predicated on any authority external to itself.[6] Indeed, it criticized and
absorbed these transcendent powers. The exchange relation, as it becomes an all pervasive market, insists that it and all it touches is
completely self-indwelling. At least momentarily it is worth being as-
tonished by the thought: the market is the power of immanence.
Whatever goes beyond this order, whatever lays claim to rising above
the exchange relation or being more than that relation is progressively
perceived as an illegitimate universal. It was, for instance, the increasingly total market of the seventeenth and eighteenth centuries that
made monism the requisite ideal of modern philosophy in Leibniz,
Spinoza, and Hegel. And the market has philosophical implications
beyond its assignments to one branch of knowledge. For the market
also prescribes nominalism as the logic of common sense: the real particular is asserted as the exclusive standard of reality and universals
are rejected as unjust and ultimately illusory forces of domination. It
is thus the market that has trained the spontaneous edginess to Tocqueville's *us*.

Much would be required to substantiate all of this. But beyond the
sensed fate of Tocqueville's *us*, further confirmation is available, even
to those who did poorly on the Tocqueville quiz, if just the mention
above of the concept of the universal prompts outrage—a "What's
that?!"—in the inner ear of the historical sensorium. And further
proof of the relation between the market as the force of immanence
and a nominalism that refuses whatever asserts itself as a universal
that goes beyond this order is evident in virtually anything else that
can be thought of on the contemporary landscape: the "he or she," for
instance, that replaced "he" did so on the basis of the criticism of a
false, dominating universal. With striking rapidity the emerging illusoriness and unpalatability of its claim brought broad swaths of even

recent texts to the verge of unreadability. And, at the same time, it is now almost impossible to posit a third person who stands for each and every person in that, by the logic of the new pronoun, he and she are strictly he or she, that is, mutually exclusive. The literalism of the critique of "he"—like the critique of Tocqueville's *us*—is itself a market force that defines the standard of reality as relentlessly singular. It should be noted that this critique of a universal, of "he," was an act in which another fraction of society found freedom by being swallowed whole into the immanence of the market.

Though the criticism rejects a false universal and lodges the power of domination in particular private interest, this act of empowerment of the particular has been partial at best. As in every other instance of this dialectic, the emancipation gained in the rise of some women to positions of power has been matched by their total subordination to the market and impoverishment as a group. Here nominalism reveals itself as a power of the dominating whole. In labor law, similarly, recent U.S. Supreme Court decisions have progressively limited the range in which individual rights can be asserted collectively. The reality of the worker as an individual is thus heightened as he or she becomes more helpless by being deprived of union recourse when resisting the demands of production. And again: right-wing Republicans have perfectly caught the historical drift in their sails with their insistence that any defense of substantive rights and efforts to ameliorate historical inequalities are based on illusory interpolations foisted on the American Constitution. If the right wing succeeds at destroying these ameliorative efforts, it will reveal the most brutal economic polarization in U.S. history.

Historically the self became powerful by developing the ability to mediate in itself its relation to the world. By confronting the world, the self became a microcosm of the tensions of the whole on which the self could then reflect and conceivably find resources within itself for asserting its own necessity. This tense relation in which the bourgeois self once stood to the universal, to the social whole, can be overheard and witnessed in every Mozart piano concerto. The sea change of the past two to three decades, now coming starkly into focus, is that the totality no longer permits any relation to it. The entrepreneurial powers that have amassed the largest fortunes they have ever controlled in proportion to the rest of the country now pursue this wealth by means of techniques of accumulation that increasingly presuppose the circumvention of the self. The telephone and the mails, which up until recently preserved elements of intimacy, have become marketing vehicles that no individual can skirt or block. The emergence of wholly owned public realms such as malls and gated communities are prototypical of the destruction of privacy in its own name in that their representatives have argued in court that within their confines basic constitutional rights including free speech are consensually abrogated. The perceptual world itself threatens to become a wholly owned subsidiary, as testified by the recent Supreme Court decision to permit the patenting and copyright registration of colors. What Herbert Marcuse described thirty years ago as "repressive desublimation," while thinking perhaps of the workings of Elvis's hips, is shy politesse compared to the libidinal spread eagle in film, music, and newspapers that no longer tolerates sublimation in the reader or viewer. Contemporary slash and gouge techniques are therefore hard to characterize as repressive because they do not in any way supplement forms of individual defense but burst through the defenses altogether. Likewise, in the case of labor, negotiation has become increasingly scarce. Conflicts, instead, are resolved by overwhelming the workers with the nonchoice between capitulation and self-impoverishment.

III

Margaret Thatcher, our contemporary, provides evidence of ears expertly trained to historical nuance. She would have no trouble pointing up where Tocqueville's maxim goes wrong. And, though she was not specifically concerned to debunk his illusions, she might as well have been when she flatly denied the existence of society: "There is no such thing as society. There are only families and individuals." Invoking the nominalist dynamic as her own power, however, does not grant her the ability to call its limits. Indeed, many readers of her renowned *bon mot* will find themselves involuntarily scrutinizing her assertion of the fundamental reality of the family. But neither does the individual—in whom all else is supposed to find its only possible justification—enjoy special dispensation. The emergence of a social totality that no longer permits any relation to it has drained the self of its substance and transformed it fundamentally. The 1994 *Diagnostic and Statistical Manual* of psychiatric illness has concluded that trauma is now so common that it can no longer be defined as an event "outside the range of normal human experience."[7] And whereas anxiety was not long ago the focus of distress, categories of panic attacks have moved to the forefront. Social phobia—the incapacitating fear of humiliation or embarrassment in social events, often combined with agoraphobia and panic anxiety—has become the single most frequent psychiatric problem. Some proportion of people with social phobia are—as a proportion of the readers of this essay are aware—housebound; others are unable to stand in a line or go to a store. Whatever reasons people give for not appearing at the polls, voting itself is clearly beyond the power of many. This is evidence that the public world has become so antipathetic to those who in some sense constitute it that it can no longer be approached, but this fact of social phobia is also evidence that, for many, the self is prohibited from rudimentary development so that even common events threaten regression and the eruption of needs and fears associated with intense vulnerability and shame.[8] Unable to engage a force that is both remote and overwhelming, prevented from developing the capacity inwardly to mediate the experience of this antagonism, the self is threatened with disintegration in the experience of panic.

IV

The need for the recovery of the public world is in a sense obvious. But if such a recovery means reaching back to what was lost, it is credulously retrospective. The public world has always served as a facade for economic manipulation. Ever since the French Revolution institutionally established the division of the individual into *citoyen* and *bourgeois*, the former's ostensibly equal political rights have served to justify the latter's right to unequal economic prerogative. Even in those exceptional periods—well documented by Habermas—in which a public world did flourish, when a degree of tact did exist between private interest and the plausible role of the citizen, this has cloaked the fact that equal exchange has always been a violent act of unequal accumulation. And, even when it is not invoked by name, the idea of the public readily functions to mask actual tensions. No better example is more commonly familiar than the program of Walter Benjamin's "The Work of Art in the Age of Mechanical Reproduction."[9]

Most everyone knows the ropes and pulleys of this essay: in it Benjamin argues that the invention of film created a new, socially critical public sphere. By its power of reproduction, film destroyed the auratic singularity of art works and thus their cult value. In the public world of the movie house, there on the screen, the world fell critically open to all in the triumph of exhibition value.[10] If this argument is almost universally familiar, it has only rarely been noticed that the thesis fully disregards the inextricability of exhibition value and exchange value. It ignores the predominance of the market over art against which all critical artists of this century have chafed as the greatest hazard to their efforts. It was, for instance, just this inextricability of exchange value and exhibition value that compelled Clyfford Still to withdraw his works from public display for decades at a time and caused Ad Reinhardt to spend the last part of his life painting works of such cunningly nuanced darkness that they would be beyond photographic reproduction. If it is striking that Benjamin's ostensibly Marxist thesis ignores the economic reality of exhibition value, it is more than startling that this has hardly ever been recognized. Though Still and Reinhardt would be dubbed hidebound from the perspective of Benjamin's essay, it is his essay that has made, and continues to make, the real contribution to socially necessary semblance. It provides resources to deny that film is a commodity and to believe, rather, that the audience is an alliance of spontaneous subjectivities finally having the chance to see the world for what it is. Once again, the ideal of the public serves as a mask, this time of the private perceptions of the film viewers who know perfectly well that ticket stubs are in their pockets and that something different from collective, critical, freedom transpires in those darkened halls.

V

The idea of the *recovery of the public world* tends toward rationalization of the same sort, as if in reaching back to better days we could pretend that the conflicts that in any case developed into the present situation were unreal. Yet the idea of the public is not simply ideological. And the project of the recovery of the public world is not ideological insofar as it implies the need for a process of criticism that wants to make good on what the concept of the public has to date deceptively promised. As ever, the only possibilities that are genuinely compelling are those that take illusory promises at their word and drive them to the limit. Thus, if formal rights have functioned to mask inequality, they are also the grounds on which the inequality of the market can be demonstrated; driven to their extreme, they no longer function as a facade but become a demand for substantive rights. Indeed, if equal exchange were truly equal it would no longer be exchange but the real freedom and bindingness of the particular that capitalism prevaricates.[11]

Yet these are dialectical thoughts, and they have necessarily shared the fate of ethical reflection. Just as it has been made obsolete by the ineluctable experience of the arbitrariness of each in an economy to which no one is necessary—and this is to bring this essay's drama of the obvious to a close—so dialectical thinking, whose only source is the relentless self-immersion of thought in the dynamic of the one and the many, has become archaic. Thus contemporary critical theory has in a sense rightly discarded dialectics. Yet the jettisoning of dialectics has not been followed by more binding critical formulations of experience. Much contemporary critical theory seeks to escape the threat of a looming nonintegration by affirming disintegration in stylized, finicky, implausible evocations of ruins, melancholy, and fragmentation. "Difference," apart from its philosophical reasoning—as a popular ideal that capitalizes on the rejection of all universals as illusory—permits ignoring the idea of the whole and suppresses dynamic, complex concepts of relationship. If it has not been noticed, the concepts of antagonism, conflict, anxiety, contrast, alienation, and opposition have disappeared from much critical discussion. The slack ideal of cultural multiplicity hovers gingerly above the guilt context of the whole, preferring the neutralization of thought to any insight into that guilt context, not least because insight implies a need for change that is sensed as beyond anyone's power. The aesthetics of this cultural moment is a postmodernism that shuns the forming of a critical microcosm by preference for a form of montage that never gets beyond juxtaposition. Especially in the arbitrarily dispersed typographical page of much—not all—contemporary poetry, this is an aesthetics that settles opportunistically for a fragile slackness where maker and reader build their secret alliance on the promise not to reveal that neither has the strength of the spontaneity that finding what is alive would require.

Suggested Reading

Jameson on Adorno

FREDERIC JAMESON is one of the great tattooed men of our times. Every inch of flesh is covered: that web of cat's cradles coiling up the right calf are Greimas and Levi-Strauss; dripping over the right shoulder, under the sign of the Cimabue Christ—the inverted crucifixion—hangs Derrida. And hardly recognizable in those many other overlapping splotches of color is just about everybody else: Lyotard, Sartre, Habermas, et al. "All One, All Different" scrolls across the panoramic chest. In *Late Marxism*[1] Jameson scouts carefully before setting portentious digit on a densely engraved quadrate of his left hip, Adorno! and falls into a roll: "Adorno you will notice is like Althusser, only more like Sartre, except the idea of totality, in my opinion, as I'll say again later, differs from Rorty, coming back to Luhman, maybe like Marxism, late, very late, minus Hegel's concept of time, perhaps, maybe, almost. . . . Take another look, another look, just not too close, please, ladies and gentleman, give the man room to breathe!"

This is mocking no doubt, but what is this: Adorno's aesthetics "can speak a variety of speculative languages, none of which ever finally freezes over . . . like Lukács's, Bloom's, Macherey's, Bakhtin's, or Derrida's"? He forgot Sartre. No worry, skip a line: "The history of

aesthetic situations is here as omnipresent and inescapable as in
Sartre." But where did de Man go? Skip again: "to use Paul de Man's
suggestive phrase" (182–183). Open to any page and the same miscellaneous cornucopia comes tumbling out, each name a distraction from
what could conceivably have been the issue at hand: "After Freud (indeed, after Marx), after Nietzsche, after Foucault on madness, after a
whole enormous enlargement in our sympathy with what people do
(this word, however, meant in Rousseau's sense as *Verstehen*)" (236).
If neither the *indeed, after Marx,* or the *whole enormous* arm flailing
adequately sharpens things up, Jameson's clarification of sympathy as
the idea of *Verstehen* in Rousseau—great German hermeneuticist—
makes every thought sparkle.

Hit and Run

Jameson is so preoccupied storing up this bounty and spilling it back
out again that paragraph by paragraph continually swerves out of its
own way to be able to throw in another garbled reference and skid
half on purpose into the next wrong topic. The excited author does
not mind; he is playing bumper cars. But if you read carefully, and still
register concussions, it is a bad experience. Consider a passage on
Adorno's style that takes up the question of Karl Kraus's influence on
him, but concludes making the point—*Watch Out!*—that Benjamin is
more important to Kraus: "What Adorno found here (in Kraus), I
want to suggest, is the very paradigm of an expressive syntax, in which
the actual *machinery of sentence structure* is itself pressed into service, in
all its endless variety, and mobilized to convey meaning far beyond its
immediate content as mere communication and denotation. To
Kraus, far more than to Adorno himself, might well apply Benjamin's
idea that speech communicates itself, and perhaps also his idiosyncratic notion of language as 'non-representational mimesis'" (64).[2]
   Every gesture of this style subserves a need for remoteness, a need
that evidently defines what thinking amounts to for this author. The
only way then to get even for reading something like this and for the
damage it has done to several generations of graduate students is to
study it close up, line by line, for what it hides. First of all, then, note
in the sentence just quoted that Jameson is barely interested in what
Adorno found of importance in Kraus. Jameson after all is a literature

professor and besides being a first-rate list maker he could not possibly believe that Kraus—rather than, say, Hoelderlin or Stefan George—was for Adorno the preeminent writer to use syntax expressively. All expressive language is in any case syntactically expressive. And whatever there is between Kraus and Adorno, the interchangeable elements of a mechanical order—that "machinery of sentence structure"—would least of all comprehend what is shared in their nuanced language. Jameson is exploiting what no one would doubt—that Adorno and Kraus are somehow inwardly related—but without in any way developing the content of this relation. Examine them closely, minutely: the bulk of the two phrases works at taking up the slack uncoiled by the contentlessness of their claim: The *very* paradigm, the *actual* machinery, the *endless* variety, the *far* beyond, the *far* more, the Adorno *himself* exalts the arbitrary by raising it to the absolute along the lines of a 'truly great vacation.' Rhetorical largess—from the "I want to suggest" to the "might well apply" to the "perhaps also"—is to supply the pomp of judicious reflection for thinking that never got a second thought.

Under even close scrutiny notice that in those places Jameson is not at all concerned with how Benjamin's ideas of speech communicating itself and "non-representational mimesis" resonate in Kraus's work, the point that should justify Jameson's skewed divigation. He has nothing to say about what either of these hardly self-evident quotations mean or how they characterize Kraus. Suspicion that conceptually not much stands back of Jameson's associations—other than the desire to fold in some lines that once caught his attention in order to keep the cant moving and all things far away—is prompted especially by the second quotation's reference to "non-representational mimesis." Benjamin never used the phrase, though he did introduce the idea of "unsinnliche Aehnlichkeiten." If "nonsensual similarities" is what Jameson meant—and noting as an aside that he subsumes it to the currently all-purpose "representation," which is not at all what Benjamin's concept is about—the nonsense clue is obvious: Benjamin's idea is said to be "idiosyncratic." Now check back to that sentence. Jameson says that this idiosyncratic idea refers to Kraus. But in what sense is one person's idiosyncrasy that which he shares compellingly with someone else? In the sense of not sharing it.

Jameson may have dubbed Benjamin's concept idiosyncratic because that serves to conveniently dismiss an idea he did not understand

and did not want to have to say two words about. This is confirmed not only by the bad translation but also by the claim that it applies more to Kraus than Adorno. In failing to comprehend what is coiled up in the concept he fails to trace it into Adorno's *Aesthetic Theory* where the concept becomes the central idea in his history of art as the transformation of external mimesis into the principle of self-likeness.

What Jameson does not understand in Benjamin and Adorno then becomes the asserted, self-evident bond between Benjamin and Kraus. The swerve in the passage follows Jameson's impulse to conjure as his own power a force to which he is subordinately uncomprehending. Those who make their way through this passage with some shudder vis-à-vis big thinking are sensing their unknowingness refractedly as Jameson's authority. This style is the manufacture of linguistic fetish in a game of blind man's bluff. It is comical and it is serious.

On the Way Down

The puzzle being examined here is that this book is widely read while making so little sense, and destructively so. Wherever the eye falls and takes seriously what it finds the molecules of print start kissing each other goodbye. It gets teary on all sides. Self-aware, the eye must decide to skirt the semiotic pulp. But then how is it possible to document the puzzle of *Late Marxism* if even its devoted readership is unlikely to allow itself to reflect on one sentence or another? For now, it will have to be on a dare: here is the elastic cable attached to the railing, this is the Golden Gate Bridge, below is *Late Marxism*. The topic is suddenly Adorno and structuralism and though the print is already swimming in all directions, Jameson is certain of one thing: "It is *certain* that Adorno is a traditional, that is to say a prestructuralist, philosopher." Adorno is a *prestructuralist*. Done. But just lines later the level of assurance named *certainty* is uncannily surpassed by *confidence:* "It can be asserted with some *confidence* that he never goes as far as the poststructuralists" (234–235). Hard! A prestructuralist does not go as far as a poststructuralist. Why not? Because he has "*some* notion of thinking . . . beyond a material embodiment in language."[3] *Some* is now followed by *almost*: "What needs to be added here is that the 'concept' functions in Adorno as a constricting and reifying system *almost* as iron-clad as language itself for poststructuralism" (234–235). With

certainty Adorno is a prestructuralist who is confidently not, somewhat not, almost a poststructuralist. Probably. But a problem remains:
Adorno did not think that the concept per se is an ultimate block to reality. If he had his writings would be chalked up to the irrationalism
against which his dialectical research took shape.[4]

The opposite direction from *certainty* to *almost* runs from *in general*
to *more exactly* by way of *indeed precisely*. Thus the brief recoil on the
elastic tether: "Art *in general*, now very much including the individual
works and *indeed precisely* consisting of them, will be opposed to
everything which is not art; or, *more exactly*, to everything 'cultural'"
(132). This could be sorted out and sense insisted on, but only for the
gullible or the hypnotized.

Always and Again

Where Jameson does come through lucidly, the question of how well
he has understood Adorno continually recurs. Note, for instance, his
comments on a passage quoted from Adorno's *Positivism Dispute* concerning the concept of totality. First, the passage from Adorno: "It is
almost tautological to say that one cannot point to the concept of totality in the same manner as one can point to the facts, from which totality distances itself as a concept" (231). Now reattach that elastic cable
and prepare to dive: according to Jameson, Adorno in this passage
wants to demonstrate in the denial of the possibility of pointing factually to the concept of totality the following self-contradiction: "The
misconception seems to be based on the idea that if you talk about
something repeatedly, you must like it; to point something out insistently turns into the advocacy of the thing, very much on the principle
of the messengers who bring bad news (and suffer the consequences)."
The tip-off to the mistakenness of Jameson's interpretation is that—
like a pop tune knotting a tail of homilies onto "Mama Said"—it tags
together a string of platitudes from *talk about it/like it* to *bad news messengers pay the consequences*. But the implicit self-contradiction that
Jameson discerns could not be what Adorno is talking about because,
as Jameson explains it, it is not a tautology, whereas Adorno emphasizes just this quality of the assertion. And Adorno's point is not so
hard to understand: he is responding to positivists who reject the concept of totality on the grounds that it cannot be factually observed.

Adorno finds a way to agree with their objection so as to undermine the criticism: To say that totality cannot be factually observed does not challenge the concept but only repeats tautologically an aspect of its definition, which is that totality is not a fact but an organization of the facts.

While the eye balks at studying the detail of *Late Marxism*, Jameson insists that this is the optimally requisite level of focus. "This book offers detailed readings" (3) of Adorno's main writings. This level of attention is coherent with what he picks out as the specific importance of Adorno's work:

> The originality, indeed, of his philosophical work ... lies in his unique emphasis on the presence of late capitalism as a totality within the very forms of our concepts or of the works of art themselves. No other Marxist theoretician has ever staged this relationship between the universal and the particular, the system and the detail, with this kind of single-minded yet wide-ranging attention.
>
> (9)

Jameson is correct that Adorno interpreted the particular as a microcosm of the whole. But this is not to be confused with a vision of infinity stored since creation in a grain of sand. Here the particular is a result. The intention of dialectics is to know this particular from within and in doing so to fulfill the Hegelian obligation that philosophy grasp time in concepts. But where Hegel's dialectic is both progressive and in principle at every point reconciled with itself, Adorno conceived a dialectic at a standstill that would potentiate in reflection the antagonistic content of history. By pursuing the mediation of the particular through the social totality, negative dialectics transforms the power of totality into the force of historical reflection by releasing the history stored in the particular as the power that vitiates it.[5] For Adorno, therefore, dialectics is, on the one hand (as he wrote), the wrong state of things and, on the other, dialectical research is the capacity to give shape in the particular to this state of things. To the extent that Adorno succeeds in this his writings are neither a metaphor, a method, a perspective, nor a system.

Though Jameson discerns the central idea of this form of interpretation, and although there are traces of many of the related concepts, the thought never becomes internal to the book. If it had, Jameson's intention to present a detailed reading of Adorno in light of what he promotes as Adorno's importance—his micrological research—would have given *Late Marxism* a dialectical turn. It did not: the reflection in which the totality is discovered in the particular never occurs. Instead of dialectical research the book is a labor of common sense: Jameson compares and contrasts, as if interpretation would result from adding and subtracting; he points weightily to paradoxes and complexity, which he confuses with dialectics; he supplants insight with the self-evidence of moral and political posturing; he names and effuses. Hardly dialectical, Jameson's stance toward these writings is what Hegel disparaged as "healthy human understanding" (*gesunder Menschenverstand*): Adorno is the topic, and—what could be more obvious?—Jameson writes about this topic. The act of abstraction—the division of the universal from the particular—that sees subject and object at opposite extremes is presumed.

This commonsensicalness lies back of much of the chaos and popularity of *Late Marxism*. Like Terry Eagleton—with whom he has much in common—Jameson is a conventional thinker whose will to occupy a front seat on the flying wedge of literary criticism, combined with an omnivorous intellectual metabolism, led him into genuinely anticonventional work, which he regularly scrambles. This does not bother his readership: anxious to share his velocity and academic promotion, they take the incoherence as the mark of authenticity embossed on ideas that they are content to let hover overhead, reserving their attention for tracking the pulse of *idées reçues* right under the surface.

The Deeper Message

Because Jameson's thought remains external to the content of his book, this content—the philosophical summaries and moral-political posturing—stands in the way of recognizing what takes place in *Late Marxism*. It is by giving attention to its impoverished detail—the non-intentional level of the book—rather than gullibly, and fruitlessly, responding at the level of argumentation and political identity, that the book can be asked to show its hand.

Consider then Jameson's *we*, the voice in which he writes. The book not only reads like, but is, an advertisement—in this case—for

Adorno. When Jameson writes that Adorno "may turn out to be just what *we* need today" (5), there is reason to suspect that this claim to political authenticity is the opportunistic, importuning "I" of mass culture solidarity. This is confirmed by the manipulativeness of what turns out to be the book's genuinely incomparable message: "The *deeper* message of my book . . . has to do with celebration of the dialectic as such" (11). Contrary to Adorno, for whom dialectics is the wrong state of things and negative dialectics its presentation, Jameson adopts the ad world's mantle of upbeat rationalization and invites everyone to come tie on a balloon to the idea of the antagonistic totality. But, his message is more significant than that; it is incomparable, literally. Scanning the page and pages of this claim, it turns out that—though the claim could be tagged onto various thoughts—the *deeper* message forms no specific comparative. It is that of the newer, better, faster type that, by being newer, better, faster than nothing ascertainable, preempts the act of discernment that might find it older, slower, worse, or more shallow. The seeming objectivity of the subjectively posited standard—surpassed by whatever is being promoted—is a measure of the degree to which the individual is willingly overwhelmed by the promotion. What is *more than* pivots on this subjectively coerced index so that what is *more than* is already part of you, your better, faster, newer, and—specifically in *Late Marxism*—your *deeper* part. Thus the technique of Jameson's call to the ghastly celebration of the perpetually antagonistic world enjoins as does any advertisement: by insinuating itself. Jameson's deeper message is that members are signed up prior to joining.

Those Crazy Texts

After introducing what he claims is Adorno's most important philosophical contribution—the interpretation of the universal in the particular—Jameson writes: "As for the current ratings of Adorno's stock . . ." (9). *We* must stop here, in this strangely echoing hollow, to consider a bit and catch our bearings. Adorno's *stock*? Its *ratings*? While these words beat about the ears, read also a few pages later that Adorno wants concepts "cashed at face value" (28). *Cashed*? Adorno wants cash for concepts? This is the language of the *tribu*, for sure. Here, at the book's trailhead, the scent is laid down for the sniffing graduate pack to follow in special disregard for any of those big ideas that are said to be as strange as they are just because common sense is in the lead. We are entering the domain of *text* and *textuality*. Here the philosophical ear must adapt to phrases such as "or, if you prefer a different kind of terminology" and "truth, however that word is used" (234). Notice, for example—in a discussion of Adorno's concept of mimesis and whether philosophy can achieve a mimetic response—how Jameson conceives the relation of the "reader's mind" to a biceps-palpating invocation of the powers of undomesticated language: "Whether philosophy can actually do that, whether the *most powerful* or formally ingenious or evocative philosophical sentence structure can intervene with (mimetic) effects of this kind in *the reader's mind*, is open to some doubt" (64). Mimesis is the affinity of subject and object as it is felt in one's knees on seeing someone else stumble on theirs. Yet the disembodied quality of Jameson's expression—"the reader's mind"—shows no familiarity at all with mimesis. Instead, he presupposes the mind as a box at the far end of the nervous system, separate as well from language. When he claims that the idea of a mimetically compelling language is "open to some doubt," he asserts, with level common sense, the diremption of subject and object that the thought of such a mimetically compelling language is beyond consideration. The presupposition is that words could never carry the distance from fingertip to cerebrum and back again. Even when he argues the contrary, this is not what he says: "A brilliant essay in literary criticism might well open up possibilities of reading, or rereading, some hitherto opaque, dull, or exasperatingly perverse text . . . and even disengaging the formation of some new aesthetic or poetic within your mind" (132). Because the power of these perverse and exasperating texts is just the ability to make it all the way into "your mind"—back behind where reading usually takes place—they hover at a fixed distance from it.

While Jameson gestures easily on all sides to strange, perverse, and ingenious texts—capable certainly of anything—his veneration serves plain dismissiveness. These texts will never rock the boat. They can be as crazy as they want just because, fully divided from manipulative mind, they are themselves meaningless counters in a cash economy of thought. Together with the textual fluidity implied by the many references to "rewriting" and "rereading," Jameson's wild texts are gathered up around something much homelier than his easy familiarity with the textual far side wants to suggest: the philosophy of language of that garden-variety skeptical empiricism that is the *sensus communis* of most of what passes for linguistic radicalism in America. Jameson considers words raw material, properly bearing a conventional denotative significance. To be meaningful, concepts must renounce all those points where Ovid starts to pass his hand over them. It is, thus, with the best of intentions that this commensensicalness wants to inspire concern that the idea of mimesis might fail the test: "It is not clear to what degree Adorno discovered the possibilities of the notion of mimesis in Benjamin's infrequent use of it: what is certain is that he went on to make it mean much more than Benjamin did—perhaps too much more" (64). Concepts that cannot be unambiguously defined are to be abandoned as magical after having first served for mysterious evocation: "These magical terms, which are evoked to explain everything without ever themselves being explained, until at length we become persuaded that they could never themselves be explained or grounded" (64).

Jameson is right that these concepts cannot be further deduced. This is not so strange: Aristotle recognized the existence of such underivative concepts without being made to feel uneasy. But Jameson's suddenly warning the reader back to dry ground severs the possibility of understanding Adorno's work: First of all, he cannot see that the problem of the whole of Adorno's writings is to follow language where it wants to go and thereby develop the critical-historical content of language in music (the concepts of development, theme, romanticism), in philosophy (beginning with the concept of enlightenment), and in literature the nonconceptual knowledge such as is coiled up in words like Stefan George's *gar*.[6] The range taken by the concepts of aura and mimesis in *Aesthetic Theory* is in the interest of lucidity and comprehension, not the confused obscurity in which Jameson's commensensicalness finds itself when actually faced with the dialectical development of a concept.

Second, the ultimate subject/object division implicit in the need to ground language means that the idea of immanent criticism escapes Jameson. *Late Marxism* barely treats of this central concept in Adorno's writings. But at one point Jameson does take up the question of what he calls the "Archimedean problems of the negative dialectic." He demands to know how this dialectic establishes a fulcrum from which to move the universe. Adorno, he claims, "needs something from outside the *system* in order to criticize it." That is not true. If the *system* were not inherently self-critical there would be no reason to criticize it. Immanent criticism turns the principle of identity, which otherwise serves the subordination of object to subject, into the power for the presentation of the way in which an object resists its subjective determination and finds itself lacking. Where this occurs it amounts to knowledge of an object from within, which for common sense is magic but for dialectical philosophy the emphatic concept of experience. Thus it is Jameson, not Adorno who requires that criticism find an Archimedean—external—leverage point. He continues in his misunderstanding: not only would the source of criticism have to be external, he writes, "but in Adorno's case this something would remain an idea," a "formal subterfuge" (235). In that Jameson cannot conceive of ideas as other than as a subjective abstraction, the formalism is on his side. Immanent criticism, on the contrary, is the development of the idea as the object's self-dissatisfaction that at every point moves toward what is not idea; it potentiates from within the requirement of an objective transformation.

Third, it is apparent why Hegel thought healthy common sense (*gesunder Menschenverstand*) was unfit for thinking. Its opinion that the movement of concepts is fruitless wandering is insisted upon reciprocally with the arbitrary and unthinking limitation of concepts. Insofar as Jameson is relentlessly levelheaded, it is no surprise that he disparages the amorphousness of the concepts of aura and mimesis and picks just the wrong moment to dig in his heals: "These concepts have nothing in common" (64). This brings him up short for understanding *Aesthetic Theory*. Central to it is the relation between aura—that which is more than is factually present in an art work—and mimesis: just by its internal mimesis of what is untrue in the world the radically anti-auratic art work becomes the negative figure of what would be other than the given and, therefore, once again becomes auratic.

"Theory"

Jameson's self-assuredness over the proper confines of thought and language is defined vis-à-vis uncertainties in which his confidence is mediated. This mediation is not hard to discern. His complaint over

the magical concepts of aura and mimesis implies the need to autho-
rize a much broader ban. For while there is a great deal to say about
mimesis and aura, there is no less to say about the concepts of experience, freedom, beauty, and so on. Jameson's worry over two concepts
must extend phobically to language altogether. This apprehension is
evident in the quotation marks in which he sets off word after word:
"Adorno certainly does have a 'style,' (like the rest of the 'modern
masters' . . .)" (11). These quotation marks express a reluctant agreement to make do with language. Words are accepted on the basis of
a peremptory gesture that means to isolate them from the guilty associations that cling to them—to "style" and "modern masters"—and
that threatens to drag them out beyond the breakers of good sense
and the writer's own purity. The neutralized word becomes terminological, a reified technical device—set between the self and the
world—over which the self claims to dispose. Bracketed in scare
quotes, words acquire a quality of obviousness, as if to say, we all
know what "style," "modern masters," "freedom," and "belief" are
about and just what must be excluded for these words to be usable.
But separated from their inherent attributions they are meaningless,
and the *bien entendu* is without content other than a self-assertion
that demands nodding along. The bracketed words are technical yet
suggestively self-promoting language. As such, language is a facade
behind which an isolated self finds a fulcrum—that pivot requisite of
all theory, according to Jameson—for manipulation. This dynamic is
not limited to the words Jameson sets in quotations marks. It is the
idea of theory throughout his work and the one that makes him an
ideal thinker for MLA theoreticians: the tattooed body of total theory
is a character mask that, though it cannot speculate philosophically, is
adequate for speculation of all other kinds.

Suggested Reading

Whatever else it is, *Late Marxism* is professorial: Each page opens to a
jowly: "So it is . . ." "To be sure . . ." and "It is surely . . ." Showing his
radical credentials, he does not hesitate to reach for maxims that ring
somberly from the lecture hall: "It is, indeed, not people who change
but rather situations." This maxim is a clue to the nature of the pro-

fessorial throughout the book and to the book as a whole. What does Jameson's apothegm mean? That people stay the same while the world changes? No, because as he draws on its wisdom he continues: "This can also account for the alterations of my own views" (4). How could the claim to the unchangingness of people explain Jameson's change? It cannot. Though his comment does make plain what he was trying to say with his maxim, which is that it is not people who change situations but the reverse. And while it is important to notice that he did not trouble to get his thought as far as logical coherence, it is more important to notice that he did not need to. His concern was the production of the semblance of a maxim in a book that is a Potemkin village of thought. Its illusoriness is the standard of the linguistic architecture: the *in my opinion* and the *perhaps* that pepper line after line, the *I want to suggest*, and, most frequently, the *seems*, which on word count alone would need be recognized as the substance of the book, larding as it does whole pages with variants on *it seems clear* and *it would seem to suggest* and *mass culture seems to demand* (150). Throughout, rudiments of academic judiciousness—that controlled suspension of conclusion—become one of the forces of the Jamesonian as if. Its appeal is not hard to locate: Since the contemporary relativism to which this as if thinking speaks is less a matter of philosophy than an indifference shaped by a panicky fear of knowing and the need to protect a self that insists on believing that it can somehow keep pulling the strings, all resignation of knowledge in the name of illusion can expect to be met with applause and relief.

The illusion Jameson means to provide is of a particular sort. Just as nineteenth-century photographers regularly used *gommage*—working over the negative with an eraser—to instill the false aura of spirit around a face or across a landscape,[7] Jameson has a dozen techniques for smearing a damp cloth across the page—beginning with the exploitation of the Adorno-Kraus relation to the incomparable comparative, to all that *seems* to be, and so on—and his aim is a related aura: *Late Marxism* manufactures the familiar. This is the halo effect produced by every name Jameson lists. Whenever he falls into a roll of Lyotard, Gramsci, Sappho, and Schelling or intersperses a sentence with "(Heidegger!)" and ends another with "so far Kant!" he transforms thought into rungs for academic arboreals arcing their way to success making lists of their own. The subordination of thought to the functional order of self-promotion—the abstracting power of the social totality—assures that the gutted, self-evident, and interchange-able results cannot help but shine. Above each of these names—and now among them Adorno—it reads: "Your choice!" The mass culture betrayal is the same as always: what appears as the familiar in *Late Marxism* is at every point the genuinely estranged.

Introduction to T. W. Adorno's
"The Idea of Natural-History"

Missing Background

Theodor W. Adorno presented "The Idea of Natural-History"[1] on July 15, 1932, as a lecture at a meeting of the Frankfurt chapter of the Kant Society.[2] The society's yearly register, published in its journal *Kant-Studien,* is an important document. That year its register lists Paul Tillich, who supervised Adorno's inaugural dissertation, as the local director. Along with a variety of details, the society's business address appears as "Horkheimer, Viktoria Allee 17." A year later the register's column for Frankfurt is blank except under the heading for local directors. There, in parentheses, catastrophe takes pains to prove its alliance with discretion: "(Director to be chosen.)"[3]

Original History of Style

The style of Adorno's early essay can be understood from the perspective of his mature work, which is emphatically artificial. His last writings, particularly *Negative Dialectics* and *Aesthetic Theory*, are written at the limits of German syntax: articles are often deleted;[4] the reference of pronouns is frequently obscure and sometimes irreducibly ambiguous; prepositional objects are almost as a rule elliptical; the subject of a clause may be deleted and reappear in the form of a relative clause;[5] the reflexive pronoun—*sich*—is deferred until the end of the sentence; the negation—*nicht*—may appear, unconventionally, at the beginning of the sentence;[6] foreign, classical, and archaic terms recur regularly; adverbs are positioned ungrammatically and accordingly accented. All these techniques break the normal rhythm of the sentence and not only demand persistently reconstructive labor on the reader's part, but bring concepts into otherwise unavailable association.[7] In agreement with Benjamin's dictum that "argumentation is fruitless," the entire structure of assumption, development, proof, and conclusion is discarded in favor of a dialectic of the object itself.[8] Any subjectively imposed order, Adorno wrote, is a mask for chaos. This critique extends to the usual apparatus of transitions. Every variation on phrases such as "now we can see" becomes an index of a loss of the matter at hand. These transitions rarely occur in Adorno's writings with the result that the progression of thought may initially appear fragmented and abrupt.[9] In "The Idea of Natural-History" this ultimately paratactical style had not yet been mastered. The artificial appears under its regressive aspect; it has a degree of rigidity, a trace of which could always be found in Adorno's personal manner, which Bloch once summed up as his "mandarin formality."

Philosophical Costume

This linguistic posture establishes the continuity between Adorno's early and later style and makes this early essay immediately recognizable to readers of his mature works. But the internal dynamic of this stylistic posture also explains the aspect of this essay that will be least familiar. Many will be surprised by phrases calling for an "ontological reorientation of history" or promoting "ontological dignity." These lines must appear extraordinarily compromising with that same Heidegger who was later drawn and quartered in the *Jargon of Authenticity*. To compare these two works from opposite ends of Adorno's career in just one regard: where the call to "dignity," just quoted, copies rhapsodic appeals in *Being and Time* to the sublimity of being, the same phrase in Adorno's later work is an object of analysis: "Dignity was never anything more than the attitude of self-preservation aspiring to be more than that."[10] These two positions vis-à-vis Heidegger are not, however, as utterly distinct as they at first appear. Imitation and rejection are more than opposites. While Adorno had been directly involved in the neo-ontological movement in the mid-twenties, he had fully separated from it by the time that he presented his lecture on natural-history. Why he nevertheless ended up on this occasion cloaked partially in conceptual Heideggerian lederhosen is initially indicated by Leo Strauss in his description of the situation of philosophy in the early 1930s:

> One has to go back to Hegel to find another professor of philosophy who affected in a comparable manner the thought of Germany. . . . His domination grew almost continuously in extent and in intensity. . . . Eventually a state was reached which the outsider is inclined to describe as paralysis of the critical faculties: philosophizing now seems to have been transformed into listening with reverence to the incipient mythoi of Heidegger.[11]

Heidegger's philosophy was the philosophical form of mythic terror taken by the disaster of the 1930s. This is what Adorno wanted to present, as well as find a way to survive, in those passages of "The Idea of Natural-History" in which he developed the conceptual synonymity of myth and nature in Heidegger. As Adorno writes, neo-ontology is nothing "other than what I mean by 'nature.'"[12] Neo-ontology is a fateful—and in this sense "natural"—structure of existential invariables. And just as all of Adorno's writings became a struggle with myth, which he analyzed with great perspicacity in his study of the *Odyssey* in *Dialectic of Enlightenment*, his own study of Ulysses' tactics in the later work reveals aspects of Adorno's resistance to Heidegger. There Adorno shows that in Homer the course of Ulysses' voyage is the production of a second natural immanence. The self—Ulysses—develops in this voyage by becoming like what it masters at the same time that it dissolves its affinity to its object. In this voyage the moment that most illumines the relation of Adorno to Heidegger is the moment when, blinded, Polyphemus demands the name of his attacker, and the cunning Ulysses replies "*Udeis*," discovering a pun on his own name meaning "nobody." This is the name that the furious titan then helplessly bellows in calling his brothers to his assistance: "Nobody" has hurt him, he cries, and his brothers mockingly fail him in his plight.

In his interpretation of this passage Adorno shows that Ulysses made this punning discovery in fright, becoming "nobody" as a model of Polyphemus's undifferentiated chthonic nature. As elsewhere in the episode with the titan, Ulysses asserts himself through self-sacrifice. He takes Polyphemus's side against himself, at one point offering him wine to better enjoy a slaughter that would have eventually included Ulysses himself: "Take Cyclops and drink. Wine goes well with human flesh." Ulysses exploits this self-sacrificial regression to find the opportunity to blind the Cyclops and escape. By making himself like Polyphemus, in answering to his needs, he gains power over him, destroys first nature, and differentiates himself from what would overwhelm him. Yet this differentiation is apocryphal. Ulysses emerges from the struggle a self-identical, invariable, force of nature as the power of self-preservation, a second immanence, that does to itself and first nature, by self-control, what it once feared from first nature: it destroys particularity. He has become "nobody." The historical voyage itself has become a natural event. External mimicry of the natural force of the cyclops becomes internal self-identical mimesis, ultimately the order of the *ratio*, which is itself a structure of the self-sacrifice of particularity to universality. Thus, in its conscious control of nature, the self has triumphed by becoming opaque to its self-reproduction as second nature.

A similar process of enlightenment can be observed in Adorno's early lecture. In those moments where Adorno mirrors the threat of Heidegger it is in the attempt, familiar as much from the *Odyssey* as from vaudevillian slapstick mime routines, to draw his opponent into movements that he would have otherwise resisted: Adorno wants to transform neo-ontology's mythically reconciling formulation of the interwovenness of nature and history into a dialectic in which their mutual and antagonistic conflict will collide and collapse. This is the conscious part of the maneuver, but it demonstrates deeper realities. For like the wooden gestures of the hypercultivated muscle that exalts the tension of its own fear, the rigidity of Adorno's essay mimics the menace it faces. The rigidified self, structured by internalized sacrifice, pays for its survival by forgetting that it has renounced itself in the process. The nemesis of the ruse of the dialectic of enlightenment is that the control gained over the other amounts to the forfeiture of true self-control. It becomes understandable, then, that Adorno comes closest to following Heidegger's lead at the central point in the essay where Adorno seeks to present himself most emphatically as himself. It is this point, to be discussed, that gives insight into a fundamental problem with the essay.

"The Idea of Natural-History" was published only posthumously.[13] There are good reasons why Adorno might have withheld its publication. The essay is awkwardly constructed, at points repetitive, at others opaquely desultory; it also relies bulkily on lengthy quotation. Much of what is said of importance appears, and better said, in works that Adorno published soon after.[14] Yet the essay independently contains several important formulations, and Adorno was not generally reluctant to substantially revise and publish his early works, especially one that he would continue to refer back to and quote right up through his very last major works. It may be, then, that he refrained from publishing the essay because of compromising Heideggerian elements in the context of what became a lifelong struggle with the ontologist. But, if so, the Heideggerian phraseology so far discussed would not have been decisive. Adorno could have edited it out without changing the essay's organization, just as he dropped several positive references to Heidegger from his essays of the mid-twenties before allowing their republication. Moreover, there are points in Adorno's mature works where somewhat similar formulations can be found.[15] A crucial element of the essay, however, that could not have been excised, and in which a positive regard for Heidegger is condensed, is the term *natural-history* (*Naturgeschichte*) itself.

Philosophical Terminology

"Natural history," in both German and English, translates *historia naturalis,* literally "the history of nature." In the Latin and Greek sense of history it means much that it occasionally, and confusingly, continues to mean in modern English: the report of an inquiry into nature having nothing necessarily to do with any temporal dimension.[16] The German term was coined in the eighteenth century as part of a nationalist movement to supplant the foreign terminology that then dominated philosophical and scientific language. The new term, however, immediately acquired pressing ambiguity as the result of the changing concepts of nature and history. When nature was conceived in scientific literature as historical, in the modern sense, natural history acquired a new literal sense that conflicted with its classical meaning. The two developments, the terminological and the conceptual, coincide importantly in Kant's work. For Kant was the first to write a scientific history of nature as a process of unending, infinite creation; he was responsible for discovering the origins of the Earth in the "dark abyss of time," arguably the most crucial scientific event in the development of romanticism in that romanticism is predicated on the perception of nature as being historical.[17] But Kant was also the most significant figure, perhaps the first, to promote the formal limitation of the ambiguity of the term *natural history*. He proposed that its meaning be restricted to the investigation of nature's self-development from primitive chaos to rational order.[18]

As Adorno points out in his lecture, he himself is not concerned with natural history in either the classical or the Kantian sense. Rather, his interest in the term is made clear by what he explains as the "idea of natural-history": to comprehend an object as natural where it appears most historical and as historical where it appears most natural. The idea of natural-history, then, is the dialectic that can be extracted from a literal analysis of the term's ambiguity: the history of nature is nature grasped as historical; natural history is the historical grasped as natural.

This formal decomposition of the term, a pun, gives a historical concept a neologistic turn. When Adorno recognized this, he would have rejected it and the essay to which it was central. It is easy to imagine that Benjamin, who may well have heard the lecture presentation, would have criticized it on just this basis. This criticism was a constant element of Benjamin's often reformulated works: in his early writings it appears, for example, as a critique of romantic reflection; in the later works it can be found in his critique of the ahistorical aspect of Mallarmé's *correspondences* by contrast with those of Baudelaire. Throughout, this critique was that of arbitrary signification that is the linguistic form of the Fall, or, less theologically, the vitiation of experience. What would have made Adorno's recognition of the neologistic character of this term particularly biting is that it would have converged with his own critique of Heidegger, whose work is built out of neologisms and terms transformed into neologism by means of often spurious etymologizing. By the time that Adorno presented "The Idea of Natural-History," he had in fact already developed this critique of Heidegger's language in the "Theses on the Language of Philosophy" (1930).

"Freely posited language"—Adorno could be referring to terms like *Dasein* that claim to gain the word's depth by pursuing a literal content (*Da-sein*, being-there)[19]—"advances the philosopher's pretension to freedom from the compulsion of history."[20] Adorno repeatedly analyzes the illusoriness of this form of linguistic manipulation. In *Dialectic of Enlightenment,* in particular, Adorno shows this to be the linguistic form of Ulysses' regressive escape from Polyphemus. Ulysses eludes death by outwitting the fatefulness of the mythical name in which the word commands the object: Ulysses exploits the distinction between sign and intention in the discovery that *Udeis* has multiple meanings. He is able to elude Polyphemus on the basis of a legalism. Yet this maneuver, while it prevails over myth, does not dissolve it. The immutable mythic word, a formula of unchanging nature, is replaced by a second formalism: "From the formalism of mythic names and ordinances, which would rule men and history as does nature, there emerges nominalism—or the prototype of bourgeois thinking."[21] The form of the nominalist term is as indifferent to its content as was the mythical word that ruled its content. The nominalist separation of form and content reappears in the idealist theory of language in which "concepts and with them words are abbreviations of a multiplicity of characteristics whose unity is constituted solely by consciousness."[22] Idealism does not solve the nominalist separation of form and content, but both camouflages and potentiates the division by positing subjectivity as the ultimate unity of language, one fully indifferent to the content of language. Hegel's own readiness to decompose terms according to their literal content, when it suited him—the best-known instance is his analysis of *er-innern*—is evidence that Heidegger's linguistic innovations, rather than criticizing the idealist tradition, follows in its wake. Thus in his early essay on language Adorno could claim that "Heidegger's language flees from history but never escapes it,"[23] on the same basis that he later showed that while Odysseus flees mythical nature he only reproduces it.

At the end of the essay on language Adorno writes that the philosopher may "no more take a word as simply given as invent one himself."[24] Yet "natural-history" effectively becomes such an invented term; its content is developed in the same literalizing fashion that Ulysses extracted the content of *Udeis.* It stands implicitly allied with such arch Heideggerian terms as *Dasein.* Its position in Adorno's essay, then, would correspond to the concept of *Aufklaerung* in *Dialectic of Enlightenment* if Adorno had developed the term according to the potential of *aufklaeren* to mean "to empty" as well as "to illuminate" rather than developing it according to the philosophical experience sedimented in the word. "Natural-history," as an unconscious reflection of Heidegger, is an unreflected mythical element in Adorno's essay. It is the form of the young Adorno's autonomy: quintessential dialectic of enlightenment, that is, self-assertion as self-denial.

Natural-History and Natural History

Just as Adorno left this essay unpublished, he also dropped the term *natural-history* in the form of a double entendre. In all of his later writings the concept *natural history* bears the sense that it has in Marx's later works, in Benjamin's study of the Baroque, and occasionally in Hegel: it is history in a natural condition. In his late essay, "Theory and Practice," for example, Adorno characteristically writes of the situation "in which natural history perpetuates itself."[25] In *Negative Dialectics* natural history occurs as society's "prolonged natural history."[26] The reason, however, that Adorno's early essay has been of particular interest is not because it and its central term were left behind, but because it contains central elements of Adorno's mature works in a still molten stage. In this regard the most casual comment in "The Idea of Natural-History" is portentous. Where Adorno writes in this lecture that what he has to say "will remain on the level of an attempt (*Versuch*) to solve the problem," in his later writings he names the essay (*Versuch*) itself as the singular modern form of philosophical consciousness. He once summarized this form as follows: "The essay as form consists in the capacity to perceive the historical, that is, manifestations of objective spirit, 'culture,' as if they were nature."[27] In "The Idea of Natural-History" Adorno developed this form of philosophical insight for the first time by following in this essay precisely the same plan that he used in *Negative Dialectics*, one of his last works: a critique of Heidegger is followed by the presentation of the central concepts of the form of the critique—respectively, the idea of natural-history and the idea of negative dialectics—and concludes with interpretive models ultimately directed toward the question of the recuperation of aesthetic and metaphysical contents.

Philosophy of Nature

In the first part of "The Idea of Natural-History" Adorno develops a critique of Heidegger by situating him in the context of modern German philosophy's attempt to solve the problem of historicist relativism. Adorno formulates this problem as that of conceiving the unity of history and nature. The history that he traces is paradoxical in several regards, the first being that it shows the convergence of neo-ontology with the historicism that the then contemporary philosophical development sought to annul. Neo-Kantianism, the dominant pre–World War I philosophy, attempted to rebut historical relativism by grounding individual autonomy in epistemological structures. Historical immanence was to be superseded by the pure immanence of consciousness. Adorno begins his review of the subsequent course of philosophy with phenomenology's attempt to direct philosophy away from the logical investigation of the constructive laws of consciousness, which had resulted in a subjective formalism, toward the investigation of essential, ultimately ontic structures of being.[28] Adorno argues that in this phenomenology failed to overcome the neo-Kantian aporia, however, for it also took the *ratio* as the starting point of its investigations. Like the neo-Kantians, phenomenology posits a dualism of nature and history. This is evident, as is its aporetic result, in Max Scheler's oeuvre. The question of the meaning of being could only be posed from the position of the autonomous *ratio* with the result that the meanings subsequently produced were necessarily subjective. The attempt to assure a historical meaning only asserts the historically given, which may, furthermore, turn out to be meaningless. Up to this point neo-ontology and historicism were fully antagonistic. Historicism rejected neo-ontology for dragging arbitrary philosophical elements into history. Neo-ontology, on the other hand, objected that historicism was unconscious of its ontological presuppositions. Heidegger's critique of phenomenology transformed this antagonism. For him essences cannot be sought beyond history. Being is not the antithesis of history, rather they converge in *Dasein*'s fundamental structure of historicity. Since the understanding transforms every element of life into a project (*Ent-wurf*) of possibility, in principle absorbing "the fullness of being's determinations," both the opposition of nature and history and of ontology and historicism should disappear along with the problem of relativism.

For Adorno, however, this is no solution. Heidegger does not overcome the problem of relativism, but simply organizes several tactics for obscuring an inability to interpret the empirical in its full multiplicity. Adorno only hints at an example of neo-ontology's limitations, briefly referring to the difficulty that Heidegger would have understanding any aspect of the French Revolution. In keeping with Adorno's comments, he might have argued that while existential historiography could, for example, follow through the authenticity of Danton's decisions, it would necessarily remain obtuse to what these decisions were actually about; existential interpretation would remain indifferent to political and economic mediations falling outside the immediate context of Danton's understanding. Or, to expand Adorno's argument by pointing out another sphere that is lost to neo-ontology: however much neo-ontology is proud of solving the problem of the opposition of mind and body by arguing that this problem is only an abstraction from Dasein's primordial being-in-the-world, whenever Dasein appears unclouded by these inauthentic categories, it has lost its body. For Dasein is never hungry, sleepy, or sexually aroused.[29] Not only must these areas of historical-biological facticity somehow be reeled up into the "project" in the category of contingency—a tautological procedure—but the structure of Dasein, in existentials such as being-toward-death, is simply the sedimentation of conceptually impenetrable empirical elements. The empirical is not actually interpreted but only set up as a nexus of absolutes.

Thus, where Heidegger claims to overcome idealism, Adorno is able to demonstrate that neo-ontology's fundamentally tautological mastery of contingency reveals an idealist core. The starting point of Heidegger's philosophy, like neo-Kantianism, remains autonomous reason. This is evident in neo-ontology's intention to analyze being in its totality, effectively the claim of an absolute subject and, second, in the priority of possibility over actuality that is implicit in the claim to totality. The superiority of the category over its elements explains the abstractness of neo-ontological interpretation and the tautological direction of its language, which amounts to the assertion of the identity of subject and object. This tautological form prohibits ontology from being able to "interpret itself as that which it is: namely, a product of, and internally related to, the idealist *ratio*."

Historicity, then, Adorno concludes, is only an "illusory solution to the problem of the reconciliation of nature and history." In the tradition of subjectivistic idealism, it actually assumes their division at the point where categorical thought excludes facticity. Heidegger simply reduces history to nature by subsuming it under historicity. Rather than the reduction of history to a natural fact, Adorno urges, it is necessary to be able to grasp history itself as nature and nature itself as history. This capacity would overcome the subjectivistic predominance of thought over its object and amount to an actual solution to the problem of relativism.

Immanent Criticism and Memory of Nature

Brief as this critique of Heidegger is, there is obviously a great deal to be said about it: while Adorno criticizes Heideggerian ontology as idealist given the priority of the *ratio* evident in the pretention to totality—a critique that in its focus on the problems of contingency, actuality, and the glorification of the status quo importantly parallels Marx's critique of Hegel—the form of Adorno's study is itself part of the idealist tradition. It is immanent criticism that has carried out a critique of idealism's claim to totality: Heidegger's work is measured according to its own concept, historicity, yet, in contrast to the Hegelian movement of the concept, no systematic hierarchy of concepts emerges. Not only is Heidegger treated immanently, but so is the modern history of philosophy. It is measured against its claim to objectivity. As is evident in Heidegger in particular, the course of this history is altogether one in which the *ratio* consumes its relation to its object. However the *ratio* attempts to establish objectivity, it seals itself off from objectivity. Historically, the *ratio* produces a second nature— ultimately, the mythical, invariable existentials of neo-ontology.

These absolutes are nothing else than meanings inserted into reality that are rebarbative to interpretation because their starting point is itself the *ratio*. Precisely here Adorno potentially has his greatest contribution to make by indicating an approach to the interpretation of these fragments of second nature as allegorical elements conceived as part of the "original history of signification," which Adorno will explain in the second section of his essay.

But it is first worth noting that if the philosophical history Adorno has so far sketched seems familiar to readers of *Dialectic of Enlightenment*, this is because "The Idea of Natural-History" is proleptically a sustained reflection on this dialectic. The history of German philosophy that Adorno has presented closely models his later interpretation of Ulysses' voyage as the development of the *ratio* in which history becomes second nature, unconscious of itself as nature as a result of the repression of mimesis in its metamorphosis into the *ratio*. What Adorno terms the "original history of signification" in the early essay will become the "original history of subjectivity"[30] traced in *Dialectic of Enlightenment*. At the same time that Adorno presents his basic model of history in the study of Heidegger, he also states the central problem of his philosophy: if the *ratio* consumes its relation to its object and thus produces a pseudo-objectivity, how can thought justify its own process and continue to think? Or, in the terms that Adorno developed in *Dialectic of Enlightenment*, if mimesis as a process of identification with the aggressor results in the repression of mimesis that knowledge to be knowledge requires, how is it possible to recuperate mimesis without simply reenacting the dialectic of enlightenment? Memory of nature in the subject is the answer that runs throughout Adorno's work. In "The Idea of Natural-History" this form of memory is conceived as the problem of perceiving transience within meaning, that is, as revealing the content of second nature. Meaning is the ruins of nature: "When the world of convention approaches, it can be deciphered in that its meaning is shown to be precisely its transience."

One of the several obscure aspects of Adorno's essay is that in it he does not actually explain how this form of interpretation is to occur. He only says that Walter Benjamin showed this perception of nature as history to be the form of allegory and indicates that this form is somehow related to the organization of constellations of concepts. But how are allegory and constellations related? This can only be briefly answered here by pointing to a central aspect of Adorno's essay already referred to. While Adorno cites Georg Lukács and Benjamin as the origin of the idea of natural-history, the major characteristic of the essay is its Hegelian form, beginning with the initial intention of developing the internal mediation of nature and history. The Hegelian intention extends right into the presentation of the origins of the idea of natural-history in the second section. Adorno introduces Lukács by giving him credit for having conceived the transformation of history into nature. Yet Adorno did not have to introduce Lukács for this purpose; the thought is equally central to Benjamin's work. In a much later essay, in fact, Adorno wrote that Benjamin had the power to regard history as nature, "as scarcely another."[31] The decisive reason for Lukács in the essay is Adorno's interest in introducing the concept of "second nature" as a Hegelian concept that does not occur as such in Benjamin's writings.[32] This concept allowed Adorno to set up a symmetrical group of concepts of nature, history, and second nature amenable to a Hegelian treatment. It would be possible to show that, in the Hegelian intention of this essay, Adorno was already at work on a critique of ontological elements in Benjamin's thought. Benjamin's study of the Baroque is a research of origins, which Adorno distantly criticizes. The problem of interpretation, he wrote, "can not simply be a matter of demonstrating that in history itself original-historical themes constantly turn up." Adorno overcame the ontological impulse of Benjamin's work while maintaining the intention of all allegory and constellative thought in the form of immanent critique, in the Hegelian movement of concepts freed from the claim to totality. It is this form of thought, evident in the first section of Adorno's essay, that Adorno made explicit in *Dialectic of Enlightenment*. There he writes that the concept per se "does not merely distance men from nature, but as the self-consideration of thought . . . allows the distance which perpetuates injustice to be measured. By virtue of this remembrance of nature in the subject . . . enlightenment is universally opposed to domination."[33] This negative dialectic is the form in which the *ratio* may continue to be pursued, albeit transformed. The allegory of the *Odyssey* is interpreted according to this intention. Measuring the distance between what an object claims to be and is, between Ulysses as what he presents himself, that is, as the bearer of culture, and as second nature, gains the content of Ulysses' voyage: the repression of internal and external nature. At this point Adorno's dialectic converges again with Benjamin. For Benjamin the idea is to its phenomena as is an expression to a face: the idea is expressive. For Adorno, likewise, the idea is not the Hegelian totality, in which expression is sublated, rather it is perceived with *thaumazein*. Here the Platonic *shock,* the ecstatic intuition of the idea, becomes the transformation of history into nature, in other words, the release of transience in the apparently inert fragments of second nature. It is distinguished from the Platonic *shock,* however, in that it is the perception of a particular rather than of a universal.

Critique of Natural-History and the Recuperation of Mimesis

Memory of nature in the subject, then, is a critique of illusion. Philosophy, Adorno wrote, "has no other measure than the collapse of illusion (*Schein*)."[34] It is a process of opening up concepts whose content is "memory of suffering." Concepts have this content only because of the experience of the process of domination that is layered in them. This determines the direction of philosophy. As Adorno wrote in "The Idea of Natural-History," concepts must be treated "as they occur in the language of philosophy," that is, according to their historical content: the nature that has passed away within them. As has already been seen, however, the term *natural-history* is not developed in this fashion in Adorno's essay. Yet the form of the term is not unallied with that of immanent criticism. In an essay on Hegel Adorno treats identification with the aggressor as the core of Hegel's dialectic, the model of the ruse of reason; reminiscent of Ulysses' skill, it is "peasant cunning": "instructed so long to humble itself in front of the powerful and to dedicate itself to their needs till it succeeds in winning away power for itself."[35] This form can be traced into the most microscopic details of Hegel's work. In his *Philosophy of Nature*, for instance, in which spirit develops through every stage of its otherness, sound—as a unity within the element of externality—is described as "the cry of the ideal under foreign power, but withal its triumph over this power since it preserves itself therein."[36] Adorno reproduces this thought in his model of the name as "the gasp of surprise that accompanies the experience of the extraordinary. It fixes transcendence of the unknown in relation to the known."[37] The gasp of surprise is mimesis of the overwhelming object. In terror, however, the self nevertheless establishes its victory. The name initiates the distinction of sign and image that is the origin of the explanation and control of nature.[38] Adorno is a critic of this ruse insofar as, in winning power for itself, the subject makes itself into a model of its former oppression. Yet while the name originates in the dialectic of enlightenment, the recovery of mimesis is in the name that is radical identification with the aggressor, thought that follows its objects to the point that "the inherent consequence of the object is transformed into its own criticism"[39]—to the point, that is, that the object destroys its own illusion. By immanent critique the object names itself. This is rational mimesis, the recovery of the name from the course of domination. Its ultimate aspiration is reconciliation with myth. The intentional form of Adorno's "The Idea of Natural-History," then, is the transformation of the regressive form of the term, *natural-history.*

Second Nature and the Recuperation of Illusion

Immanent criticism, as the critique of illusion, could not be the strict rejection of illusion. For the strength of this form of criticism lodges nowhere else. Immanent criticism can only break illusion by the strength of illusion itself, in other words, by the strength of the concept's claim to identity, for only identity has the capacity to criticize identity. Adorno's philosophy is for this reason the dialectical reflection on the critique and recuperation of semblance. In this reflection Adorno's negative dialectics and his sociological studies converge with his aesthetic writings. This is the mediation that Adorno develops in the third section of "The Idea of Natural-History" where these dimensions of his thought appear in their mutually implicating complexity. This final section begins by developing the thought that is at the core of the historical study of part 1 and which, with the slightest modification, includes the central concepts of *Dialectic of Enlightenment:* myth is shown to be not simply a static foundation but, on the contrary, in it the new and the repetitive are mediated in one another. The historical is mythical and the mythical historical. Not only are they intertwined, but the historically new appears in the mythical. This is apparent in the phenomenon of the semblance of second nature, which is a semblance because it is the mere appearance of meaning. Although it is historically produced, this semblance appears mythical: that is, as archaic, as emphatically expressive, as an engulfing whirlpool.[40] "The Idea of Natural-History" begins to explain this phenomenon in order to elucidate mythical semblance as implicitly containing the possibility of reconciliation: "the definitive transcendent element of myth, reconciliation, also inheres in semblance." Adorno hardly explains himself: "I refer you to the structure of the original-historical in semblance itself, where semblance, in its thusness (*Sosein*), proves itself to be historically produced." In other words, the element of reconciliation in semblance appears when its content of transience is expressed, there where the archaic reveals itself as the historical. In its transience, second nature presents itself as first nature.

Thus second nature proves to be, in Benjamin's terms, an allegorical object: a *facies hippocratica*.

Adorno is here developing the full content of the concept of second nature. In opposition to both Benjamin and the early Lukács, Adorno did not reify the critique of reification. In alliance with Hegel spirit can only come to itself by way of its other, and therefore reification is not conceived as strictly negative. In art, myth becomes its opposite. Convention and its meaninglessness would come to term in the release from the spell of false meaning. The obscurity of Adorno's brief early passage is repeatedly clarified by innumerable discussions in his later work. To quote just one, "Art's truth appears guaranteed more by its denial of any meaning in organized society, of which it will have no part—accomplished by its own organized absence of meaning—than by any capability of positive meaning within itself."[41] Through complete control over the material, at the limit of convention, the mythical becomes expressive, "passions are no longer simulated, but rather genuine emotions of the unconscious—of shock, of trauma—are registered without disguise through the medium of music."[42] Only by way of illusion, in other words, is art able to destroy illusion. "The radicalism with which the technical work of art destroys aesthetic illusion makes illusion responsible for the technical work of art."[43]

Art is semblance that, by its completion, causes semblance to collapse. The fundamental problem of art, then, is that it is the critique of reification by way of reification. This thought was the basis of Adorno's polemic against engaged art: in spite of its dogged clearheadedness, engaged art would actually return art to magic by wanting to strip off art's illusoriness.[44] Engaged art, which thinks it is opposed to abstractionism, fails to recognize its affinity with all modern art's attempt to do away with its semblance. For Adorno the problem of aesthetics becomes the attempt to justify semblance. This is the content of his *Aesthetic Theory*. It seeks the validation of art through the justification of its semblance as the capacity to criticize semblance.

Second nature, then, is not only convention, but potentially a new nature. In his study of *Brave New World* Adorno criticizes Huxley's disdain for Lenina, a robotic, test-tube creation, the quintessence of mechanically inhibitionless sexuality and artificial charm, with whom the novel's protagonist falls in love. According to Adorno, Huxley misunderstood his creation: "Because she is at one with convention down to her very core, the tension between the conventional and the natural dissolves, and with it the violence in which the injustice of convention consists. . . . Through total mediation . . . a new immediacy, a new humanity would arise."[45] Adorno has the same to say of Anton Webern's tonal invention: the purely artificial tone becomes a new natural tone.[46] Similarly, Ulysses' voyage, a work of artifice, is not only a course of regression. Even though artifice is shown to be "the means by which the adventuring self loses itself in order to preserve itself,"[47] Adorno does not allow these concepts to become static. Ulysses' artifice is also seen to become its own opposite: after returning home, Ulysses must again set out to appease Poseidon, who was enraged with Ulysses for having blinded his son Polyphemus. Ulysses is instructed to carry an oar inland until he meets someone who will mistake the oar for a winnowing fan. This will make the god laugh and in this laughter wounded nature will surrender its rage.[48] Adorno emphasizes the significance of this passage of the epic, and it is important to understand why. The oar that has been brought inland has renounced its function. The artifice of self-preservation has, like Lenina, become pure artifice, related to art, whose problem, Adorno writes, is "to make things of which we do not know what they are."[49] Similarly, the artificiality of Adorno's language can irritate because at every point it rejects the possibility of grasping the immediate as anything but the illusion of nature.[50] Adorno's style, in other words, aspires to be the completion of the ruse of immanent criticism, ultimately the model of a second nature.

Postscriptum

Readers of Adorno's essay will discover that in it Adorno develops a concept of dialectical nature—a code word for Marxism in his lecture—as a form of interpretation that delineates the possibility for the comprehension of all signification precisely in its meaninglessness. This meaninglessness turns out not to be an arbitrariness of reference, but rather fragments in which suffering nature can be presented. Nature and history, in other words, are not presented as shifting one magically into the other. Rather they are dialectically mediated in each other in an antagonism whose emerging irreducibility presents what Adorno would later term, in *Dialectic of Enlightenment*, "memory of nature." In this early lecture, then, Adorno presented an idea of the truth of nature in a way that would grasp all that the neo-ontologists of the so-called Frankfurt discussions were claiming to arrive at as the truth in history in their ascent to the primordial meanings that were to be sifted out of history.

Adorno developed this concept of materialism from a critique of Benjamin's early, non-Marxist work on Baroque German drama and in "The Idea of Natural-History" it is possible to watch this transformation of Benjamin's thought, which Adorno carries out through an introduction of psychoanalytic thinking. In a single sentence Adorno summarizes the results of his early dissertation on Freud: "I would like to recall that psychoanalytic research presents this antithesis [of nature and history] with full clarity in the distinction between archaic symbols, to which no associations may attach themselves, and inter-subjective, dynamic, inner-historical symbols, which can all be eliminated and transformed into psychical actuality and present knowledge." The psychoanalytic model of interpretation thus became for Adorno a form in which mythical nature could be critically comprehended. This then allowed him to translate Benjamin's concepts into a form of Hegelianism that has been deprived of the possible affirmation of the course of history while, at the same time, demonstrating that neo-ontology itself inherited the Hegelian identity of subject and object in its actual, mythologizing obtuseness to historical reality— one version, really, of Adorno's thesis on Kierkegaard.

The whole of Adorno's philosophy, therefore, right through *Negative Dialectics*, stood before him in this brief talk as a capacity to present the reality of history with an unprecedented starkness of philosophical consciousness. In many regards, it is evident, the development of this model of interpretation compelled Adorno to leave psychoanalysis and much of Benjamin behind. What was abandoned in this seminally productive philosophical development, however, is also worthy of consideration, and it too is available to be studied here in Adorno's brief lecture.

The Idea of Natural-History

Theodor W. Adorno

ALLOW ME TO PREFACE MY REMARKS today by saying that I am not
going to give a lecture in the usual sense of communicating results or
presenting a systematic statement. Rather, what I have to say will remain on the level of an essay; it is no more than an attempt to take up
and further develop the problems of the so-called Frankfurt discussion.[1] I recognize that many uncomplimentary things have been said
about this discussion, but I am equally aware that it approaches the
problem correctly and that it would be wrong always to begin again at
the beginning.

First permit me a few words on terminology. Although the topic is
natural-history, it is not concerned with natural history in the traditional, prescientific sense of the history of nature, nor with the history
of nature where nature is the object of natural science. The concept of
nature employed here has absolutely nothing to do with that of the
mathematical sciences. I cannot develop in advance what nature and
history will mean in the following context. However, I do not overstep
myself if I say that the real intention here is to dialectically overcome
the usual antithesis of nature and history. Therefore, wherever I oper-
ate with the concepts of nature and history, no ultimate definitions are
meant, rather I am pursuing the intention of pushing these concepts to

a point where they are mediated in their apparent difference. The concept of nature that is to be dissolved is one that, if I translated it into standard philosophical terminology, would come closest to the concept of myth. This concept is also vague, and its exact sense cannot be given in preliminary definitions but only in the course of analysis. By it is meant what has always been, what as fatefully arranged predetermined being underlies history and appears in history; it is substance in history. What is delimited by these expressions is what I mean here by "nature." The question that arises is that of the relationship of this nature to what we understand by history, where history means that mode of conduct established by tradition that is characterized primarily by the occurrence of the qualitatively new; it is a movement that does not play itself out in mere identity, mere reproduction of what has always been, but rather one in which the new occurs, it is a movement that gains its true character through what appears in it as new.

I would like to develop what I call the idea of natural-history on the basis of an analysis or, more correctly, an overview of the question of ontology within the current debate. This requires beginning with "the natural." For the question of ontology, as it is formulated at present, is none other than what I mean by "nature." I will then begin at another point and attempt to develop the concept of natural-history out of the problematic of the philosophy of history. In the course of discussion this concept will already substantially gain its content and concreteness. After the formulation of these two questions has been sketched out, I will attempt to articulate the concept of natural-history itself and analyze the elements by which it appears to be characterized.

I

To consider, then, first of all, the problem of the present ontological situation: if you pursue the question of ontology as it has been formulated in the context of so-called phenomenology and indeed especially in the context of post-Husserlian phenomenology, that is, from Scheler on, one can conclude that its initial intention was to overcome the subjectivistic standpoint of philosophy. It meant to replace a philosophy that aims at the dissolution of all categories of being into categories of thought, and that believes itself able to ground all objectivity in certain fundamental structures of subjectivity, by an approach that establishes another kind of being, a region of being that is different in principle, a transsubjective, an ontic region of being. And ontology is at issue so long as the logos is to be developed from this ὄν (being). It is indeed the fundamental paradox of all modern ontological thought that the means with which the attempt is made to establish transsubjective being is none other than the same subjective reason that had earlier erected the infrastructure of critical idealism.[2] Phenomenological-ontological thought presents itself as an attempt to secure transsubjective being by means of autonomous reason and its language since other means and another language are not available. Now, the ontological question of being can be articulated in two forms: In one form it is the question of being itself, what, since Kant's first critique, as the thing in itself, has been pushed back beyond the reach of philosophical inquiry and then drawn back out again. At the same time, however, this question becomes that of the *meaning* of being, the meaningfulness of the existing or of the meaning of being as, simply, possibility. It is precisely the double form of the question that argues powerfully for the thesis that I am propounding, that the ontological question with which we are today concerned, holds to the starting point of autonomous reason: only when reason perceives the reality that is in opposition to it as something foreign and lost to it, as a complex of things, that is, only when reality is no longer immediately accessible and reality and reason have no common meaning, only then can the question of the meaning of being be asked at all. The question of meaning is determined by the starting point of reason, but at the same time the question of the meaning of being, the axis of the early phases of phenomenology (Scheler), produces a broadly encompassing range of problems through its subjectivistic origin. For this production of meaning is none other than the insertion of subjective meanings as they have been posited by subjectivity. The insight that the question of meaning is nothing more than the insertion of subjective meaning into the existing leads to the crisis of phenomenology's first stage. The drastic expression of this crisis is the obvious instability of fundamental ontological categories that reason has to experience in its attempt to secure an order of being. As it has been shown that the factors accepted as fundamental and meaningful, as for example in Scheler's work, stem from a different sphere and are in no way themselves possibilities within being but have been derived from the existing and are indeed imbued with all the dubiousness of the existing, so the whole question of being becomes insoluble within phenomenology.[3] So far as the question of meaning can still occur, it does not imply the establishment of a sphere of significations isolated from the empirical that would be valid and always accessible; rather the question of meaning is really none other than the question τί ἦν ὄν, the question of what being itself properly *is*. The expressions: meaning and signification are ambiguous in these contexts. Meaning can be a transcendent content that, lying behind being and signified by it, can be developed by analysis. On the other hand, meaning can also be the interpretation of the existing itself with regard to what characterizes it as being, but without this interpreted being thereby having been proven meaningful. It is therefore possible to pose the question of the meaning of being as the signification of the *category* of being, as that which being really is, but that, in terms of the initial question, the existing will turn out to be not meaningful but meaningless, as is increasingly the case today.

If this reversal of the question of being has occurred, then the single initial intention of the original ontological reversal disappears, namely, that of the turn toward the ahistorical. This was the case with Scheler's work, at least in his early work (which has remained the more influential) where he attempted to construct a heaven of ideas on the foundation of a purely rational intuition of nonhistorical and eternal content that radiates over and above everything empirical and has a normative character to which the empirical allows access. But, at the same time, there is a basic tension between the meaningful and essential that lies behind the historically manifested and the sphere of history itself. In the origins of phenomenology there is a dualism of nature and history. This dualism ("nature" in this context means that which is ahistorical, Platonically ontological), and the original intention of the ontological reversal that it embodies, has corrected itself. The question of being no longer has the significance of the Platonic question of the extent of the static and qualitatively different ideas that stand in contrast to the existing, the empirical, in a normative relationship or in a relationship of tension. Rather, the tension disappears; the existing itself becomes meaning, and a grounding of being beyond history is replaced by a project (*Entwurf*) of being as historicity.

This displaces the problem, and, for the moment, at least, the issues dividing ontology and historicism apparently disappear. From the perspective of history, of historical criticism, ontology seems to be either a merely formal framework that has nothing to say about the content of history and can be arbitrarily set up around the concrete, or, in the Schelerian form of material ontology, it appears as the arbitrary production of absolutes out of inner-historical facts that, perhaps for ideological purposes, are raised to the level of eternal and universal values. From the ontological point of view the problem is just the reverse, and it is this antithesis that has dominated our Frankfurt discussions: according to the ontologists all radically historical thought, all thought that aims at reducing content exclusively to historical conditions, must presuppose a project of being by which history is already given as a structure of being: only within the framework of such a project is the historical organization of particular phenomena and contents in any way possible.

Now the most recent turn of phenomenology, if one may still call it that, has carried out a correction at this point by eliminating the pure antithesis of history and being. By, on the one hand, renouncing the Platonic heaven of ideas and, on the other, by, in observing being, regarding it as life, false stasis and formalism have been eliminated. For the project (*Entwurf*) appears to absorb the fullness of the elements of being and even the suspicion of the transformation of the accidental into the absolute disappears. History itself, in its most extreme agitation, has become the basic ontological structure. At the same time, historical thought itself appears to have undergone a fundamental reversal. It is reduced to a philosophically based structure of historicity as a fundamental quality of human existence (*Dasein*). This structure is responsible for there being any history in the first place without, however, that which history is being set up in opposition to it as a finished, fixed, and foreign object. This is the point that the Frankfurt discussion has reached and where I may begin to introduce critical themes.

It appears to me that the starting point that we have arrived at here and that unifies the ontological and historical questions likewise fails to master the concrete issues or does so only by modifying its own logic and by incorporating as its content themes that do not necessarily derive from the outlined principle. I will demonstrate this with regard to just two points.

First of all, even this project is limited to general categories. The problem of historical contingency cannot be mastered by the category of historicity. One can set up a general structural category of life, but if one tries to interpret a particular phenomenon, for example, the French Revolution, though one can indeed find in it every possible element of this structure of life, as for instance that the past returns and is taken up and one can verify the meaning of the spontaneity that originates in man, discover causal context, etc., it is nevertheless impossible to relate the facticity of the French Revolution in its most extreme factual being to such categories. On the contrary, in the full breadth of the material one will find a sphere of "facticity" that cannot be explained. This is of course not my own discovery but has long since been demonstrated within the framework of ontological discussion. But it has not been previously enunciated so sharply, or, rather, it has been worked over in an expedient fashion: all facticity that will not, on its own, fit into the ontological project is piled into one category, that of contingency, of the accidental, and this category is absorbed by the project as a determination of the historical. However logically consistent this may be, it also includes the admission that the attempt to master the empirical has misfired. At the same time, this turn in the theory offers a schema for a new turn within the question of ontology. This is the turn toward tautology.

I mean nothing else than that the attempt of neo-ontological thought to come to terms with the unreachability of the empirical continually operates according to one schema: precisely where an element fails to dissolve into determinations of thought and cannot be made transparent but rather retains its pure thereness, precisely at this point the resistance of the phenomenon is transformed into a universal concept and its resistance as such is endowed with ontological value. It is the same with Heidegger's concept of being-toward-death as well as with the concept of historicity itself. The structure of historicity, in the neo-ontological formulation of the problem, only offers an apparent solution to the problem of the reconciliation of nature and history. Even though history is acknowledged to be a fundamental phenomenon, its ontological determinations or ontological interpretation is in vain because it is transfigured directly into ontology. This is the case for Heidegger, for whom history, understood as an all embracing structure of being, is equivalent to his own ontology. This is the basis of such feeble antitheses as that of history and historicity, which contain nothing but qualities of being that have been gleaned from human existence and transposed into the sphere of ontology by being subtracted from the existing and transformed into ontological determinations, aids for the interpretation of that which is basically only being repeated. This element of tautology is not due to the coincidences of the linguistic form, rather it is necessarily embedded in the ontological question itself, which holds to the ontological endeavor, but because of its rational starting point it is unable to ontologically interpret itself as what it is: namely, a product of and internally related to the starting point of the idealist ratio. This requires explanation. If there is a path that leads farther, then it can in fact only be adumbrated by a "revision of the question." Of course this revision is not only to be applied to the problem of history but also to the problem of neo-ontology itself. At least some indication may be given here why it appears to me that this problem stems from the fact that the idealist starting point has not been abandoned even by neo-ontological thought. Specifically: neo-ontology is characterized by two elements that it owes to idealism.

The first is the definition of the encompassing whole vis-à-vis the particularities included in it; it is no longer held to be a systematic whole, but rather a structural whole, a structural unity or totality. In conceiving the possibility of encompassing all reality unambiguously, even if only in a structure, a claim is implicit that he who combines everything existing under this structure has the right and the power to know adequately the existing in itself and to absorb it into the form. The moment that this claim can no longer be made, it becomes impossible to talk about a structural whole. I know that the contents of the new ontology are quite different from what I have just asserted. The most recent turn in phenomenology, it would be said, is precisely not rationalistic, but rather an attempt to adduce the irrational element in a totally new way under the category of "life." It makes, however, an enormous difference whether irrational contents are inserted into a philosophy that is founded on the principle of autonomy or whether philosophy no longer assumes that reality is adequately accessible. I only need to point out that a philosophy like Schopenhauer's came to its irrationalism by no means other than strict adherence to the fundamental theme of rational idealism—the Fichtean transcendental subjectivity. To my mind this is evidence for the possibility of an idealism with irrational content.

The second element is the emphasis on possibility in contrast to reality. Actually it is this problem of the relationship of possibility and reality that is perceived as the greatest difficulty in the context of neo-ontological thought. I want to be careful here not to attribute positions to neo-ontology that are still being disputed within it. But it is consistently agreed that the project (*Entwurf*) of being at least takes priority over the subsumed facticity, a facticity that is to be fitted in as an afterthought and is subject to criticism when it does not fit in. I find idealist elements in the predominance of the sphere of possibility because in the context of the critique of pure reason the antithesis of possibility and reality is none other than that of the categorical subjective structure and empirical multiplicity. This relation of neo-ontology to the idealist position not only explains its formalism, the unavoidable generality of its categories, to which facticity can not conform, but is also the key to the problem of tautology. Heidegger says that it is no mistake to move in a circle, the only concern is to enter it in the proper fashion. I am inclined to agree with him. But if philosophy is to remain true to its task, then entering the circle correctly can only mean that being, which determines or interprets itself as being, makes clear in the act of interpretation the element through which it interprets itself as such. The tautological tendency, as I see it, can only be clarified through the old idealist theme of identity. It has its origin in the subsumption of a being that is historical by the subjective category of historicity. The historical being that has been subsumed by the subjective category of historicity is supposed to be identical with history. Being is to conform to the categories with which historicity stamps it. The tautology appears to me to be less a self-grounding of the mythical depths of language than a new camouflage of the old classical thesis of the identity of subject and object. Heidegger's most recent turn toward Hegel seems to confirm this interpretation.

Given this revision of the problem, the starting point itself remains to be revised. We have established that the division of the world into nature and spirit or nature and history, a tradition set by subjectivistic idealism, must be overcome and that its place must be taken by a formulation that achieves in itself the concrete unity of nature and history. A *concrete* unity, however, is not one modeled on an antithesis of possible and real being, but a unity developed from the elements of real being itself. The neo-ontological project of history only has a chance of winning ontological dignity, of achieving an actual interpretation of being, if it is directed not at possibilities of being, but radically at the existing itself in its concrete inner-historical definition. Every exclusion of natural stasis from the historical dynamic leads to false absolutes, every isolation of the historical dynamic from the unsurpassably natural elements in it leads to false spiritualism. The achievement of the neo-ontological formulation is that it has radically demonstrated the insuperable interwovenness of natural and histori-cal elements. On the other hand, this formulation of the problem must be purged of the idea of an all encompassing whole, and it is necessary, furthermore, to criticize the separation of the real and possible from the point of view of reality, whereas they were previously quite dis-parate. These are in the first place general methodological require-ments. But much more is to be postulated. If the question of the rela-tion of nature and history is to be seriously posed, then it only offers any chance of solution if it is possible *to comprehend historical being in its most extreme historical determinacy, where it is most historical, as natu-ral being, or if it were possible to comprehend nature as a historical being where it seems to rest most deeply in itself as nature.* It is no longer simply a matter of conceptualizing the fact of history as a natural fact *toto caelo* (inclusively) under the category of historicity, but rather to re-transform the structure of inner-historical events into a structure of natural events. No being underlying or residing within historical be-ing itself is to be understood as ontological, that is, as natural being. The retransformation of concrete history into dialectical nature is the task of the ontological reorientation of the philosophy of history: the idea of natural-history.

II

I go back now to the question of the philosophy of history that has al-ready led to the construction of the concept of natural-history. The concept did not fall from heaven. Rather it has its binding identity in the context of historico-philosophical work on particular material, till now above all on aesthetic material. The simplest way to give an idea of this type of historical conception of nature is to cite the sources in which the concept of natural-history originates. I am referring to the works of Georg Lukács and Walter Benjamin. In the *Theory of the Novel* Lukács applied a concept that leads in this direction, that of a second nature. The framework of the concept of second nature, as Lukács uses it, is modeled on a general historico-philosophical image of a meaningful and a meaningless world (an immediate world and an alienated world of commodities), and he attempts to present this alienated world. He calls this world of things created by man, yet lost to him, the world of convention. "Where no aims are immediately given, the structures that the spirit in the process of becoming human finds amongst men as the scene and substrate of its activity lose their evident enrootedness in supra-personal ideal necessities; they are simply existent, perhaps powerful, perhaps frail, but they neither carry the consecration of the absolute nor are they the natural containers for the overflowing inwardness of the world. They form the world of convention, a world from whose all-embracing power only the innermost recesses of the soul are safe; a world that is present everywhere in boundless multiplicity and whose strict lawfulness, both in becoming and in being, is necessarily evident to the cognizant subject. But for all its lawfulness this world supplies neither meaning for the subject in search of a goal nor sensuous immediacy as material for the acting subject. This world is a second nature; like the first—"first nature" for Lukács is likewise alienated nature, nature in the sense of the natural sciences—"it can only be defined as the embodiment of well-known yet meaningless necessities and therefore it is ungraspable and unknowable in its actual substance."[4] This fact of a world of convention as it is historically produced, this world of estranged things that cannot be decoded but encounters us as ciphers, is the starting point of the question with which I am concerned here. From the perspective of the philosophy of history the problem of natural-history presents itself in the first place as the question of how it is possible to know and interpret this alienated, reified, dead world. Lukács already perceived this problem as foreign to us and a puzzle to us. If I should succeed at giving you a notion of the idea of natural-history you would first of all have to experience something of the θαυμάζειν (shock) that this question portends. Natural-history is not a synthesis of natural and historical methods, but a change of perspective. The passage in which Lukács comes closest to this conception runs as follows:

> The second nature of human constructs has no lyrical substantiality, its forms are too rigid to adapt themselves to the symbol creating moment; the content of its laws is far too rigidly defined ever to free itself from those elements that in lyric poetry must give rise to essayistic impulses; these impulses, indeed, live so exclusively by the grace of laws and have in fact so little valency of sensual existence independent of them that without them they would collapse into nothing. This nature is not mute, corporeal and foreign to the senses like

first nature: it is a petrified estranged complex of meaning that is no longer able to awaken inwardness; it is a charnel-house of rotted interiorities. This second nature could only be brought back to life, if ever, by a metaphysical act of reawakening the spiritual element that created or maintained it in its earlier or ideal existence, but could never be experienced by another interiority.[5]

The problem of this awakening, which Lukács grants to be a metaphysical possibility, is the problem that determines what is here understood by natural-history. Lukács envisioned the metamorphosis of the historical qua past into nature; petrified history is nature or the petrified life of nature is a mere product of historical development. The reference to the charnel house includes the element of the cipher: everything must mean something, just what, however, must first be extracted. Lukács can only think of this charnel house in terms of a theological resurrection, in an eschatological context. Benjamin marks the decisive turning point in the formulation of the problem of natural-history in that he brought the resurrection of second nature out of infinite distance into infinite closeness and made it an object of philosophical interpretation. Philosophy has succeeded in refining the concept of natural-history by taking up this theme of the awakening of an enciphered and petrified object. Two passages from Benjamin's *The Origin of the German Play of Lamentation*[6] are germane to those quoted above from Lukács. "In nature the allegorical poets saw eternal transience, and here alone did the saturnine vision of these generations recognize history."[7] "When, as is the case in the German play of lamentation, history comes onto the scene, it does so as a cipher to be read. 'History' is writ across the countenance of nature in the sign language of transience."[8] The deepest point where history and nature converge lies precisely in this element of transience. If Lukács demonstrates the retransformation of the historical, as that-which-has-been into nature, then here is the other side of the phenomenon: nature itself is seen as transitory nature, as history.

The problem of natural history can not be correctly formulated in terms of general structures, but only as interpretations of concrete history. Benjamin shows that allegory is no composite of merely adventitious elements; the allegorical is not an accidental sign for an underlying content. Rather there is a specific relation between allegory and the allegorically meant, "allegory is expression." Allegory is usually taken to mean the presentation of a concept as an image and therefore it is labeled abstract and accidental. The relationship of allegory to its meaning is not accidental signification, but the playing out of a particularity; it is expression. What is expressed in the allegorical sphere is nothing but a historical relationship. The theme of the allegorical is, simply, history. At issue is a historical relationship between what appears—nature—and its meaning, i.e, transience. This is explained as follows:

> The worldly, historical breadth . . . of the allegorical intention is, as natural history, as the original history of signification or of intention, dialectical in character.[9] The relationship of symbol and allegory may be incisively and formally determined by means of the decisive category of time, whose introduction into this sphere of semiotics was the great romantic insight of these thinkers. Whereas in the symbol, with the glorification of death and destruction, the transfigured face of nature reveals itself fleetingly in the light of redemption, in allegory the observer is confronted with the *facies hippocratica*[10] of history, a petrified primordial landscape. Everything about history that, from the beginning, has been, ultimately, sorrowful and unsuccessful, is expressed in a face—or rather in a death's head. And although such a thing lacks all "symbolic" freedom of expression, all classical proportion, all that is human, nevertheless not only the nature of human existence in general but the biographical historicity of an individual is enunciated in this figure of the most extreme subjugation to nature, in the form of a riddle. This is the heart of the allegorical vision, of the Baroque, secular exposition of history as the passion of the world; it is only meaningful in the stations of its prostration. The greater the signification, the greater the subjugation to death, for death digs most deeply the jagged demarcation line between *physis* and signification.[11]

What is the meaning here of "transience" and "original history of signification"?[12] I cannot develop these concepts in a traditional fashion. What is at issue is of an essentially different logical form than that of a scheme of thought based on a project (*Entwurf*) whose foundation is constituted by a general conceptual structure. The alternative logical structure cannot be analyzed here. This structure is a constellation. It is not a matter of clarifying concepts one out of another, but of the constellation of ideas, namely, those of transience, signification, the idea of nature and the idea of history. One does not refer back to these ideas as "invariants"; the issue is not to define them, rather they gather around a concrete historical facticity that, in the context of these elements, will reveal itself in its uniqueness. How do these elements cohere? According to Benjamin, nature, as creation, carries the mark of transience. Nature itself is transitory. Thus it includes the element of history. Whenever a historical element appears it refers back to the natural element that passes away within it. Likewise the reverse: whenever "second nature" appears, when the world of convention approaches, it can be deciphered in that its meaning is shown to be precisely its transience. As Benjamin has understood this—and here the discussion must be pushed farther—there are certain fundamental original-historical phenomena, which were originally present, have passed away and are signified in allegory, return in the allegorical, return as script. It cannot simply be a matter of demonstrating that in history itself original history as transience contains within itself the theme of history. The basic quality of the transience of the earthly signifies nothing but just such a relationship between nature and history: all being or everything existing is to be grasped as the interweaving of historical and natural being. As transience, all original history is absolutely present. It is present in the form of "signification." "Signification" means that the elements of nature and history are not fused with each other, rather they break apart and interweave at the same time in such a fashion that the natural appears as a sign for history and history, where it seems to be most historical, appears as a sign for nature. All being, or at least all being that has been or become what it is, transforms itself into allegory; in these terms allegory is no longer merely a category of history. Likewise "signification" itself is transformed from a problem of the hermeneutics of the philosophy of history, from a problem of transcendental meaning into the element whose character it is to transubstantiate history into original history. Hence "original history of signification." So, for example, in the language of the Baroque, the fall of a tyrant is equivalent to the setting of the sun. This allegorical relationship already encompasses the presentiment of a procedure that could succeed in interpreting concrete history as nature and to make nature dialectical under the aspect of history. The realization of this conception is once more the idea of natural-history.

III

Having sketched out the origin of the idea of natural-history, I would like to carry the discussion farther. The positions of Lukács and Benjamin with regard to the idea of natural-history are related in the problem of the image of the charnel house. For Lukács it is something simply puzzling; for Benjamin it is a cipher to be read. For radical natural-historical thought, however, everything existing transforms itself into ruins and fragments, into just such a charnel house where signification is discovered, in which nature and history interweave and the philosophy of history is assigned the task of their intentional interpretation. A double turn, therefore, is made: on one hand I have reduced the ontological problematic to a historical formula and tried to show in what way ontology is to be concretely and historically radicalized. On the other hand, I have shown, under the aspect of transience, how history itself in a sense presses toward an ontological turn. What I mean here by ontological turn is something entirely different from that which is presently understood by the term.[13] Therefore I will not try to appropriate the expression for my own purposes, but will introduce it dialectically. What I have in mind with the idea of natural-history is not "historical ontology," not an attempt to isolate a group of historical elements and to hypostatize them ontologically, force them, as for example Dilthey did, to encompass the totality of an epoch as its sense or fundamental structure. Dilthey's attempt at a historical ontology ran aground because he did not engage facticity with sufficient seriousness; he remained in the sphere of intellectual history and, in the fashion of vague categories of styles of thought, entirely failed to grasp material reality. Instead of intellectual history, instead of trying to reconstruct basic images of history epoch by epoch, the issue is to grasp historical facticity in its historicity itself as natural-historical.

To articulate the idea of natural-history I will take up a second problem from the opposite side. (This is a direct continuation of the Frankfurt discussion.) One might object that I am proposing a sort of bewitchment of history and passing off the historical, in all its contingency, as the natural and then original-historical. The historical is to be transfigured as something meaningful because it appears allegorical. That is, however, not what I mean. Certainly the starting point of the problem's formulation, the natural character of history is disconcerting. But if philosophy wanted to be nothing more than the shock that the historical presents itself at the same time as nature, then such a philosophy would be subject to Hegel's criticism of Schelling's philosophy as the night of indifferentiation in which all cats are grey. How does one avoid this night? That is something that I would like to clarify.

The starting point here is that history, as it lies before us, presents itself as thoroughly discontinuous, not only in that it contains disparate circumstances and facts but also because it contains structural disparities. If Riezler enumerates three opposing yet interrelated categories of historicity (i.e., *tyche, ananke, spontaneity*),[14] I myself would not attempt to synthesize this division of the structure of history into a so-called unity. I believe, indeed, that the neo-ontologists have performed something very fruitful in their conception of this structure. Now this discontinuity, which, as I said, can not be legitimately transformed into a structural whole, presents itself in the first place as one between the mythical archaic, natural material of history, of what has been, and that which surfaces as dialectically and emphatically new. The problematic character of these categories is clear to me. The differential procedure required to arrive at natural-history, without anticipating it as a unity, consists, first, in accepting these two problematic and indeterminate structures in their contradictoriness, as they occur in the language of philosophy. This is legitimate in that it appears that the philosophy of history increasingly comes to just this sort of intertwining of the originally existing and the newly becoming in the findings presented by research. I would like to recall that psychoanalytic research presents this antithesis with full clarity in the distinction between archaic symbols, to which no associations may attach themselves, and intersubjective, dynamic, inner-historical symbols, which can all be eliminated and transformed into psychical actuality and present knowledge. Now the first task of the philosophy of history is to distinguish these two elements, separate them, and set them out in mutual opposition. Only where this antithesis is made explicit is there a chance of succeeding in the complete construction of natural-history. Pragmatic findings, which turn up when one observes the archaic-mythical and the historical-new, indicate the direction of this process. It is evident that the foundation, the mythical-archaic, the supposedly substantial and enduring mythical, is in no way a static foundation. Rather, there is an element of the historically dynamic, whose form is dialectical, in all great myths as well as in the mythical images that our consciousness still carries. The mythical fundamental elements are in themselves contradictory and move in a contradictory manner (recall the phenomenon of the ambivalence, the "antithetical sense" of primal words).[15] The myth of Kronos is just such a myth in which the most extreme godly power of creation is coupled with the fact that he is the god who annihilates his creations, his children. Likewise, the mythology that underlies tragedy is in every instance dialectical because it includes the subjugation of the guilty man to nature at the same time that it develops out of itself the reconciliation of this fate: man raises himself up out of his fate as man. The dialectical element here is that the tragic myths contain at one and the same time subjection to guilt and nature and the element of reconciliation that transcends the realm of nature. This notion not only of a static undialectical world of ideas, but of undialectical myths that break off the dialectic, points back to its origins in Plato.[16] In Plato the world of appearances lies fallow; it is abandoned, but visibly ruled by the ideas. Yet the ideas take no part in the world of appearances, and since they do not participate in the movement of the world, as a result of the alienation of the ideas from the world of human experience, they are necessarily transferred to the stars in order to be able to maintain themselves in the face of the world's dynamic. The ideas become static: frozen. This is, however, already the expression for a level of consciousness in which consciousness has lost its natural substance as immediacy. In Plato's moment consciousness has already succumbed to the temptation of idealism: spirit, banned from the world, alienated from history, becomes the absolute at the cost of life. The misconception of the static character of mythical elements is what we must free ourselves from if we want to arrive at a concrete representation of natural-history.

On the other hand, "the new," the dialectically produced, actually presents itself in history as the archaic. History is "most mythical where it is most historical." This poses the greatest problems. Rather than pursuing the thought in general terms, I will give an example, that of semblance (*Schein*)—and I mean semblance in the previously established sense of second nature. This second nature is a nature of semblance in that it presents itself as meaningful and its semblance is historically produced. Second nature is illusory because we have lost reality, yet we believe that we are able to meaningfully understand it

in its eviscerated state or because we insert subjective intention as signification into this foreign reality, as occurs in allegory. Now what is
remarkable is that the inner-historical essence is itself semblance of a
mythical kind. Just as the element of semblance is an aspect of every
myth, indeed just as the dialectic of mythical fate is in every instance
inaugurated by semblance in the forms of hubris and blindness, so the
historically produced elements of semblance are always mythical.
This is so not only in that they reach back to the archaic original-
historical and that in art every illusory element has to do with myth
(one thinks of Wagner), but rather because the mythical character itself returns in the historical phenomenon of semblance. Its clarification would be an authentic problem of natural-history. This would
involve demonstrating, for example, that if you sense an aspect of
semblance in certain houses, then along with this semblance there is
the thought of that-which-has-always-been and that it is only being
recognized. The phenomenon of déjà vu, of recognition, is to be analyzed at this point. The mythical model of anxiety returns vis-à-vis
such inner-historical alienated semblance. An archaic anxiety de-
scends everywhere that the illusory world of convention appears in
front of us. The element of foreboding is also an aspect of this semblance; one of its mythical elements is to have the character of drawing
everything into itself as into a funnel. The element of the actuality of
semblance in contrast to its simple pictorialness, that we perceive semblance as expression everywhere that we come up against it, that it can
not be sloughed off as merely illusory but expresses something that
can not be described independently of its semblance—this is also a
mythical element of semblance. To make a final point: the definitive
transcendent element of myth, reconciliation, also inheres in semblance. It is worth remembering that emotion always accompanies the
lesser, not the greatest art works. I am referring to that element of reconciliation that is present wherever the world appears most as semblance: the promise of reconciliation is most perfectly given where at
the same time the world is most firmly immured from all "meaning."
With this I refer you to the structure of the original-historical in semblance itself, where semblance in its thusness (*Sosein*) proves itself to
be historically produced or, in traditional philosophical terms, where
semblance is the product of the subject/object dialectic. Second nature
is, in truth, first nature. The historical dialectic is not simply a renewed interest in reinterpreted historical materials, rather the histori-

cal materials transform themselves into the mythical and natural-historical.

I wanted to speak about the relationship of these matters to historical materialism, but I only have time to say the following: it is not a question of completing one theory by another, but of the immanent interpretation of a theory. I submit myself, so to speak, to the authority of the materialist dialectic. It could be demonstrated that what has been said here is only an interpretation of certain fundamental elements of the materialist dialectic.

Notes

Introduction

1. "God told me to strike at al Qaida and I struck them, and then he instructed me to strike at Saddam, which I did." The president of the United States, in a speech quoted from *Haaretz* in Justin A. Frank, *Bush on the Couch* (New York: Regan, 2004), p. 72.

2. The German, *Ursprung ist das Ziel,* of course involves a host of ideas and associations that are not apparent in the English, "Origin Is the Goal," and vice versa. To note just the most important, *Ziel* means both *goal* and *aim*. *Goal* and *aim* each also imply the other and can be used with partial synonymity, but while juggling the English alternatives against each other allows for more precise differentiation of the several meanings, the German makes it possible to better comprehend their unity. The limits to plausible translation of the epigram require the English reader to imagine *aim* into every occurrence here of *goal*.

3. Theodor W. Adorno, *Negative Dialektik,* in *Gesammelte Schriften,* henceforth *GS*, ed. Rolf Tiedemann, with the assistance of Gretel Adorno, Susan Buck-Morss, and Klaus Schultz, 20 vols. (Frankfurt: Suhrkamp, 1997), 6:158; *Negative Dialectics,* trans. E. B. Ashton (New York: Continuum, 1983), p. 155.

   Translations throughout this volume are exclusively for the purposes of their specific contexts; they will not necessarily conform to published editions of these same texts. This may amount to amendment, but as frequently it is a matter of developing possibilities of syntax that can be constrained by the obligations of full translation. It is a truism that, free of their own circumstance, the translation of individual lines can be improved, though they of course at the same time forfeit the informing coherence of the passage they are drawn from. Word choice in these translations is also sometimes influenced by the opportunity to accent a meaning that might not be the preferred solution in an authoritative edition.

4. Henry David Thoreau, *Walking* (New York: HarperCollins, 1994), p. 1 (emphasis added).

5. Adorno, *Negative Dialectics*, p. 155.

6. Theodor W. Adorno, "Veblen's Attack on Culture" (1941), in *Prisms,* trans. Samuel and Shierry Weber (Boston: MIT Press, 1981), p. 88; *GS* 10.1:88.

7. Adorno, *Negative Dialectics*, p. 155.

8. Adorno's interpretation of Kraus's epigram owes much to Walter Benjamin's *Origin of the German Play of Lamentation*. Adorno and Benjamin's differences, however, over the concept of origin are dauntingly complex. See "Title Essay: Baroque Allegory and 'The Essay as Form'" (this volume).

See especially Walter Benjamin, *The Origin of German Tragic Drama,* trans. John Osborne (London: NLB, 1977), pp. 44–48.

A further note on language is relevant here: *Ursprung* and *Origin* share etymologically in the images of *arising* and *coming forth*, but this is much more on the surface in the German since one can directly comprehend an *Ur-*, a primordial, *sprung,* leap or sprouting, much in the spirit of what is thought in the English "spring has sprung." The past participial quality of *Ursprung*, however, while it demonstrates the activity of a verb, is a noun that does not—unlike so many German nouns—have the vernacular capacity to exist as a verb; there is no *urspringen* in modern German. The English noun, *origin*, however is matched by *originate*, which in German would be the infinitive *entspringen*. In wanting to unscramble the puzzle of Kraus's elusive phrase, an informed English reader of the German may therefore freely speculate on how the phrase's potential took shape out of certain asymmetries of German and then experiment with various translations beginning with something like: *origination is the aim*, which is revealing close to Pound's *Make it new*—a phrase Adorno never quoted—or Rimbaud's *Il faut être absolument moderne*—a phrase that was always on Adorno's mind. The self-evidence of such a translation, however, obviously falls short of much that is at stake now in the Krausian phrase.

9. The theologoumenon of utopia as a smallest difference was common to Adorno and Benjamin. See Theodor W. Adorno, *Alban Berg: Master of the Smallest Link*, trans. Juliane Brand and Christopher Hailey (New York: Cambridge University Press, 1991).

10. See Robert Spaemann, *Die Frage Wozu?* (Muenchen: Piper, 1981).

11. See Emile Meyerson, *Identity and Reality* (1908), authorized translation by Kate Lowenberg (New York: Dover, 1962). One way of formulating the dialectic of enlightenment—though Adorno did not develop this thesis—is specifically in terms of the development of this mechanical spatialization of nature.

12. See J. Laplanche and J. B. Pontalis, *The Language of Psychoanalysis*, trans. Donald Nicholson-Smith (New York: Norton, 1973), p. 387.

13. See Theodor W. Adorno, "Der Begriff des Unbewussten in der transzendentalen Seelenlehre" (1927), in *GS* 1:79–324.

14. See Theodor W. Adorno, "Die revidierte Psychoanalyse," in *GS* 8:20 ff.

15. Theodor W. Adorno, "The Meaning of Working Through the Past," in *Can One Live After Auschwitz?* ed. Rolf Tiedemann, trans. Rodney Livingstone and others (Stanford: Stanford University Press, 2003), p. 3 ff.

16. The German psychoanalytic term for "working through" is *Durcharbeitung*.

17. See Theodor W. Adorno, *Was bedeutet Aufarbeitung der Vergangenheit*, in *GS* 10.2:552 ff.

18. See Theodor W. Adorno, "Stravinsky or Restoration," *Philosophy of New Music,* ed. , trans., and intro. Robert Hullot-Kentor (Minnesota: University of Minnesota Press, 2006).

19. For some orientation see R. Horacio Etchegoyen, *The Fundamentals of Psychoanalytic Technique* (London: Karnac, 1991).

20. Governor Jeb Bush, quoted in Frank, *Bush on the Couch*, p. 1.

21. See Theodor W. Adorno, "Psychology and Sociology," trans. Irving Wohlfarth, in *New Left Review*, no. 46, pp. 63–80 and no. 47, pp. 79–97.

22. Sacrifice is inevitably tautological: sacrifice made for the sacrifice already made. This presents its identitarian aspect. Reporting on the president's intention to pursue the war in Iraq, a recent headline reads: "Citing Sacrifice, President Vows to Keep Up Fight," *New York Times*, Tuesday, August 23, 2005, p. A1. To date, in Mayan reminiscence, all allegiance demands the hand over the heart. See *Popul Vuh,* trans. Dennis Tedlock (New York: Touchstone, 1996).

23. Theodor W. Adorno, *Aesthetische Theorie,* in *GS* 7:104, and *Aesthetic Theory*, ed., trans., and intro. Robert Hullot-Kentor (Minnesota: University of Minnesota Press, 1997), p. 66.

24. The commonplace then, of contemporary art study that preoccupies itself with the discussion of the function, e.g., of literature in "the devel-

opment of national identity," would be transformed by the consideration that if a nation fully had an identity it would no longer have one
and that art, in so far as it is art, and is shaped by the same problems as
national identity, can only be distinguished from other ideological
mechanisms in that art's own self-identity drives it toward exactly that
identity in which nation would dissolve. What is presumed in the current discussion of the place of art in national identity has usurped the
lion's share of what was in other decades discussed in terms of political
commitment. See Theodor W. Adorno, "Commitment," in *Notes to
Literature,* ed. Rolf Tiedemann, trans. Shierry Weber Nicholsen (New
York: Columbia University Press, 1992), 2:76–94.

Back to Adorno

1. Max Horkheimer and Theodor W. Adorno, *Dialectic of Enlightenment,*
   trans. John Cumming (New York: Continuum, 1978).

   The situation of the translation of Adorno's work has been considerably transformed since this essay was written. In particular, an excellent
   new translation of the *Dialectic of Enlightenment* now exists, ed. Gun-
   zelin Schmid Noerr, trans. Edmund Jephcott (Stanford: Stanford University Press, 2002). The remarks on the old translation, however, are
   presented below in note 67, in part because the old translation continues
   to circulate and also because these remarks may be of use to readers interested in questions of the translation of these concepts and understanding why the older translation was replaced.
2. This summary is based on G. S. Noerr, "Nachwort des Herausgebers,"
   pp. 423–542, especially pp. 443–444, published, along with "Nachwort
   von Juergen Habermas," as appendixes to Max Horkheimer and
   Theodor W. Adorno, *Dialektik der Aufklaerung* (Frankfurt: Fischer,
   1986), and on conversations with Rolf Tiedemann in July 1987.
3. Habermas, "Nachwort," p. 277.
4. Noerr, "Nachwort," p. 449.
5. Juergen Habermas, "Bemerkungen zur Entwicklung des Horkhei-
   merischen Werkes," in *Max Horkheimer heute: Werk und Wirkung,* ed.
   Alfred Schmidt and Norbert Altwicker (Frankfurt: Fischer, 1986),
   p. 171.
6. Habermas, "Nachwort," p. 277.
7. See, for instance, Erich Kahler's *Man the Measure* (1947) (Ohio: Meridian, 1967) and the last chapter and epilogue to Erich Auerbach's *Mimesis* (1945) (Princeton: Princeton University Press, 1968), which also presents a kind of dialectic of enlightenment.

8. Horkheimer, Letter to Pollock, cited by Noerr, "Nachwort," p. 432.

9. Ibid., p. 507.

10. Ibid., p. 508.

11. Habermas, "Nachwort," p. 278.

12. Ibid., p. 277.

13. Ibid., p. 282.

14. Ibid.

15. The *Zeitschrift fuer Sozialforchung,* edited by Horkheimer, was discontinued after 1941 and the move to California.

16. Habermas, "Nachwort," p. 280.

17. There are many variants on the theme of Adorno the pessimist, and they almost always pair—as does Habermas—the charge of pessimism with an attack on modern art: "Adorno's advocacy of modernism, it must be remembered, springs from a social pessimism that is unable to identify any contemporary agent of political change; given the prevailing technocratic logic of an administered society, the dissonant, fragmentary nature of modem art offers passive resistance to the all-pervasive commodification of experience.... Feminism, however, rejects such pessimism in its identification of women as an oppressed class." Rita Felski, *Beyond Feminist Aesthetics* (Cambridge: Harvard University Press, 1989), p. 189. The language here draws distantly on Marx, but at the vanishing point: Marx's interest in the proletariat was not because he could not find other oppressed groups, but because its claims, he held, were universal. In the passage quoted above, however, this universality is sloughed for a modest "Je suis la revolution," phrased in a sociologese in which disempowerment takes shape as a Robinsonade, on which Adorno comments: "These prototypical figures of the shipwrecked make out of their weakness, the weakness of individuality separated from the collective, their social strength. Thrown to the mercy of the sea, helplessly isolated, their isolation dictates the ruthless pursuit of their self-interest." As to shipwrecked, there is no limit today to people in this position, whereas an inability to recognize the content of modern art means an inability to know this. Adorno, the "pessimist," wary of vanguards, though hardly obtuse to the situation of women, wrote in the last lines of the "Concept of Enlightenment": "While bourgeois economy multiplied violence through the mediation of the market, it also multiplied its objects and forces to such an extent that for their administration not just the kings, not even the middle classes are necessary, but everyone. They learn from the power of things to dispense at last with power" (Horkheimer and Adorno, *Dialektik der Aufklaerung*, p. 60).

18. The conversation begins with Horkheimer irritated by the metaphysical quality of Adorno's thought. The conversation is formal; they address one another as *Sie*.

19. "Little drum: three rapid little beats of a single instrument awaken the feeling of a crowd marching in the distance. Thus is remembered that all music, and even the most lonely, concerns the many, whose gesture the sound of the drum preserves." Theodor W. Adorno, "Motive," in *Gesammelte Schriften,* henceforth *GS*, ed. Rolf Tiedemann, with the assistance of Gretel Adorno, Susan Buck-Morss, and Klaus Schultz, 20 vols. (Frankfurt: Suhrkamp, 1997), 16:280.

20. Horkheimer and Adorno, *Dialektik der Aufklaerung*, pp. 506–8.

21. Habermas's relation to Horkheimer is complex. The two men certainly did not see eye to eye; and Habermas's identification with him in the context of the "Nachwort" to the *Dialectic of Enlightenment* is restricted to his criticism of Adorno.

22. This was Rolf Tiedemann's assessment of the situation in Frankfurt in July 1987.

23. Horkheimer and Adorno, *Dialectic of Enlightenment,* p. xvi.

24. Habermas, "Nachwort," p. 289.

25. Theodor W. Adorno, "Geschichtsphilosophie" (1957), unpublished lecture series, p. 19.

26. Habermas, "Nachwort."

27. Horkheimer and Adorno, *Dialectic of Enlightenment,* p. xiv (translation modified).

28. Theodor W. Adorno, "Einleitung in die Moralphilosophie," unpublished lecture series, p. 157.

29. George Schrader, "Hegel's Contribution to Phenomenology," *Monist* 48 (1964), p. 24.

30. Friedrich Schiller, *On the Aesthetic Education of Man,* trans. E. Wilkinson and L. Willoughby (London: Oxford, 1982), p. 27. I have generally used this translation, but have modified it when needed.

31. Ibid., p. 19.

32. Ibid., p. 27.

33. Ibid., pp. 28–29.

34. Ibid., p. 61.

35. Theodor W. Adorno, *Kierkegaard: Construction of the Aesthetic,* ed., trans., and intro. Robert Hullot-Kentor (Minnesota: University of Minnesota, 1989), p. 131.

36. Adorno reflects explicitly on this: "The myths are sedimented in the thematic layers of the *Odyssey;* the account given of them, however, the unity wrested from the diffuse legends, is at the same time the de-

scription of the flight of the individual from the mythic powers" (Horkheimer and Adorno, *Dialectic of Enlightenment*, p. 46 [translation modified]).

37. Ibid., p. 48 (translation modified).

38. Ibid., p. 79 (translation modified).

39. "Knowledge . . . can now become the dissolution of domination," ibid, p. 42.

40. Horkheimer and Adorno, *Dialectic of Enlightenment*, p. 461.

41. Ibid.

42. G. W. F. Hegel, *Encyklopaedie*, vol. 8, in *Theorie Werkausgabe* (Frankfurt: Suhrkamp, 1971–1978), p. 265.

43. G. W. F. Hegel, *Reason in History,* translated by Robert S. Hartman (Indianapolis: Bobbs Merrill, 1953), p. 41. Quoted by Shlomo Avenieri, "Consciousness and History," in *New Studies in Hegel's Philosophy* (New York: Holt, Rhinehart, and Winston, 1971), p. 110.

44. Horkheimer and Adorno, *Dialectic of Enlightenment*, p. 50 (translation modified).

45. Ibid., p. 10 (translation modified).

46. Ibid., p. 55 (translation modified).

47. Habermas, "Nachwort," p. 282.

48. See H. S. V. Ogdan, "The Rejection of the Antithesis of Nature and Art in Germany, 1700–1800," *Journal of English and German Philosophy,* no. 38 (1939).

49. Immanuel Kant, *Critique of Judgment,* trans. by Werner Pluhar (Indianapolis: Hackett, 1987), p. 182.

50. Schiller, *On the Aesthetic Education of Man,* p. 147.

51. Adorno, "Moralphilosophie," p. 168.

52. Horkheimer and Adorno, *Dialectic of Enlightenment*, p. 75 (translation modified).

53. Ibid., p. 78 (translation modified).

54. Ibid., p. 56 (translation modified).

55. Ibid., p. 51 (translation modified).

56. Adorno, "Moralphilosophie," p. 157.

57. Horkheimer and Adorno, *Dialectic of Enlightenment*, p. 54 (translation modified).

58. Ibid. (translation modified).

59. Adorno, "Moralphilosophie," p. 193.

60. See Adam Carse, *The History of Orchestration* (New York: Dover, 1964), p. 335.

61. Horkheimer and Adorno, *Dialectic of Enlightenment*, p. 44 (translation modified).

62. Ibid., p. 45 (translation modified).

63. Walter Benjamin, "The Storyteller," in *Illuminations,* trans. by Harry Zohn (New York: Schocken, 1969), p. 90.

64. Ibid., pp. 79–80.

65. Theodor W. Adorno, *Aesthetic Theory,* ed. Rolf Tiedemann and Gretel Adorno, trans. Robert Hullot-Kentor (Minnesota: University of Minnesota Press, 1997); Theodor W. Adorno, *GS,* 7:278.

66. Horkheimer and Adorno, *Dialectic of Enlightenment,* p. 79 (translation modified).

67. Juergen Habermas, "The Entwinement of Myth and Enlightenment: Horkheimer and Adorno," in *The Philosophical Discourse of Modernity,* trans. F. Lawrence (Cambridge: MIT Press, 1987), p. 121.

For those who grew up with the first English edition of the *Dialectic of Enlightenment* and thought they knew what was in it, it may come as hard news to learn that the words of this text are the wrong ones. Some examples from the second excursus of the volume, "Odysseus or Myth and Enlightenment" will produce a needed suspicion about the translation as a whole. There are, however, two drawbacks to this catalogue of mistranslations. The first is that it may give the impression that there is nothing right about Cumming's translation. This is not the case. Much of it is good, and at a couple of points it even improves on the original. The second drawback to this *corrigenda* is that it hardly makes compelling reading. However, there is no other way to document the translation's inadequacy other than by pushing a sort of attentiveness farther than anyone might want to read.

Focusing, then, on what is wrong with the translation, taking sentences by the handful, here is what one comes up with: The first phrase of the essay, "As we have seen"—though a seemingly convenient bridge from the lead essay, "The Concept of Enlightenment"—does not occur in the original, or for that matter, anywhere in Adorno's writings. The book is only able to organize adequately its complexity because of its paratactical structure, which eschews all such bridges. Though this particular translator's interpolation does not block comprehension, it implies a general misunderstanding of the text, and, in the face of the book's intricacies, this misunderstanding consistently catches sentences going the wrong direction. Thus, for example: Adorno did write—as the translation has it—that "through laughter blind nature becomes *aware* of itself." But he could not have written, as the translation continues—that, as a result of this self-consciousness, nature "thereby surrenders itself to the powers of destruction." If reflection were the catalyst of destructiveness, the whole of Adorno's thought would be senseless. Adorno in fact wrote the opposite: in the self-consciousness of its laughter blind nature "gives up its destructive force." The translation is full of similar misconstruals: In the context of a discussion of marriage, Cumming has it that "the wife *denotes pleasure* in the fixed order of life and property." According to the original, the wife "*betrays pleasure.*" In the discussion of the Circe episode, the sorceress for some reason conjures not with "wine and *herbs*" but "wine and *cabbage.*" Odysseus is not the man "for whom all *reasonable things are alike,*" but the man "whom *all rational thinkers once resembled.*" Magic does not use "the fixed order of time to attack the fixed will of the subject;" rather, "along with the fixed order of time, this power [magic] seizes the fixed will of the subject." Polyphemous does not trust "in the power of *immortality,*" but in the "power of *immortals,*" the Olympian gods. Adorno's essay is a study of the origin of the epic as form. The epic develops as it organizes the tribal, mythical legends into one coherent narrative of adventure; according to the existing translation, the *Odyssey* *pulls* "myth into time," thus "*concealing* the abyss that separates it [myth] from homeland and reconciliation." But this is once more a reversal of the sense of the passage: In the original the abyss is not concealed but "*revealed*"—a reversal of sense that threatens to unhinge the whole of Adorno's discussion of the relation of epic to myth.

Cumming's single most important failing, however, is his translation throughout of *Vertretung* and its derivatives as "representation" rather than "substitution." Choosing between the two English terms is not simple; "representation" is correct but misleading. It is only possible to get the sense of the essay by beginning from "substitution." This can best be shown by comparing two versions of a crucial passage which at the same time will give an idea of what even the most diligent reader is up against in the current translation: "Just as the capacity of *representation* is the measure of domination, and domination is the most powerful thing that can be represented in most performances, so the capacity of *representation* is the vehicle of progress and regression at one and the same time." Compare this: "Just as *substitutability* is the measure of domination, and that person is most powerful who can have others *substitute* for him or her in the majority of tasks, so *substitution is* at once the vehicle of progress and regression." In this passage Adorno and Horkheimer begin to reconceive the commonplace that domination is the power to have others do one's own work; they reformulate this idea as part of the history of sacrifice in which an object of lesser value is cunningly *substituted* for another of greater value. The misunderstanding of this concept and the theory of sacrifice of which it is part has far-reaching consequences, producing distortions and blind spots throughout Cumming's translation. Thus, for example, one reads that *"The mythic folk religions* must have been shown to be illusory long before they acquired a civilized form." But it turns out that it is the *rationality of sacrifice* that "must have shown itself to be illusory long before the development of the mythical folk religions." These mistranslations will somehow have to be sorted out before any real discussion of this pivotal text of critical theory can proceed in the English-speaking world.

Things Beyond Resemblance

1. *Adorno: Eine Bildmonographie,* ed. Theodor W. Adorno-Archiv (Frankfurt: Suhrkamp, 2003), p. 190.
2. The reader is asked to tolerate the German title here until the question of its correct translation is discussed, below, in "Marginal Translation."
3. Vladimir Nabokov, *Lolita* (New York: Vintage, 1997), p. 148.
4. Mark Landler, "Viacom to Buy German Rival to MTV," *New York Times,* June 25, 2004, p. W1.
5. Ibid.
6. Susanne K. Langer, "Speculations on the Origins of Speech and Its Communicative Function," in *Philosophical Sketches* (Baltimore: John Hopkins Press, 1962), pp. 26–53. Cf. also Suzanne K. Langer, *Feeling and Form* (New York: Scribner's, 1953) and *Mind: An Essay on Human Feeling,* vol. 1 (Baltimore: John's Hopkins University Press, 1967).
7. Sir James Jeans, *Science and Music* (New York: Dover, 1968; repr. Cambridge: Cambridge University Press, 1937), esp. p. 231.
8. *Luftdruckmelodien*: melodies composed out of atmospheric pressure.
9. An expression of Guenter Anders.
10. Theodor W. Adorno, *Philosophy of Modern Music*, trans. Anne G. Mitchell and Wesley V. Blomster (New York: Seabury, 1973).
11. This is the same text a copy of which Thomas Mann studied in 1943 in preparation for *Doctor Faustus*. Cf. *Briefwechsel 1943–1955: Th. W. Adorno/Thomas Mann,* ed. Christoph Goedde and Thomas Sprecher (Frankfurt: Suhrkamp, 2002), p. 10; also Thomas Mann, *The Story of a Novel*, trans. Richard and Clara Winston (New York: Knopf, 1961), especially pp. 42–48; and Jo-Ann Reif, "Adrian Leverkuhn, Arnold Schoenberg, Theodor Adorno: Theorists real and fictitious in Thomas Mann's Doctor Faustus," *Journal of the Arnold Schoenberg Institute* 7.1 (1983): 102–106.
12. See "Second Salvage: Prolegomenon to a Reconstruction of 'Current of Music'" (this volume). As Adorno wrote in a letter on July 14, 1942, to Leo Lowenthal, whom he often relied on in practical matters: "I want to bring you up to date today on the following: As you'll remember, last

spring Runes had the idea of publishing *Philosophie der neuen Musik* in his journal and had me do a rough translation, which I finished in December. Now he suddenly writes me, blatantly breaking a verbal and written commitment, to say that several experts have decided the work can not be published, and returned it to me. I have responded very sharply to him and held my alternatives in reserve; still haven't heard from him. I'd be very appreciative for your advice." Letter, Adorno to Loewenthal, August 14, 1942, unpublished; in possession of Dr. Rolf Tiedemann.

13. Quoted in *A Schoenberg Reader*, ed. Joseph Auner (New Haven: Yale University Press, 2003), p. 335.

14. Adorno to Hans Eisler, January 8, 1942, Archiv der Akademie der Kuenste, Berlin.

15. *A Schoenberg Reader*, p. 331.

16. Cf. Theodor W. Adorno, *Kierkegaard: Construction of the Aesthetic*, trans. Robert Hullot-Kentor (Minnesota: University of Minnesota Press, 1989).

17. See Theodor W. Adorno, "Reversal Into Unfreedom," in *Philosophy of New Music*, ed. and trans. Robert Hullot-Kentor (Minnesota: University of Minnesota Press, 2006).

18. Adorno's comment here is perhaps not to be accepted totally at face value. *Philosophy of New Music* does pursue the fundamental ideas of *Dialectic of Enlightenment*. But it is a question why, if the musical work was meant to be an excursus to the philosophy of history, the first half on Schoenberg—written several years before the philosophy of history—and the part on Stravinsky, written some years after it, were not rewritten and unified in the actual language of *Dialectic of Enlightenment*. Adorno gives his reasons, and they are consistent. Yet it is striking that the dialectic of "myth" and "enlightenment" only remotely appears in the pages of this musical study and that, in place of the concepts of myth and enlightenment, a kind of euphemism broadly predominates for them: the "ever same" and "domination." If anything, a revision of the text employing the concepts of *Dialectic of Enlightenment* might have helped articulate the polarizing directions of the presentation; it certainly would not have impeded it. One might speculate, then, that *Dialectic of Enlightenment* stands between the two parts of the book not only as a development of thought but also as what *Philosophy of New Music* did not want to refer to. This would be confirmed by the fact that the moment of the publication of *Philosophy of New Music*, when Adorno and Horkheimer had planned to return to Germany, was the same moment at which they prudently decided—certainly with much ambivalence, most of all on Adorno's part—to suppress the circulation

and republication of *Dialectic of Enlightenment* on the basis of hesitations, if not toward the actual theses of their philosophy of history, then toward the dangers posed by the work's extreme formulations of the critique of enlightenment, which might well have been exploited for irrationalist purposes by a renewed fascism in Germany, had that occurred.

19. See Theodor W. Adorno, "Twelve-Tone *Melos* and Rhythm," in *Philosophy of New Music*.

20. *A Schoenberg Reader*, pp. 337–338.

21. See Theodor W. Adorno, "Break from the Material," in *Philosophy of New Music*.

22. Ibid.

23. Wallace Stevens, "Prologues to What Is Possible," in *Collected Poetry and Prose* (New York: Library of America, 1997), pp. 437–438.

24. Wallace Stevens, "Of Mere Being," ibid., pp. 476–477.

25. Stevens, "Prologues to What Is Possible."

26. See Theodor W. Adorno, "Music as Knowledge," in *Philosophy of New Music*.

27. Ibid.

28. Theodor W. Adorno, "Palace of Janus," in *Minima Moralia*, trans. E. F. N. Jephcott (London: NLB, 1974), pp. 146–148.

29. Adorno, of course, nowhere dealt with *postmodernism*, not in so many words. But, in spite of the fact that "Stravinsky and the Restoration" is easily the most reviled and automatically dismissed of anything he wrote—and while there is no reason to deny its deficiencies, in particular the almost corny psychoanalytic amateurishness of the musical symptomatology Adorno adduced almost straight off the page of Otto Fenichel's *Psychoanalytic Theory of Neurosis*—all the same, Adorno's treatment of *neoclassicism* amounts, *avant la lettre,* to what may be the most incisive critique of postmodernism written to date. The essay deserves to be recognized and studied as such. In many ways it may speak more to developments in the United States than does the compositionally more important essay on Schoenberg. What Adorno discerned in Stravinsky is an appeal to authenticity that is fundamentally a desideratum of authority, achieved by obliterating subjective intention. Adorno develops this thesis in his remarks on Stravinsky's use of pastiche—a kind of abstract diversity—musical quotation, self-reproduction, willful fragmentation, imitation of ancient forms, and so on.

30. Adorno, "Palace of Janus," p. 147.

31. See Theodor W. Adorno, "New Conformism," in *Philosophy of New Music*.

The Philosophy of Dissonance

This essay was first presented at a conference at the Arnold Schoenberg Institute, University of Southern California, in honor of Leonard Stein, entitled "Constructive Dissonance: Arnold Schoenberg and Transformations of Twentieth-Century Culture," November 16, 1991.

1. Arnold Schoenberg, *Theory of Harmony*, trans. Roy E. Carter (Berkeley: University of California Press, 1983), p. 415.

2. Dika Newlin, *Schoenberg Remembered* (New York: Pendragon, 1980), p. 30.

3. Theodor W. Adorno, *Minima Moralia*, trans. E. F. N. Jephcott (London: NLB, 1974), p. 164.

4. Theodor W. Adorno, "On Popular Music," in *Zeitschrift fuer Socialforschung* 9 (1941): 28.

5. Theodor W. Adorno, *Philosophy of Modern Music,* trans. Anne Mitchell and Wesley Blomster (New York: Seabury, 1973), p. 5.

6. Ibid., p. 6.

7. This passage is indebted throughout to Richard Hennessy's brilliant paper "What's All This About Photography," *Artforum,* May 1979, pp. 22–25.

8. These comments are reported from the preconcert talk by Christopher Rouse to the San Francisco Symphony's performance of Mahler's Symphony no. 6 in A Minor, October 11, 1991.

9. In *Theorie des Expressionismus*, ed. Otto F. Best (Stuttgart: Reklam, 1971), p. 86.

10. Adorno, *Philosophy of Modern Music,* p. 162.

Critique of the Organic

1. Max Horkheimer and Theodor W. Adorno, *The Dialectic of Enlightenment*, trans. John Cumming (New York: Herder and Herder, 1972), p. 51.

2. Theodor W. Adorno, *Aesthetische Theorie,* in *Gesammelte Schriften,* henceforth *GS*, ed. Rolf Tiedemann, with the assistance of Gretel Adorno, Susan Buck-Morss, and Klaus Schultz, 20 vols. (Frankfurt: Suhrkamp, 1997), 7:84.

3. Theodor W. Adorno, *Kierkegaard: Konstruktion des Aesthetischen,* in *GS* 2:293.

4. Theodor W. Adorno, *Kierkegaard: Construction of the Aesthetic*, trans. Robert Hullot-Kentor (Minnesota: University of Minnesota Press, 1989), p. 131.

5. Ibid., 118.

6. Ibid., 110.

7. Ibid., 131.

8. Leo Lowenthal, "Recollections of Adorno," *Telos* 61 (1984): 160–161.

9. Theodor W. Adorno, "Kierkegaard's Doctrine of Love," *Zeitschrift fuer Sozialforschung*, 8, 413–429.

10. Adorno, *Kierkegaard, GS* 2:294–295.

11. Walter Benjamin, "Kierkegaard: Das Ende des philosophischen Idealismus," in *Gesammelte Schriften,* ed. Hella Tiedemann-Bartels (Frankfurt: Suhrkamp, 1991), 3:383.

12. F. J. Brecht, *Kant Studien* 40 (1935): 327.

13. Helmut Kuhn, *Zeitschrift fuer Aesthetik und allgemeine Kunstwissenschaft* 28 (1934): 104.

14. Anonymous, *Koelner Vierteljahrschrift fuer Soziologie* 12 (1934): 198.

15. Karl Loewith, *Deutsche Literaturzeitung* 4 (1934): 28.

16. Adorno, "The Essay as Form," trans. Robert Hullot-Kentor and Frederic Will, *New German Critique* 32 (1984): 141–143.

17. Theodor W. Adorno, *Minima Moralia,* trans. E. F. N. Jephcott (London: NLB, 1974), p. 71.

18. See Robert Hullot-Kentor, "Adorno's Aesthetics: The Translation," *Telos* 65 (1986): 143–147.

19. Adorno, *Minima Moralia*, p. 71.

20. Adorno, *Kierkegaard: Construction of the Aesthetic*, p. 29.

21. Theodor W. Adorno, "Vers une musique informelle," in *GS* 16:500.

22. Adorno, *Minima Moralia,* p. 71.

23. The effect in English would be like saying "He takes seriously himself."

24. Adorno, "Vers une musique informelle," in *GS* 16:528–530.

25. Theodor W. Adorno, "Der wunderliche Realist: Ueber Siegfried Kracauer," in *GS* 11:388.

26. This review got as far as being typeset before it was blocked by the National Socialist censors. It is currently to be found among Kracauer's posthumous papers at the Deutsches Literatur Archiv am Neckar, Marbach.

27. Adorno, *Kierkegaard: Construction of the Aesthetic*, p. 85.

28. How interpretation is to proceed was the question that ultimately divided Adorno from Benjamin. Benjamin wanted to present montages of images; they would speak out of their dense juxtaposition. In the vast quotations assembled in *Kierkegaard*, this book stands closest of all of Adorno's writings to Benjamin's ideal: many of its passages are expected to speak for themselves. A good part of the obscurity of the book originates here. Adorno ultimately rejected montage as a form that would only relive the dream, not interpret it, and return the

work to the historicism that it was his and Benjamin's aim to overcome. In Adorno's later studies quotations become sparser and the weight of interpretation increasingly falls to the work of dialectical concepts.

29. Adorno, *Kierkegaard: Construction of the Aesthetic*, p. 11.

30. Ibid.

31. Ibid., p. 14.

32. See Susan Buck-Morrs, *The Origins of Negative Dialectics* (New York: Free Press, 1977), and Carlo Pettazzi, "Studien zu Leben und Werk Adornos bis 1938," *in Text/Kritik* (special Adorno issue), ed. H. L. Arnold, pp. 28–37.

33. See Fred R. Dallmayr, "Adorno and Phenomenology," *Cultural Hermeneutics* 3 (1976): 367–405.

34. Adorno, "Der Begriff des Unbewussten in der transzendentalen Seelenlehre," in *GS* 1:156.

35. Hanns Eisler, *Composing for the Films* (Oxford: Oxford University Press, 1947), pp. 77–78. As Adorno mentions in a note appended to the German edition of this volume, he was the principal author of the English edition as well, but renounced coauthorship to avoid American political entanglements, which he feared would result in legal complexities that would interfere with his desire to return to Europe.

36. Adorno, *Vers une musique informelle*, in *GS* 16:538.

37. Theodor W. Adorno, "Faellige Revision: Zu Schwepperhaeusers Buch ueber Kierkegaard und Hegel," in *GS* 20.1:258.

38. Adorno, *Kierkegaard: Construction of the Aesthetic*, p. 39.

39. Ibid., 37.

40. Ibid., 48.

41. Ibid., 52.

42. Ibid., 53.

43. Ibid., 52.

44. Ibid.

45. Walter Benjamin, *The Origin of the German Play of Lamentation* [title corrected], trans. John Osbourne (London: NLB, 1977), p. 180.

46. Marcel Proust, *Swan's Way,* trans. C. K. Moncrieff (New York: Mondern Library), p. 100.

47. Ibid.

48. Ibid., 101.

49. Ibid.

50. Adorno, "The Idea of Natural-History" (this volume).

51. Ibid.

52. Adorno, *Philosophische Terminologie*, ed. Rudolf zur Lippe (Frankfurt: Suhrkamp, 1974), 1:34–35.

53. Ibid., 1:83.

54. Theodor W. Adorno and Ernst Krenek, *T. W. Adorno und Ernst Krenek: Briefwechsel*, ed. Wolfgang Rogge (Frankfurt: Suhrkamp, 1974), pp. 34–35.

55. The manuscript of Adorno's *Habilitationsschrift* is among his papers at the Theodor W. Adorno-Archiv in Frankfurt.

56. Adorno, *Kierkegaard: Construction of the Aesthetic*, p. 3.

57. Adorno, "Introduction to the Writings of Walter Benjamin," trans. R. Hullot-Kentor, in *Walter Benjamin: Critical Essays and Reflections* (Cambridge: MIT Press, 1980), p. 16.

58. Adorno, *Kierkegaard: Construction of the Aesthetic,* p. 126.

59. Adorno's effort to document hope perhaps explains the important distortion late in the book where, in a discussion of Kierkegaard's famous revision of the story of the Merman and Agnes, Adorno mistakes the Merman for a "guardian angel," who is, in fact, Agnes.

60. Adorno, *Aesthetische Theorie*, p. 245.

Second Salvage

1. Theodor W. Adorno, *Minima Moralia*, trans. E. F. N. Jephcott (London: NLB, 1974), p. 19. Also, *Minima Moralia,* in *Gesammelte Schriften,* hereafter *GS*, ed. Rolf Tiedemann, with the assistance of Gretel Adorno, Susan Buck-Morss, and Klaus Schultz, 20 vols. (Frankfurt: Suhrkamp, 1997), 4:20.

2. Compare Evelyn Wilcock, "Adorno's Uncle: Dr. Bernard Wingfield and the English Exile of Theodor W. Adorno 1934–8, "*German Life and Letters* 49, no. 3 (July 1996): 329–335.

3. Max Horkheimer to T. W. Adorno, October 20,1937, in Theodor W. Adorno, Max Horkheimer *Briefwechsel 1927–1969,* ed. Christoph Goedde and Henri Lonitz (Frankfurt: Suhrkamp, 2003), 1:440.

4. Adorno to Horkheimer, October 21, 1937, ibid., 1:442.

5. Adorno to Benjamin, November 27, 1937, in *Theodor Adorno and Walter Benjamin: The Complete Correspondence*, trans. Nicolas Walker (Cambridge: Harvard University Press, 1999), p. 227. Also *Theodor W. Adorno/Walter Benjamin Briefwechsel 1928–1940,* ed. Henri Lonitz (Frankfurt: Suhrkamp Verlag, 1994), p. 296 (emphasis added).

6. Adorno to Lazarsfeld, January 1, 1938, Theodor W. Adorno-Archiv.

7. Adorno sketched the proposed volume in letters to several colleagues and editors. The most important of these letters, because it gives the clearest statement of Adorno's plans for the book, is that of May 17, 1940, to Phillip Vaudrin, an editor at Oxford University Press:

Dear Mr. Vaudrin:

In addition to the three sections of my book, *Current of Music,* which I have already sent you, I am listing below a provisional table of contents:

1. Introduction (paper on the elements of a social critique of radio music).
2. The Radio Voice (effect of electric transmission on serious music).
3. Analytical Study of NBC's Music Appreciation Hour.
4. What a Music Appreciation Hour Should Be (based on my WNYC material).
5. Likes and Dislikes in Light-Popular Music.
6. Theory of Jazz.
7. Hit Analyses.
8. Program Making: The Future of Music on the Air.

In *Adorno: Eine Bildmonographie*, ed. Theodor W. Adorno-Archiv (Frankfurt: Suhrkamp, 2003), p. 170.

8. Gleason Archer, *History of Radio to 1926* (New York: Ayer, 1938), pp. 131–146.
9. Dickson Skinner, "Music Goes Into Mass Production," *Harper's Monthly Magazine*, April 1939, p. 485.
10. James F. Evans, *Prairie Farmer and WLS: The Burridge D. Butler Years* (Urbana: University of Illinois Press, 1969), p. 155.
11. Leopold Stokowski, "New Vistas in Radio," *Atlantic Monthly*, January 1935, p. 12.
12. Evans, *Prairie Farmer and WLS*, p. 162.
13. Barnett Newman, "On the Need for Political Action by Men of Culture," in *Selected Writings and Interviews*, ed. John P. O'Neill (Berkeley and Los Angeles: University of California Press, 1990), p. 5.
14. Joshua B. Freeman; *Working-Class New York* (New York: New Press, 2000), p. 67.
15. Alton Coor, "Mayor Mild in Music Talk," *World-Telegram*, December 1937, *WNYC Scrapbook for 1937*, Municipal Archive of New York City.
16. Skinner, "Music Goes Into Mass Production," p. 487.
17. Ibid., p. 488.
18. Kathleen Ann Moran, "From a Toy to a Tool: The Emergence and Growth of WOI to 1940" (master's thesis, State University of Iowa, Ames, 1981), p. 164.
19. Skinner, "Music Goes Into Mass Production," p. 487.
20. Ben Hamilton, "Listen and Learn," *WNYC Scrapbook for 1938*, Municipal Archive of New York City.

21. *New York Panorama: Federal Writers' Project 1938* (New York: Pantheon, 1984), p. 298.

22. Compare Theodor W. Adorno, "Analytical Study of the NBC *Music Appreciation Hour,*" *Musical Quarterly* 78, no. 2 (Summer 1994): 325–377.

23. Hamilton, "Listen and Learn."

24. Skinner, "Music Goes Into Mass Production," p. 487.

25. Daily statistics on radio stations in the United States, by format, taken from *100000 Watts: U.S. Radio and TV Directory*, www.l00000Watts .com.

26. Gunther Schuller, "A Stranglehold on the Arts," *Keynote*, May 1982, p. 25.

27. See Jacques Lautmann and Bernard-Pierre Lécuyer, *Paul Lazarsfeld* (1901–1976), *La sociologie de Vienne à New York* (Paris: l'Harmattan, 1998).

28. Letter by Frank Stanton to John Marshall, January 17, 1940, Rockefeller Archive Center.

29. Ibid.

30. Lazarsfeld wrote to Robert J. Havighurst at the Rockefeller Foundation, "Dr. T. W. Adorno is in charge of the conceptual analysis of this field [the Music Study section]. His qualifications for such work stem from the fact that he is a musician of rank as well as a former professor of Social Philosophy at the University of Frankfort." Lazarsfeld to Havighurst, October 21, 1939, Rockefeller Archive Center.

31. It is for this reason that the title of Benjamin's most famous essay is correct as "mechanical reproduction," contrary to the new translation of this essay as "The Work of Art in the Age of Its Technological Reproducibility" (in Walter Benjamin, *Selected Writings*, vol. 4: *1938–1940*, trans. E. F. N. Jephcott et al. [Cambridge: Harvard University Press, 2003], pp. 251–283). What is at stake in this essay is specifically the concept of mechanism.

32. See note 21.

33. Lazarsfeld to Adorno, February 26, 1940, Theodor W. Adorno-Archiv.

34. Lazarsfeld to Frank Stanton, December 14, 1938, Rockefeller Archive Center.

35. Theodor W. Adorno, "Scientific Experiences of a European Scholar in America," in *Critical Models*, trans. Henry Pickford (New York: Columbia University Press, 1999), p. 227.

36. This exchange of motifs, it must be noted, involved Adorno taking the side of Benjamin's early, neo-Platonic messianism against the later Brechtian-Marxist thinking of the "The Work of Art in the Age of Its Mechanical Reproduction."

37. Adorno to Benjamin, May 4, 1938, in *Theodor Adorno and Walter Benjamin: The Complete Correspondence*, p. 251. The date of this letter (no. 103) has been mistranscribed as March 4 in the otherwise excellent translation of these letters.

38. In Thedor W. Adorno, *Essays on Music: Theodor W. Adorno*, selected and with introduction, commentary, and notes by Richard Leppert, trans. Susan Gillespie et al., pp. 288–317. See also Theodor W. Adorno, *Dissonanzen: Musik in der verwalteten Welt*, in *GS* 14:14–50.

39. Theodor W. Adorno-Archiv manuscript, 23 pages. Another, earlier version exists with the important title "Aesthetic Aspects of Radio," 18 pages.

40. Theodor W. Adorno-Archiv manuscript, 157 pages, with handwritten corrections by unnamed American editor. A separate manuscript contains 91 pages of additional materials to this draft.

41. Theodor W. Adorno-Archiv manuscript, 86 pages.

42. Theodor W. Adorno-Archiv manuscript, 35 pages.

43. Adorno, "Music in Radio," p. 151, Theodor W. Adorno-Archiv.

44. Ibid., 153.

45. Adorno, "Music and Radio," p. 22.

46. *Theodor W. Adorno und Ernst Krenek Briefwechsel*, ed. Wolfgang Rogge (Frankfurt: Suhrkamp, 1974), p. 126 (emphasis added).

47. Adorno, "Scientific Experiences of a European Scholar in America," p. 228 (emphasis added).

48. Theodor W. Adorno, *Philosophy of New Music*, trans. Robert Hullot-Kentor (Minneapolis: University of Minnesota Press, 2006); see also Theodor W. Adorno, *Philosophie der neuen Musik*, in *GS* 12:44.

49. Ibid; also, ibid. 12:15.

50. This is the Cartesian structure that Benjamin unconsciously inherited when he thought he was invoking a messianic structure in his "The Work of Art in the Age of Its Mechanical Reproduction" and that Adorno better understood as the model of all pretense to authenticity ever since—so to speak—the beginning.

51. Though it is implicit in his thinking, Adorno himself did not conceive the problematic of the dialectic of enlightenment in precisely these terms of the critique of space. It should be considered, in fact, that his formulation of the dialectic of enlightenment—certainly in these early radio studies—was restricted by what might be called a residual Kantianism in the presumed parameters of transcendental consciousness. If this is the case, then Adorno's own critique of the mechanical universe—and in many regards this defines the impulse the whole of his philosophy consistently cast in an unwavering antiorganicism (see "Critique of the Organic," this volume)—failed to discern a definitive pre-

supposition of the process of mechanization. Here Adorno clearly knew less about the history of science than he might have. This lack of a fundamental discernment between the concepts of nature and space is the same (effectively managerial) blind spot that can vitiate the historical value of the insight sought by the contemporary vogue of studies along the lines of the "production of space," for it consigns these investigations to the superficiality of the study of convention as social construction. It might be possible to pick up on this problem beginning with Adorno's "The Idea of Natural-History" (this volume), where he writes in the final paragraph that "second nature" is also "first nature" and to conceive this as a dialectic of space and nature. The degree to which the neo-Thomistic framework of Yves R. Simon's *The Great Dialogue of Nature and Space* (Indiana: Carthage Reprint, 2001) is at odds with Adorno's thinking makes Simon's diligently lucid scholarship provocatively all the more valuable in this context.

52. See "Things Beyond Resemblance" (this volume).

53. Adorno, "Scientific Experiences of a European Scholar in America," p. 227.

54. *The 1940 Journal of Clifford Odets*, introduction by William Gibson (New York: Grove, 1988), p. 60.

55. Adorno would have understood the degree to which he was mistaken had he studied a work that was certainly available to him, Sir James Jeans's *Science and Music*, first published in 1937 (New York: Dover, 1968). Jeans there explains that even rudimentary radio speakers effectively transmit sound beyond their own frequency range because the ear itself produces the missing tones. Jeans wrote of just the kind of radios Adorno studied: "Many are designed deliberately to cut out all frequencies below about 250, the frequency of about middle C, and so transmit no bass or tenor tones at all. Yet we hear the double bass strings, the basses of the brass, and male voices with absolute clearness. The explanation is, of course, that all these sources of sound are rich in harmonics. Out of these our ears create the missing fundamental tones and lower harmonics as difference tones, and the combination of these with the higher harmonics, which come through unhindered, restores for us the tone played by the orchestra" (241).

56. Adorno, *Philosophy of New Music*.

57. Adorno, "Scientific Experiences of a European Scholar in America," p. 227.

58. All of these essays are now available in *Essays on Music*.

59. *Theodor W. Adorno: Briefe an die Eltern 1939–1951,* ed. Christoph Goedde and Henri Lonitz (Frankfurt: Suhrkamp, 2003), p. 484.

60. Ibid., p. 496.

61. Theodor W. Adorno, *Der getreue Korrepetitor,* in *GS* 15:163–187.

62. Ibid., pp. 369–401.

63. Theodor W. Adorno, "On Popular Music," in *Introduction to the Sociology of Music*, trans. E. B. Ashton (New York: Continuum, 1988), pp. 21–38; also *Einleitung in die Musiksoziologie,* in *GS* 14:199–218.

64. After a delay of some years, *Current of Music,* edited by Robert Hullot-Kentor, is being published by the Theodor W. Adorno-Archiv and Suhrkamp Verlag in 2006.

Title Essay

1. This title, *Metacritique of Epistemology*, has been mistranslated—perhaps on the insistence of the publisher's marketing division—as *Against Epistemology*, adapting it to Heidegger's critique of epistemology and movieland's obligatory double punch.

2. Theodor W. Adorno, *Gesammelte Schriften,* henceforth *GS*, ed. Rolf Tiedemann, with the assistance of Gretel Adorno, Susan Buck-Morss, and Klaus Schultz, 20 vols. (Frankfurt: Suhrkamp, 1974), 11:28.

3. Ibid.

4. See Theodor W. Adorno, "The Essay as Form," trans. Robert Hullot-Kentor and Frederic Will, *New German Critique* 32 (1984): 151–171.

5. Paul Tillich, *Mysticism and Guilt-Consciousness in Schelling's Philosophical Development,* trans. Victory Buovo (Lewisberg: Bucknell University Press, 1974), pp. 1–42.

6. Theodor W. Adorno, *Philosophische Terminologie,* 2 vols. (Frankfurt: Suhrkamp, 1973), 2:62–67.

7. Walter Benjamin, *The Origin of the German Play of Lamentation*, trans. John Osbome (London: NLB, 1977), pp. 36–37.

8. Gérard Lebrun, *La Patience du Concept* (Paris: Gallimard. 1972), pp. 71–123. This preeminent study of Hegel's aesthetics deserves to be better known in this country.

9. Benjamin, *The Origin of the German Play of Lamentation*, p. 47 (emphasis added).

10. Ibid., p. 223.

11. Ibid., p. 184.

12. Max Horkheimer and Theodor W. Adorno, *Dialectic of Enlightenment,* trans. John Cumming (New York: Herder and Herder, 1972), p. 15.

13. Ibid., p. 5.

14. Ibid., p. 33.

15. Theodor W. Adorno, *Aesthetische Theorie,* in *GS* (Frankfurt: Suhrkamp, 1970), 7:363.

16. Ibid., 7:364.

17. Theodor W. Adorno, *Vorlesung zur Einleitung in die Erkenntnistheorie* (Frankfurt: Junius Druck/Hesa Druck, n.d.), p. 317.

18. This section relies on Charles Rosen, *Schoenberg* (New York: Viking, 1975), pp. 23–62.

19. Many of these techniques are to be found in Benjamin's work. Yet Benjamin developed them more by way of a religious appropriation, with reference to the *tractatus,* than to aesthetic form. They are legitimated by their reference to the research of *origin,* which protects them from the charge of artificiality and "artiness" that falls on Adorno.

20. Translation amended.

21. Karl Marx, *Doktordissertation,* in MEGA, 1, 1/1, p. 64.

What Is Mechanical Reproduction?

1. This essay was initially solicited for a Stanford University publication, *Mapping Benjamin: The Work of Art in the Digital Age,* ed. Hans Ulrich Gumbrecht and Michael Marinen (Stanford: Stanford University Press, 2003), pp. 293–312.

2. Walter Benjamin, "The Work of Art in the Age of Mechanical Reproduction," in *Illuminations,* trans. Harry Zohn (Boston: Schocken, 1976); further page references appear in brackets in the text.

3. At the several points where the English translation reverts to the literal out of a sense of responsibility to the original, the obvious indeterminateness of "technical reproduction" compels the translation to seek modifying expressions that would give the phrase some content. But the absence of any compact adequate English phrase instead drives the translation into greater obscurities. This is what happens in the following passage in which "process reproduction" is to somehow help elucidate "technical reproduction." "Confronted with its manual reproduction, which was usually branded as a forgery, the original preserved all its authority: not so vis-à-vis technical reproduction [*technische Reproduktion*]. The reason is twofold. First, process reproduction [*technische Reproduktion*] is more independent of the original than manual reproduction" (220).

4. See Theodor W. Adorno, *Aesthetic Theory,* ed. Rolf Tiedemann and Gretel Adorno, trans. Robert Hullot-Kentor (Minnesota: University of Minnesota Press, 1997).

5. *Arnold Schoenberg and Wassily Kandinsky: Letters, Pictures, Documents,* ed. Jelena Hahl-Koch, trans. John C. Crawford (London: Thames and Hudson, 1984), p. 26.

6. See Walter Benjamin, *The Origin of the German Tragic Drama,* trans. John Osborne (London: NLB, 1977), p. 182.

7. *The Correspondence of Walter Benjamin*, ed. Gershom Scholem and Theodor W. Adorno, trans. Manfred R. Jacobson and Evelyn M. Jacobson (Chicago: University of Chicago Press, 1994), p. 595.

8. Benjamin, *The Origin of German Tragic Drama,* pp. 165–166.

9. Theodor W. Adorno and Max Horkheimer, "Odysseus or Myth and Enlightenment," from *Dialectic of Enlightenment,* trans. Robert Hullot-Kentor, *New German Critique* 56 (1992): 109–142.

Adorno Without Quotation

1. This essay is also published in German, as "Adorno ohne Anfuehrungszeichen," trans. Elisabeth Lenk and Gesa Lolling, in *Philologie und Scham: Texte von, ueber und fuer Rolf Tiedemann* (Frankfurt: Die Buechse der Pandora, 2006).

2. The instances are too frequent to quote here. See, for example, the editorial, *New York Times,* September 9, 2003, p. A28.

3. See Juliet Schor, *The Overworked American* (New York: Basic, 1993).

4. Theodor W. Adorno, *Minima Moralia* ("Das Ganze ist das Unwahre"), trans. E. F. N. Jephcott (London: NLB, 1974), p. 50.

5. Wallace Stevens, *Collected Poetry and Prose* (New York: Library of America, 1997), p. 277.

Popular Music and "The Aging of the New Music"

The epigraph to this essay is from David A. Sheldon. "The Philosophy of T. W. Adorno," *Current Musicology* (Spring 1965), p. 90.

1. See Theodor W. Adorno, "Uber Einige Relationen zwischen Musik und Malerei," in *Anmerkungen zur Zeit* (Berlin: Akademie der Kunste, 1967), especially pp. 5–9, and "Vers une musique informelle," in *Gesammelte Schriften,* henceforth *GS,* ed. Rolf Tiedemann, with the assistance of Gretel Adorno, Susan Buck-Morss, and Klaus Schultz, 20 vols. (Frankfurt: Suhrkamp, 1997), 16:498–540.

2. See Theodor W. Adorno, "The Aging of the New Music," trans. Robert Hullot-Kentor and Frederic Will, *Telos* 77 (1989): 95–116. References below are to this translation.

3. See Heinz-Klaus Metzger, "Just Who is Growing Old?" in the *Reihe,* no. 4 (1958): 63–82. Metzger went so far as to draw up a juxtaposition of lines from Adorno's essay with those of another, conservative music critic known for his complete rejection of new music.

4. Theodor W. Adorno, *Die Philosophie der neuen Musik*, in *GS* 12:38–39. See Theodor W. Adorno, *The Philosophy of Modern Music*, trans. Anne Mitchell and Wesley Blomster (New York: Seabury, 1973), p. 32.

5. In "The Idea of Natural-History" (this volume) Adorno writes: "If the question of the relation of nature and history is to be seriously posed, then it only offers any chance of solution if it is possible *to comprehend historical being in its most extreme historical determinacy, where it is most historical as natural being, or if it were possible to comprehend nature as a historical being where it seems to rest most deeply in itself as nature."*

6. Adorno's thesis of the transformation of expression in new music is a reformulation of Benjamin's distinction between symbol and allegory in the second part of *The Origin of the German Tragic Drama.*

7. For a full account of this movement see Paul Griffiths, *Modern Music: The Avant-Garde Since 1945* (New York: Braziller, 1981), pp. 19–88.

8. Cf. Gyoergy Ligeti, "Metamorphoses of Musical Form," in the *Reihe* (London: Universal, 1960), p. 5.

9. Ibid. Ligeti agreed with Adorno in regard to total serialism as a movement, but thought Adorno was wrong in the case of Boulez and several other important composers.

10. Quoted in Griffiths, *Modern Music,* p. 98.

11. The central letters of this correspondence are in *Aesthetics and Politics*, trans. Harry Zohn (London: NLB, 1977). pp. 126–141.

12. Ibid., p. 129.

13. Ibid., p. 130.

14. In "The Aging of the New Music" nature is equivalently the "material" to which the compositional self is subordinated.

15. Theodor W. Adorno, *Kierkegaard: Construction of the Aesthetic,* trans. Robert Hullot-Kentor (Minnesota: University of Minnesota Press, 1989).

16. Adorno, "Vers une musique informelle," in *GS* 16:537–538.

17. Theodor W. Adorno, *Composing for the Films* (London: Athlone, 1994), p. 130.

18. Theodor W. Adorno, "Marginalien zu Theorie und Praxis," in *GS* 10.2:764.

The Impossibility of Music

1. See "Popular Music and 'The Aging of the New Music'" (this volume).

2. Vincent Persichetti, *Twentieth-Century Harmony* (New York: Norton, 1961), p. 13.

3. See "Introduction to T. W. Adorno's 'The Idea of Natural-History'" (this volume).

4. Adorno discusses tradition as "the presence of the forgotten" in *Philosophy of New Music* (Minnesota: University of Minnesota Press, 2006). For Adorno's discussion of the aesthetic shudder, see *Aesthetische Theorie* in *Gesammelte Schriften,* henceforth *GS,* ed. Rolf Tiedemann, with the assistance of Gretel Adorno, Susan Buck-Morss, and Klaus Schultz, 20 vols. (Frankfurt: Suhrkamp, 1997), 7:124–125 and 489–490.

5. Theodor W. Adorno, "Klassik, Romantik, neue Musik," in *GS* 16:126–130.

6. Charles Rosen, *Schoenberg* (New York: Viking, 1975), pp. 28–29.

7. Theodor W. Adorno, "Vers une musique informelle," in *GS* 16:324.

8. Theodor W. Adorno, "Die gesellschaftliche Lage der Musik," in *Zeitschrift fur Sozialforschung* 1 (1932): 103–124, 356–378.

9. See Michael Fink, *Inside the Music Business* (New York: Schirmer, 1989), pp. 224–225.

10. Popular music, with its angry posturing, harmonic reversals, secret lyrics, and obscenity also lays claim to the critique of semblance, though without ever wanting to carry it out. This is, as Glenn Gould explained, one of its perfections: "Each of the songs . . . emphasizes some aspect of that discrepancy between an adolescent's short-term need to rebel and long range readiness to conform"; *Glenn Gould Reader* (New York: Vintage, 1984), p. 303.

11. See the discussion with David Sylvester in the film *The Brutality of Fact,* BBC, November 16, 1984, which contains some material not found in the interviews published as *The Brutality of Fact,* ed. David Sylvester (New York: Thames and Hudson, 1988).

12. Adorno discusses Kafka in this regard in "Standort des Erzahlers," in Theodor W. Adorno, *Noten zur Literatur,* in *GS* 11:41–48. *Aesthetic Theory* is, as a whole, devoted to the presentation of this antinomy of aesthetic semblance.

13. Theodor W. Adorno, "Kriterien der neuen Musik," in *GS* 16:184–187.

14. Gould, *Glenn Gould Reader,* p. 110.

15. This is the same process that occurred socially. Social integration resulted in the dissolution of conventionally binding relations and the arbitrariness of the constituents of society. See Adorno, "Kriterien der neuen Musik," in *GS* 16:170–182.

16. Adorno, *Philosophy of New Music,* p. 39.

17. Ibid.

18. Adorno, "Klassik, Romantik, neue Musik," in *GS* 16:141.

19. Adorno, "Vers une musique informelle," in *GS* 16:537.

Apple Criticizes Tree of Knowledge

Karl-Otto Apel, "Normatively Grounding 'Critical Theory' Through Recourse to the Lifeworld: A Transcendental-Pragmatic Attempt to Think with Habermas Against Habermas," in Axel Honneth, Thomas McCarthy, Claus Offe, and Albrecht Wellmer, eds., *Philosophical Interventions in the Unfinished Project of Enlightenment*, trans. William Rehg (Cambridge: MIT Press, 1992).

Right Listening and a New Type of Human Being

1. David Sylvester, *The Brutality of Fact: Interviews with Francis Bacon* (New York: Thames and Hudson, 1987), p. 22.
2. Wallace Stevens, "Of Modern Poetry" in *Collected Poetry and Prose* (New York: Library of America, 1997), p. 219.
3. Wallace Stevens, "Credences of Summer," ibid., p. 324.
4. Alexis de Toqueville, *Democracy in America,* trans. George Lawrence (New York: Harper Collins, 2000), p. 429.
5. Ibid., p. 437.
6. Ibid., p. 439.
7. Theodor W. Adorno, *Minima Moralia,* translated by E. F. N. Jephcott (Verso, 1978), p. 247.
8. See Erich Kahler, *Man the Measure* (New York: Meridian, 1967), p. 488.
9. Wilhelm Heinrich Wachenroder and Ludwig Tieck, *Outpourings of an Art-Loving Friar,* trans. Edward Mornin (New York: Ungar, 1975), p. 26.
10. And, as Walter Benjamin points out, even in the film age European critics aspired to pray to these images: "Alexandre Arnoux concludes his fantasy about the silent film with the question: 'Do not all the bold descriptions we have given amount to the definition of prayer?'" Walter Benjamin, "The Work of Art in the Age of Mechanical Reproduction," in *Illuminations,* trans. Harry Zohn (New York: Schoken, 1969), p. 227. Benjamin quotes Arnoux from *Cinéma pris*, 1929, p. 28.
11. Again, Tocqueville was the first to document this, and—in a chapter entitled "The Industry of Literature"—did so a full century before Adorno wrote on the "culture industry." In that chapter Tocqueville writes, "Democracy not only gives the industrial classes a taste for letters but also brings an industrial spirit into literature" (p. 475).
12. Theodor W. Adorno, "What National Socialism Has Done to the Arts," in *Gesammelte Schriften,* ed. Rolf Tiedemann, with the assistance

of Gretel Adorno, Susan Buck-Morss, and Klaus Schultz, 20 vols. (Frankfurt: Suhrkamp, 1997), 20.2:419.

13. See "Second Salvage" (this volume).

14. "Problem des neuen Menschentypus," manuscript dated June 23, 1941, Theodor W. Adorno-Archiv, Frankfurt am Main.

15. Stevens, *Collected Poetry and Prose,* p. 665. See also "Adorno Without Quotation," this volume, section 2.

16. Stevens, *Collected Poetry and Prose,* p. 662.

17. Adorno, *Minima Moralia*, pp. 75–76.

18. Theodor W. Adorno, *Current of Music,* ed. Robert Hullot-Kentor, (Frankfurt: Theodor W. Adorno-Archiv and Suhrkamp, 2006), chapter 4.

19. Ibid.

Ethics, Aesthetics, and the Recovery of the Public World

1. "Ethics, Aesthetics, and the Recovery of the Public World" was first presented at a conference on "The Recovery of the Public World," at Simon Fraser University, Spring 1995.

2. This essay draws throughout on Theodor W. Adorno's lecture series, *An Introduction to Moral Philosophy* (*Zu einer Einleitung in die Moralphilosophie*), 1957, an unauthorized transcription by Peter Tumarkin. Mimeograph.

3. Theodor W. Adorno, *Minima Moralia*, trans. E. F. N. Jephcott (London: NLB, 1974), p. 184.

4. Erich Kahler, *Man the Measure* (Ohio: Meridian, 1967), pp. 79–80.

5. Alexis de Tocqueville, *De la Démocratie en Amérique* (Paris, 1864), 2:151. Quoted in Max Horkheimer and Theodor W. Adorno, *Dialectic of Enlightenment,* trans. John Cumming (New York: Herder and Herder, 1972), p. 133.

6. See C. B. Macpherson, *The Political Theory of Possessive Individualism* (Oxford: Oxford University Press, 1962), pp. 87–90.

7. See Anthony LaBruzza and Jose Mendez-Villarrubia, *Using DSM-IV: A Clinician's Guide to Psychiatric Diagnosis* (Northvale, NJ: Aronson, 1994), p. 303.

8. Ibid., pp. 298–303.

9. In Walter Benjamin, *Illuminations*, ed. Hannah Arendt, trans. Harry Zohn (New York: Schocken, 1969), pp. 219–251.

10. Theodor W. Adorno, *Aesthetische Theorie*, in *Gesammelte Schriften*, ed. Rolf Tiedemann, with the assistance of Gretel Adorno, Susan Buck-Morss, and Klaus Schultz, 20 vols. (Frankfurt: Suhrkamp, 1997), 7:336.

11. Theodor W. Adorno, *Negative Dialectics*, trans. E. B. Ashton (New York: Seabury, 1973), p. 300 ff.

Suggested Reading

1. Fredric Jameson, *Late Marxism: Adorno, the Persistance of the Dialectic* (London: Verso, 1990).
2. Emphasis has been added in quotations throughout this discussion.
3. Jameson is superficial: Since the distinction of thought and language is already in language, the argument that thought and language are identical can only be made on the basis of the assumption—suppressed yet determinate—that they are different in a nonlinguistic fashion. Whether Jameson is right that the denial of the distinction is essential to poststructuralism, his own formulation amounts to a rediscovery of Watson's behaviorism.
4. See "Critique of the Organic," this volume.
5. Totality in Adorno's writings means the functional context developed in various ways through the exchange relation. Totality is no more or less real than this functional order. It should not be thought that totality means a system that is simply closed. It is closed and disorganized by its principle of closure. This relation is misunderstood by the usual argument that Adorno exaggerated the idea of the totally administered society. The origin of this misunderstanding is a credulousness for administration. Those who think Adorno overestimated the functional web do so because they imagine that, if the world were so tightly organized as Adorno claims, planes would leave on the minute. Adorno's point, rather, is that administration is a principle of disorganization.
6. See Theodor W. Adorno, "On Lyric Poetry and Society," trans. Bruce Mayo, in *Telos* (1974), pp. 56–71. Now also in Theodor W. Adorno, *Notes to Literature,* trans. Shierry Weber Nicolsen (New York: Columbia University Press, 1991), pp. 50–53.
7. Walter Benjamin, *Gesammelte Schriften,* ed. Rolf Tiedemann (Frankfurt: Suhrkamp, 1972), 2.1:368 ff.

Introduction to T. W. Adorno's "The Idea of Natural-History"

1. A hyphen distinguishes two terms in this essay: *natural-history* and *natural history.*
2. Adorno's essay has already received substantial attention. See Susan Buck-Morss, *The Origins of Negative Dialectics* (New York: Free Press, 1977), chapter 3; Fred R. Dallmayr, *Twilight of Subjectivity* (Amherst: University of Massachusetts Press, 1981), pp. 211–219; Friedemann

Grenz, "Die Idee der Naturgeschichte," in *X. Deutscher Kongress fuer Philosophie,* ed. Kurt Huebner and Albert Menne (Hamburg: Mohr, 1973), pp. 344–350; W. Martin Luedke, *Anmerkungen zu einer Logik des Zerfalls* (Frankfurt: Suhrkamp, 1981), pp. 69–85.

3. *Kant-Studien* 38 (1933): 498.

4. See, for example, Theodor W. Adorno "Kritik am ontologischen Beduerfnis treibt zur immanenten der Ontologie," *Negative Dialektik,* in *Gesammelte Schriften,* henceforth *GS,* ed. Rolf Tiedemann, with the assistance of Gretel Adorno, Susan Buck-Morss, and Klaus Schultz, 20 vols. (Frankfurt: Suhrkamp, 1997), 6:104. How to translate this line and many others in *Negative Dialectics* is puzzling. E. B. Ashton's current translation of the work is admirable for having dragged the book into English, but culpable for having half strangled it on arrival. His translation drops clauses and whole lines (e.g., pp. 35, 76, 99, 143), translates terms arbitrarily (e.g., *Vermittlung* as transmission), and changes hard thought into simple incomprehensibility by dividing the text into paragraphs where there are none. Altogether it is a model of conformist translation. Adorno's sentence might be rendered: "Critique of the ontological need leads to an immanent one of ontology." Ashton makes it both homey and pedantic. "Our critique of the ontological need brings us to an immanent critique of ontology itself." Theodor W. Adorno, *Negative Dialectics,* trans. E. B. Ashton (New York: Continuum, 1983), p. 97.

5. "Ueber die Seinsphilosophie hat keine Gewalt, was sie generell, von aussen her abwehrt, anstatt in ihren eigenen Gefuege mit ihr es aufzunehmen, nach Hegels Desiderat ihre eigene Kraft gegen sie zu wenden"; Adorno, *Negative Dialektik,* in *GS* 6:104. The "das" requisite to the first clause, which would normally correspond to the "was" of the second clause, is missing. It is perhaps not possible to translate this sentence into English and maintain the discomfiture of that first clause. A plausible translation, however, might run: "What would reject ontology, generally, from an external position, instead of taking it on in its own structure, turning its own force against itself according to Hegel's desideratum, has no power over the philosophy of being"; Adorno, *Negative Dialectics,* p. 97.

6. "Nicht reicht dabei aus, der Seinsphilosophie zu demonstrieren so etwas gebe es nicht wie das, was sie Sein nennt." Adorno, *Negative Dialektik,* p.104; cf. *Negative Dialectics,* p. 97.

7. This discussion and examples of Adorno's style come primarily from Hermann Deuser, *Dialektische Theologie* (Munich: Gruyter, 1980), pp. 118–128.

8. Cf. Adorno, *Negative Dialectics,* p. 403.

9. Where this type of phrase does occur in English editions it usually indicates faulty translation; cf. "As we have seen" (Max Horkheimer and Theodor W. Adorno, *Dialectic of Enlightenment,* trans. John Cumming [New York: Continuum, 1978], p. 43). But this is not always the case. Neither is the abruptness of Adorno's language always justified. It does not always lead into the object. The abandonment of argumentative form turns the text's integrity over to its density, a particularly vulnerable form that magnifies any slightest loss of tension. Transitional sentences, where they do occur in Adorno's writing, have just this diluting effect. Adorno will occasionally try to take up the slack by increasing the abruptness of the sentence. The sentence quoted in footnote 4, for example, begins a new section and actually has a transitional function. Adorno tries to cover up its function by heightening the abruptness of the rhetoric. Whereas the sentence implies some form of criticism in apposition to immanent criticism and gains its tension from this implied apposition, no apposition is actually involved.

10. Theodor W. Adorno, *Jargon of Authenticity,* trans. Knut Tarnowski and Frederic Will (Evanston: Northwestern University Press, 1973), p. 161.

11. Leo Strauss, "Kurt Riezler," in *Social Research,* 23 (1956): 17

12. See Adorno, "The Idea of Natural-History" (this volume).

13. Theodor W. Adorno, "The Idea of Natural-History," was first published in *GS* 1:345–365.

14. I am particularly referring to Adorno's *Kierkegaard: Construction of the Aesthetic.* It will be a matter of dispute whether this work actually precedes or postdates Adorno's "Idea." The Kierkegaard manuscript was first completed in 1930. But the edition that was eventually published was the result of massive revisions undertaken during the summer and fall of the period during which Adorno presented the "Idea." The degree to which the published edition differs from the original was something that Adorno emphasized to Ernst Krenek in a letter of September 1932: "Each sentence has been newly formulated and many and precisely central parts are being fully reworked." Theodor W. Adorno and Ernst Krenek, *Briefwechsel* (Frankfurt: Suhrkamp, 1974), pp. 34–35. It would be necessary to compare the two versions to actually know the extent of the revisions. Unfortunately, Adorno's estate is unable to make the only known copy available for research.

15. E.g., Theodor W. Adorno, *Noten zur Literatur,* in *GS* 11:400.

16. Karl Loewith, *Nature, History, and Existentialism* (Evanston: Northwestern University Press, 1966), p. 139.

17. Steven Toulmin and June Goodfield, *The Discovery of Time* (London: Hutchinson, 1965), p. 129; and Paolo Rossi, *The Dark Abyss of Time,* trans. L. G. Cochrane (Chicago: University of Chicago Press, 1987).

18. Rudolf Eisler, *Kantlexikon* (Hildesheim, 1961), p. 380.

19. For further examples from an extensive repertoire, see Heidegger's development of *Ver-haeltnis* and *Ge-Stell* in *Die Technik und die Kehre* (Tuebingen: Klett-Cotta, 1976), pp. 27 and 39.

20. Theodor W. Adorno, "Thesen ueber die Sprache des Philosophen," in *GS* 1:368. Adorno's view of Heidegger's language is condensed in his admiration for Kracauer's untranslatable parody: "Eifersucht ist the Leidenschaft die mit Eifer sucht, was Leiden schafft."

21. Horkheimer and Adorno, *Dialectic of Enlightenment*, p. 27.

22. Adorno, "Thesen ueber die Sprache des Philosophen," in *GS* 1:366.

23. Ibid., 1:368.

24. Ibid., 1:369.

25. Adorno, *Stichwoerte* (Frankfurt: Suhrkamp, 1970), p. 178.

26. Adorno, *Negative Dialectics*, p. 321.

27. Theodor W. Adorno, "Charakteristik Walter Benjamins," in *GS* 10.1:242.

28. Cf. F. J. Rintelen, *Contemporary German Philosophy* (Bonn: Bouvier, 1970).

29. Gunter Anders, "On the Pseudo-Concreteness of Heidegger's Philosophy," *Philosophy and Phenomenological Research* 8:337–370. This essay is brilliantly compelling and in some regards surpasses Adorno's commentary on Heidegger.

30. Horkheimer and Adorno, *Dialectic of Enlightenment*, p. 78.

31. Adorno, "Charakteristik Walter Benjamins," in *GS* 10.1:242.

32. *Second nature* would, in Benjamin's terms, simply be the *natural historical* carrying a sense conflicting with Adorno's development of the term.

33. Horkheimer and Adorno, *Dialectic of Enlightenment*, p. 33.

34. Adorno, *Zur Metakritik der Erkenntnistheorie,* in *GS* 5:47.

35. Ibid., 5:286.

36. G. W. F. Hegel, *Werke* (Frankfurt: Suhrkamp, 1970), 9:174.

37. One of the most significant conflicts between Adorno and Benjamin is that for the latter the name is prelapsarian; for Adorno, it is postlapsarian.

38. Horkheimer and Adorno, *Dialectic of Enlightment,* p. 15.

39. Theodor W. Adorno, *Philosophy of Modern Music,* trans. Anne Mitchell and Wesley Blomster (New York: Seabury, 1979), p. 27.

40. Adorno's description of the mythical character of second nature should be read as completing Strauss's description of the historical moment.

41. Adorno, *Philosophy of Modern Music*, p. 42; translation modified.

42. Ibid., p. 39.

43. Ibid., p. 70.

44. Theodor W. Adorno, *Aesthetische Theorie,* in *GS* 7:154 ff.

45. Theodor W. Adorno, "Aldous Huxley and Utopia," *Prisms,* trans. Samuel and Shierry Weber (Boston: MIT Press, 1981), pp. 105–106.
46. Adorno, *Aesthetische Theorie,* in *GS* 7:122 ff.
47. Horkheimer and Adorno, *Dialectic of Enlightenment,* pp. 48–49.
48. This point is hard to get from the English version of *Dialectic of Enlightenment,* which translates the passage in question as "through laughter blind nature becomes aware of itself as it is, and thereby surrenders itself to the power of destruction" (p. 77). This should read: ". . . and thereby forgoes its destructive power."
49. Adorno, *Aesthetische Theorie,* in *GS* 7:178.
50. To choose one example of this irritation that is of particular interest for its perception of a thicket of nature, one critic wrote that Adorno came "to the conclusion that neo-classicism was intrinsically reactionary, a theme that he was to pursue through the thickets of his prose for the next forty years." Peter Heyworth, *Otto Klemperer* (Cambridge: Cambridge University Press, 1983), p. 263.

The Idea of Natural-History

1. There are various opinions on this reference, but none authoritative. Cf. W. Martin Luedke, *Anmerkungen zu einer Logik des Zerfalls* (Frankfurt: Suhrkamp, 1981), p. 74; and Hermann Moerschen, *Adorno und Heidegger* (Stuttgart: Klett, 1982), p. 34. (Translator's note.)
2. Neo-Kantianism. (Translator's note.)
3. This was a general critique of Scheler current in the late 1920s. One student put it: "Whatever happens in the real world . . . the assassination of a dictator, or the failure of such a plot . . . either can be explained by Scheler's sociology and metaphysics. His philosophy is adapted to account for any situation; like the barber's stool, as one of Shakespeare's fools says, it's designed for any ass." Quoted in J. R. Staude, *Max Scheler* (New York: Free Press, 1967), p. 239. (Translator's note.)
4. Georg Lukács, *The Theory of the Novel,* trans. Anna Bostock (Monmouth: Merlin, 1978), p. 62, translation corrected.
5. Ibid., p. 54.
6. Title amended. (Translator's note.)
7. Walter Benjamin, *The Origin of German Tragic Drama,* trans. John Osborne (London: NLB, 1977), p. 179, translation amended. (Translator's note.)
8. Ibid., p. 177, translation amended.
9. This line precedes the passage that Adorno actually quotes. It does not appear in either the published or in Adorno's manuscript. From the context, however, it is clearly required. The editor of Adorno's collected

works agrees, and it will be inserted in future editions (letter from Tiedemann). It is interesting to speculate why this line is missing. Tiedemann guesses that the essay was delivered from notes. The single manuscript that exists would be the work of a stenographer who could have easily missed a line. Unfortunately, it has not been possible to check whether a stenographer was at this meeting for, according to the present editor of *Kant-Studien,* all of the society's records from the period were destroyed (letter from Manfred Kleinschneider). One thing, however, makes it doubtful that the essay is solely the work of a stenographer, and that is its footnotes. Only Adorno could have plausibly put in footnote 16. He must have gone over the essay, perhaps preparing it for publication, and this makes the fact important that Adorno, not known for carelessness, passed over the passage's discontinuity. An explanation is possible. The line contains two important elements, one a reference to the "original history of signification" and the other to natural history, in Benjamin's sense, of course. The former was needed for the coherence of Adorno's talk. But in that, for Benjamin, it is given as a synonym for natural history, the reference would have confused the presentation.

Readers may find that substituting "primordial" for "original" helps clarify the concepts in this essay.

10. This is not one of those Latin phrases that everyone is supposed to know. The "Hippocratic face" is the physiognomy of a person suffering from "the worst." Francis Adams, in his introduction to *The Genuine Works of Hippocrates* (New York: William Wood, 1886), p. 195, cites the classical description of this countenance: "a sharp nose, hollow eyes, collapsed temples, the ears cold, contracted, and their lobes turned out: the skin about the forehead being rough, distended, and parched; the color of the whole face being green, black, livid, or lead colored." For a discussion of "the face of nature" in Greek, Hebrew, and early modern traditions, see H. A. Wolfson, *The Philosophy of Spinoza* (Cambridge: Harvard University Press, 1962), 1:244–247. (Translator's note.)

11. Benjamin, *The Origin of German Tragic Drama,* p. 166, translation amended.

12. Literally, the last part of this sentence reads, "in both cases 'transience' and 'transitoriness' occur." In fact, only the word *transience* appears in the cited passages. Nothing of importance seems to be at stake, and so the phrase has been dropped to avoid confusion. (Translator's note.)

13. Although Heidegger does not use the term *ontological turn* (*ontologische Wendung*), in the context of his work it would refer to a transformation of ontology such as occurred with Descartes. (Translator's note.)

14. Kurt Riezler, 1882–1955. Nationalist, classicist, philosopher. Once well known for his study of Parmenides and an aesthetics, more recently for

his World War I diaries. Adorno is referring to his *Gestalt und Gesetz* (1924), a "critical metaphysics" that argues that life is characterized by a fundamental dualism of law and form, unified by fate. (Translator's note.)

15. Apparently a references to Freud's "The Antithetical Sense of Primal Words" (1910), in *Collected Papers*, ed. Joan Riviere (London: Hogarth, 1950). (Translator's note.)

16. Cf. Søren Kierkegaard. *The Concept of Irony,* trans. Lee M. Capel (Bloomington: Indiana University Press, 1965), p. 112 ff.

Index

"absorption in speculation," 29

abstraction, 17, 77; existence as, 78; as mark of mythical, 81. *See also* musical abstraction

Adams, Francis, 303*n*10

administration, 298*n*5

Adorno, Gretel, 25, 96

Adorno, Theodor W., 4, 5–12, 24–32, 36, 39, 43, 45–46, 54–61, 65, 69, 70, 77–82, 85, 90–93, 95–98, 101, 111, 120, 124, 126, 133, 154, 158–61, 173, 191, 199–201, 223–25, 248, 278*n*67, 281*n*12, 281*n*18, 282*n*18, 287*n*7, 300*n*14; aesthetics of, 70, 78, 86, 88, 196, 208, 220; austerity of, 69; Benjamin and, 130, 175, 284*n*28, 301*n*37; biographies of, 95; boutique moments of, 135; citizenship of, 57; correspondence of, 69; death of, 24; ear of, 193; early work of, 79–80; as enemy of enlightenment, 32; English works of, 96–97; on essay, 132; followers of, 162; German repatriation of, 123; Horkheimer and,

29–30; ideal form of, 80–81; intellectual development of, 163–64; isolation of, 123, 163, 196; Kraus and, 221–23; language of, 27, 82, 250, 300*n*9; "mandarin formality of," 235; musical aesthetics and, 53, 170, 178, 181, 185; naturalization of, 45; in New York City, 95–96; as optimist, 29; as pessimist, 29, 275*n*17; philosophy of, 119, 130, 132, 161, 165, 193–94, 196, 200, 251; *physiognomic* approach of, 120; as priest, 201; as psychoanalytic researcher, 10–11, 13; quoting of, 165–66; as refugee, 96; self-preservation and, 60; style of, 10, 91; thinking of, 119, 289*n*51; as traditionalist, 223; translation of, 45, 55, 274*n*1; as uncompromising figure, 67; in United States, 10, 23, 45–46, 155, 195, 203

Adorno-Archiv, 94, 97

aesthetic(s), 219; of Adorno, Theodor W., 70, 78, 86, 88, 196, 208, 220; of Bacon, 196; comportment, 122; experi-